# Settler Tenses

# Settler Tenses

## QUEER TIME AND LITERATURES OF THE AMERICAN WEST

RYAN TAN WANDER

TEXAS TECH UNIVERSITY PRESS

This book is typeset in EB Garamond. The paper used in this book meets the minimum requirements of ANSI/NISO Z39.48-1992 (R1997). ♾

Designed by Hannah Gaskamp
Cover design by Hannah Gaskamp

Library of Congress Cataloging-in-Publication Data

Names: Wander, Ryan Tan, author. Title: Settler Tenses: Queer Time and Literatures of the American West / Ryan Tan Wander. Description: Lubbock, Texas: Texas Tech University Press, 2024. | Includes bibliographical references and index. | Summary: "Traces the discursive production of masculinities in late nineteenth and early twentieth-century literatures of the American West"—Provided by publisher.
Identifiers: LCCN 2024018994 (print) | LCCN 2024018995 (ebook) |
ISBN 978-1-68283-226-4 (cloth) | ISBN 978-1-68283-227-1 (ebook)
Subjects: LCSH: Western stories—History and criticism. | American literature—20th century—History and criticism. | Masculinity in literature. | Queer theory. | Colonists in literature. | Frontier and pioneer life in literature. | Nationalism—United States—History—20th century. | LCGFT: Literary criticism.
Classification: LCC PS374.W4 W35 2024 (print) | LCC PS374.W4 (ebook) |
DDC 813/.087409—dc23/eng/20240607
LC record available at https://lccn.loc.gov/2024018994
LC ebook record available at https://lccn.loc.gov/2024018995

Printed in the United States of America
24 25 26 27 28 29 30 31 32 / 9 8 7 6 5 4 3 2 1

Texas Tech University Press
Box 41037
Lubbock, Texas 79409-1037 USA
800.832.4042
ttup@ttu.edu
www.ttupress.org

For Ingrid, Bob, Cary, and Katherine. And for my teachers, students, and fellow scholars, past, present, and future.

# Contents

# Acknowledgments

This book owes its existence to the brilliance and generosity of so many. Hsuan Hsu deserves more credit than I can possibly give, as do Elizabeth Freeman and Mark Jerng. Their models of scholarly rigor and intellectual risk-taking are imprinted on every page of this book; any instances of laxity or timidity are mine alone. Hsuan in particular invested a heroic amount of time and effort in reading drafts and pointing me in productive directions. I'd like to think that in my as yet slim interactions with graduate students at Valdosta State University, I've been able to practice a fraction of the acuity and care that Hsuan lavished upon me. Lisa Tatonetti, Bill Handley, and Susan Bernardin have also been integral to my scholarly development. This book owes a great deal to them as well. Travis Snyder, my editor at Texas Tech University Press, saw potential in my work years ago. His guidance and encouragement made this book possible and rendered it much smarter and more coherent. The rest of the team at TTUP have been helpful and gracious throughout the process. Christie Perlmutter deserves special recognition for her expert copyediting. Peer reviewers for TTUP provided feedback that truly transformed the book's arguments and the overall story that it tells. I cannot thank them enough for their astute recommendations.

I'm exceedingly grateful for the intellectual communities that have welcomed me in over the years. My time in graduate school at UC Davis demonstrated just how sustaining intellectual camaraderie can be. I owe thanks to more people than I can name here. Molly Ball, Mike Clearwater, Matt Franks, Danny Grace, Will Hughes, Sawyer Kemp,

## ACKNOWLEDGMENTS

John Mac Kilgore, Maria Kuznetsova, Jeremy Miller, Josef Nguyen, Bonnie Roy, Damien Schlarb, Danielle Shaw, and Bryan Yazell deserve special recognition. My relationships with them have been among the great pleasures of my life. The College of Idaho provided a uniquely intimate space for my scholarship and teaching. My profound gratitude for the guidance of Dali Islam, Steve Maughan, Diane Raptosh, and Sue Schaper during my one year at the C of I. Rachel Miller, Stelios Panageotou, and Nick Underwood provided much-needed, and much-appreciated, friendship and guidance. I miss spending time with Nick, Rachel, and Stelios and wish we could have had more than just the one year together. Colleagues at my new institution, Valdosta State University, provided the support and encouragement necessary to complete this book. Adam Wood, head of the English Department at VSU, provided sage counsel in key moments. The scholarly, artistic, and pedagogical commitment, not to mention the friendship, of Eric Blix, Li-Mei Chen, Kendric Coleman, Ubaraj Katawal, Jane Kinney, Emma Kostopolus, Theresa Thompson, and Marty Williams have buoyed me during my time at VSU. The intellectual curiosity of my students at all these institutions made this a better book.

Countless audience members at the annual Western Literature Association Conference offered incisive feedback on work that eventually ended up in this book. I could not ask for a more vibrant space of exchange and collaboration. Tom Lynch, former editor of *Western American Literature*, was vital as I developed ideas that eventually turned into parts of this book. My thanks to Geoffrey Bateman, and to Krista Comer, both of whom I had the pleasure to work with as part of special issues of *WAL*. Audiences at the Rocky Mountain Modern Language Association Conference, Pacific Ancient and Modern Language Association Conference, and The American Short Story: New Horizons Conference hosted by the Obama Institute for Transnational American Studies also provided probing and deeply appreciated feedback.

Friends and family have been by my side throughout. Brett Abraham has been there for me for the majority of my life. Dana Arter and Joel Rapaport always have something flattering to say about me as a scholar, teacher, and person. I'm not convinced that they're right, but I can say that their company and conversation have been a constant source of joy and enrichment. My mom's support for my career has been unwavering, even as I've had to move far away from her to continue it. My dad could not be more proud of me; as a former academic, he understands the rigors and joys of what we do and just how important our work is. Cary, my brother, has always been eager to celebrate even my smallest of accomplishments. My partner, Katherine, has seen the highs and lows of my scholarly and pedagogical career; she's kept me going when I've felt ready to give up, and I can't thank her enough for that. Aunt, Nana, Opa, Iepoh, and Natasha have cheered me on every step of the way. I am lucky to be surrounded by friends and family who bring art, intelligence, joy, love, and wit into my life every day.

A course release from the VSU Provost's Office allowed me to focus more of my energy on completing this book, for which I am grateful. Material from chapter 1 appeared in an earlier version in "Heterochronic West: Temporal Multiplicity in Bret Harte's Regional Writing," in *Western American Literature* 51, no. 2 (Summer 2016); I thank the editors and the University of Nebraska Press for permission to reprint. Material from chapter 3 appeared in an earlier version in Ryan Wander, "The End(s) of Regeneration: Naturalist Frontier Chronotopes and the Time of US Settler Colonial Biopolitics," in *Settler Colonial Studies* 11, no. 1 (January 2, 2021); I thank the editors and Taylor & Francis, Ltd. for permission to reprint.

# Settler Tenses

# INTRODUCTION

# Queer Chronotopes of the American West

In his "Transcendental Aesthetics" (one of the main sections of his *Critique of Pure Reason*) Kant defines space and time as indispensable forms of any cognition, beginning with elementary perceptions and representations. Here we employ the Kantian evaluation of the importance of these forms in the cognitive process, but differ from Kant in taking them not as "transcendental" but as forms of the most immediate reality.

—Mikhail Bakhtin, "Forms of Time and of the Chronotope in the Novel"

[M]odern sexuality was not a product of settler colonialism, as if it came into being in the United States after settlement. Rather, modern sexuality became a method to produce settler colonialism, and settler subjects, by facilitating ongoing conquest and naturalizing its effects.

—Scott Morgensen, *Spaces between Us*

This book argues that a body of late nineteenth and early twentieth-century white male-authored texts about the frontier, by authors Bret Harte, Edward L. Wheeler,[1] Frank Norris, Jack London, Owen Wister, and Zane Grey, thematically and formally aligned queer subjectivities and bodies with the imperatives of US settler colonialism. As a field, queer studies has demonstrated the profound intellectual and political possibilities that proceed out of an

(Frances Palmer, *Across the Continent.* "*Westward the Course of Empire Takes Its Way,*" Collections: Currier & Ives Prints)

understanding of *queer* as a term that includes but is also much more than same-sex acts and desires. Queer studies has also demonstrated that *time* is an aspect of individual and social experience through which collectivities take shape in harmony with and in opposition to (middle-class) heteronormative imperatives of home, family, and (re) production. This book seeks to demonstrate that the literary narratives discussed in its pages produce (part of) the time and space of US settler colonialism, the very bedrock of settler collectivity, and that these narratives do so queerly.

In 1868, Currier and Ives, the self-proclaimed "Grand Central Depot for Cheap and Popular Prints" and purveyor of "colored engravings for the people," released a lithograph that looked forward to the imminent connection of the Atlantic and Pacific via the First Transcontinental Railroad (see figure).[2] The lithograph is the work of English-born artist Frances "Fanny" Palmer, who employs familiar frontier and settler colonial tropes of open space, providential futurity, and Native American disappearance to visually narrate the US's "manifest destiny." Palmer's lithograph, *Across the Continent.* "*Westward the Course of Empire Takes*

*Its Way,"* is composed around a set of oppositions: Native Americans versus settlers, past versus future, wilderness versus civilization. Within the lithograph's artistic chronotope, these oppositions point to an artistic merging of western North American space with the historical unfolding of US settler civilization. The open-endedness implied in the railroad's disappearance into the horizon situates viewers in the time and space of continual conquest. We might even read this endless horizon as a prescient gesture toward the burgeoning of overseas imperialism in the Pacific at the turn of the twentieth century; from the perspective of our present, little imagination is required to envision Palmer's train leading the US to the Pacific and into the Spanish-American War of 1898. Patrick Wolfe famously wrote that settler colonialism is "a structure not an event"; Palmer's lithograph visualizes this temporality of settler colonial "structure" by imagining the unending (re)production of civilization in erstwhile wilderness.[3]

In an essay titled "The *Bildungsroman* and Its Significance in the History of Realism," Mikhail Bakhtin theorized the relationship between the artistic visualization of temporality and the intentions of historical actors. He wrote of a "historical time" that is perceptible in art, technology, and human social organization. In these "visible vestiges of man's creativity, traces of his hands and his mind," wrote Bakhtin, "The artist perceives . . . the most complex designs of people, generations, epochs, nations, and social and class groups."[4] In her representation of the US's advance into western frontier space(s), Palmer had perceived what must have seemed, for proponents and opponents of expansionism alike, to be the US's ongoing historical design: to turn historical uncertainty into future inevitability. But inevitability isn't the same as linearity. Palmer's arrow-straight railroad evacuates the drama and messiness of the settler empire building that would continue to unfold in the wake of transcontinental connection. Ironically, it's in the writing of white male authors often associated with the linear teleologies of evolution, heteronormativity, History, and nationalism that the circuitousness of settlement and the queer time of settler colonialism come to the fore.

Before proceeding any further, I want to briefly outline what this book is and what this book does. *Settler Tenses* coheres around a tracing and analysis of masculinist chronotopes of late nineteenth and early twentieth-century literatures of the American West. Matters of sexuality and queerness, indigeneity and race, sociality and collectivity, and nation and nationalism are integral to this book, and concern with the artistic and phenomenological arrangement of time and space provides a connecting thread across all the analyses that this book undertakes. Another, more controversial link between these analyses is the demographic makeup of the authors under consideration: they are all white men, with the exception of Ann S. Stephens, the white female author of *Malaeska: The Indian Wife of the White Hunter* (1839), and barring the possibility that one or more of the dime novels discussed in this book were written in whole or in part by non-white and/or non-male authors. This recentering of white male voices in a scholarly book published around the end of the first quarter of the twenty-first century presents distinct risks and, I think, the possibility of distinct rewards. As a mixed-race, Asian American settler of color scholar, I am well aware of the irony of my writing a book about the white male voices that for so long have dominated the conversation from the comfort of their large, stable chairs at the literary historical table. A project like the current volume can easily appear, to borrow a concept from Frank B. Wilderson III, to be a form of Asian American junior partnership, an act of subjugated complicity in white supremacist settler colonialism.[5] I would charge myself with such complicity were this a different kind of book, written in a different spirit, engaged in a different mode of analysis. But this is a book that seeks to articulate, through the analytics and claims that I will lay out just below, how white male authors working in prominent literary genres of the late nineteenth and early twentieth centuries created a set of characters and narratives that produced US settler colonialism as a deeply *queer* territorial, discursive, and *temporal* project.

This book's archive corresponds roughly to the postbellum, 1865 to 1914 period that continues to shape the study and teaching of American literature in spite of ongoing efforts to reshape scholarship and syllabi beyond traditional periodizations. The story that this book tells about this period aims at a literary historical intervention as well as interventions in the theory and history of settler colonialism and gender and sexuality in the US. My interventions in the theory and history of settler colonialism and gender and sexuality in the US follow from my literary historical claim. That literary historical claim, in brief, is that a body of white male-authored texts from the age of realism and naturalism thematically and formally aligned queer subjectivities and bodies with the imperatives of US settler colonialism.

This alignment unfolded in literary narrative as a suturing of queer temporalities to the time and space of the nation. I am compelled to stress here that there are limits to this literary historical claim given the relative narrowness of this book's archive, composed of works by Bret Harte, Edward L. Wheeler, Frank Norris, Jack London, Owen Wister, and Zane Grey. A more comprehensive or differently-defined archive—for example, one that included the work of minority and female authors such as Sutton Griggs and Sui Sin Far—would give us a fuller and richer account of the ways in which US literature of the postbellum period participated in the making (and potential unmaking) of settler colonial hegemony. This volume's aims are more modest. It seeks to elucidate how authors and works laden with power and authority within the symbolic and material economies of white supremacist heteropatriarchy used queer affects and temporalities to write settler colonialism as a project of queer incorporation.

This book assembles an archive of works that to varying degrees have been marked and marketed by their authors, publishers, critics, and scholars as expressions of hegemonic racial, gender, and sexual identities and sensibilities. The point is not to recenter these voices so as to give them another chance to dominate the conversation. Nor is the point to articulate questionable notions of these writers' and texts' "representativeness"—Victoria Lamont's *Westerns: A Women's History* (2016), for instance, has shown that across much of the period that this book covers, women writers were involved in, and indeed central to, the making of the Western as a genre and literary and popular culture more broadly.[6] *Settler Tenses* recenters the work of Harte, Wheeler, Norris, London, Wister, and Grey because there is a striking consistency to the ways these white male settler authors staged frontier spaces as sites for the suturing of queer temporalities to the time and space of the nation.

If the use of the term *queer* to describe postbellum subjectivities and bodies seems anachronistic, that is because it is. This book uses the term to bring to the surface a host of subjective and bodily orientations whose functions vis-à-vis settler nationalism only become legible through the analytic of queerness and the analytical and conceptual tools of the queer studies work of the last three or so decades. In other words, in calling these subjective and bodily orientations queer this book is not making a claim about how its archive's literary characters and narratives would have been understood in their moment of production and initial reception. I am instead arguing that we can describe anew the relation between text and context in the postbellum period if we mobilize the analytics of queer studies, a field whose methods do not require that its objects of analysis fit into ontological categories such as the late nineteenth-century invention known as the "homosexual."[7] The interventions in the theory and history of settler colonialism and gender and sexuality in the US that follow from this literary historical claim concern the importance and periodization of queer affects, sensations, and thoughts—what this book refers to at points as queer subjective and bodily orientations—in relation to the all-encompassing historical and social formation captured in abstract form in the phrase "settler colonialism." At this level, *Settler Tenses* argues that queerness—as affects, sensations, thoughts, or, to capture it in a word, as *orientations*—was absolutely central to the project of US settler colonialism as it proceeded in the late nineteenth and early twentieth centuries. This contention in turn re-periodizes the compatibility of queerness and nationalism as a phenomenon with a history that stretches quite a bit further back in time than the post-1965, post–Civil Rights era.[8]

To make these claims, *Settler Tenses* examines late nineteenth and early twentieth-century literary texts that engage what Hsuan Hsu calls the "culturally valorized chronotope" of the frontier, a chronotope that usually features "open space, linear progression, and a regeneration of national ideals."[9] Like Bakhtin, who draws our attention to chronotopic contestation by noting the artist's perception of "the most complex designs of . . . *social and class groups*," Hsu "highlight[s] the racial specificity of chronotopic experience" and divergent experiences of the same space.[10] Bakhtin and Hsu's emphasis on how chronotopic analysis highlights the varying and often contentious "designs" of different social groups informs the readings in this book—indeed, it is nearly impossible to do otherwise given the class differences between the target audiences of, for example, Bret Harte's genteel regional writing and Edward L. Wheeler's working class–oriented dime novels. This book is also impelled, though, by my sense of the profound similarities between the chronotopes of these texts and how those similarities can enrich our understanding of how and why the frontier was (and arguably remains) central to US cultural imaginings of hegemonic and generally quite toxic forms of whiteness and masculinity. The key to a fuller and richer understanding of the death grip with which the white frontiersman held (again, arguably still holds) US culture is to recognize that one of the figure's key elaborations—namely, his transformation into the cattle range cowboy (and cognate figures suited to other kinds of frontier spaces) in the late nineteenth and early twentieth centuries—coincided with the crystallization of homosexuality, heterosexuality, and the discursive and institutional ensemble known as "modern sexuality."[11]

This book extends the temporal implications of anthropologist Scott Morgensen's reading of modern sexuality, via Michel Foucault, as the ensemble of discourses and institutions that produce "primitive and civilized gender and sexuality" alongside and against one another and that also define biopolitical relations among subjects and populations.[12] For Foucault, disciplinary and regulatory discourses and institutions work on bodies and populations to render them docile, predictable, and manageable; these discourses and institutions control, maximize, and purify individual bodies and whole populations. But there are always and necessarily resistances within these power relations, as Foucault stresses in *The History of Sexuality, Volume 1*.[13] This play of power and resistance—in other words, this constitution of biopower—is, as Dana Luciano has pointed out, "a *spatiotemporal* phenomenon": bodies and populations are disciplined and regulated in accordance with the (state) imperative to orient these (differentiated) bodies and populations toward optimal temporalities of life, death, and (re)production. Luciano's term for this temporal arrangement of life is *chronobiopolitics*.[14] As Luciano and Morgensen point out, the settler colonial US state of the late nine-teenth and early twentieth centuries orchestrated this temporal optimi-zation along taxonomies of race and indigeneity. Morgensen in particular stresses that disciplinary anatomopolitics and regulatory biopolitics took hold of bodies and populations and shaped individual and collective orientations toward time in ways that tended toward the imperatives of a settler state invested in appropriating and erasing indigeneity as well as optimizing life along racial hierarchies within and beyond North America.[15] Such temporal optimization constitutes a signal feature of a *settler tensing* whereby individuals and populations are managed in the direction of Native genocide, racialized expendability, and white settler ascendance.

The title of this book, *Settler Tenses*, is intended to encapsulate how literature representationally differentiates bodies and populations to pro-duce, reinforce, and modify a settler (bio)politics of time and racialized vitality. In the notion of settler tensing, I wish to bring Morgensen's argu-ment that modern sexuality has functioned as "a method *to produce* set-tler colonialism" to bear on Luciano's account of the nineteenth-century temporalization of the human body in the deployment of sexuality.[16] If, as Luciano discusses, Native Americans were temporalized in the antebellum cultural context as lamentably yet inevitably disappearing in the face of civilization, Morgensen's account of late nineteenth and early twentieth-century efforts to impose modern sexual discipline and regulation on Native Americans suggests a significant measure of anxious uncertainty about Indigenous peoples' presumed disappearance. This was a period, Morgensen writes, of "tense negotiations of active and contested settlement."[17] Native disappearance was a question rather than an easy or romantic assertion, and the settler production of differ-entially temporalized bodies and populations functioned as a means to discursively and materially effect the Native disappearance and settler futurity that were not yet entirely settled.

In this not yet entirely settled context and beyond, what Foucault names "bodies and pleasures"—what he at one point refers to more capa-ciously as "bodies and their materiality, their forces, energies, sensations, and pleasures"—serve as privileged sites for potentially revolutionary resistance to the grips of power.[18] Crucial here is the difference between potentiality and actuality, between resistance that leads to profound social transformation and resistance that gets folded back into and consolidates power. Bodily orientations toward time—not just in "pleasures" but also in all the modes of embodiment and orchestrations of the body that harness its "forces," its political and economic productivity—are thus key nodes through which disciplinary and regulatory mechanisms operate and resistance to the US settler state's forms of temporal optimization might be imagined and embodied. From within the power relations of the anatomo- and biopolitics of the US settler state, how might the body's "forces" be imaginatively channeled into resistance to a settler colonial hegemony that is premised on Native American disappearance and racialized domination, and what is the ultimate effect of that resistance?

*Settler Tenses* argues that the group of white male settler authors named above, who wrote Westerns, literary naturalism, and regional writing, constructed chronotopes that amount to queerly settler colonial responses to the temporal imperatives of the US settler state. These queerly settler colonial chronotopes bend the modern sexual logics of US settler colonialism but ultimately coopt temporal queerness to forecast futures of settler colonial hegemony: these chronotopes contain, for example, racialized characters who further the appropriation of Indigenous lands and genocide of Indigenous peoples as well as white cowboys who adopt sexual primitivity in order to transcend it. Writing in a critical late nineteenth and early twentieth-century period of US settler colonial consolidation, these white male authors coopted temporalities assigned to gendered, racial, and sexual others to tell stories in which not one but many timelines pointed to essentially the same outcome: the ascendance and permanence of a normatively white settler society. Put another way, US settler hegemony since at least the late nineteenth century has been about incorporating the queer timelines and orientations of settler heteropatriarchy's abjected others. It has been about protecting the turf on which cisgender heteronormative white men reign by claiming for these men the very orientations to time, history, and futurity that subject some bodies to violence and relegate some populations to extinction.

A few words about the relationship between settler tensing and literary form should clarify the theoretical and methodological framework that led to the claims above about the literary colonization of time. At first blush, literary form may seem to bear attenuated connections to the disciplinary and regulatory (re)channeling of the body's forces that Foucault lays out in, among other places, *Discipline and Punish*, *The History of Sexuality, Volume 1*, and *Society Must Be Defended*.[19] We have to turn to Bakhtin's "Forms of Time and of the Chronotope in the Novel" to understand how literary form addresses the anatomo- and biopolitics of the US settler state. A narrow reading of Bakhtin's well-known reformulation of Kant's "transcendental" categories of time and space as instead "forms of the most immediate reality" would largely leave alone the question of (re)directing the body's forces.[20] But Bakhtin's theorizing of artistic representation is emphatically about the body and the ways bodies inhabit and orient themselves toward time and space. In "Forms," Bakhtin is arguably referring quite literally to human bodies when he writes that in the literary artistic chronotope, "Time, as it were, thickens, takes on *flesh*."[21] Literature's "thickening," or enfleshment, of temporality in the bodies of characters offers concrete expressions of orientations toward time and space that are at once embodied and phenomenological. Characters in a literary text are embodied manifestations of historically and ideologically specific apprehensions of time and space, translating and condensing phenomenological experience into imagined bodies that register and respond to power-laden orchestrations of historical bodies. In the context of the late nineteenth and early twentieth-century literary texts that this book considers, such imagined bodies variously uphold settler colonial hegemony.

Like Frances Palmer, who offered up an artistic chronotope in which western frontier space and endless conquest merged into "one carefully thought-out, concrete whole," the authors considered in this book, all of whom wrote during a late nineteenth and early twentieth-century period of transcontinental settlement and continuing settler imperial expansion, offered concrete literary wholes that (re)produced historical reality in ways responsive to the era's settler colonialism.[22] These responses were often not as clear-cut as Palmer's representation of boundless conquest. To elucidate the complexities, the resistances and complicities, of these chronotopes, I work at the intersections of genre studies, sexuality studies, and settler colonial studies throughout the discussions in this book. *Settler Tenses* puts US literary studies scholarship on the articulation of temporalities in nineteenth and twentieth-century literature and culture—the strategic as well as the ostensibly accidental joinings of divergent relationships to time as they assume form in the disciplining of bodies and the movements of narrative—into conversation with scholarly and theoretical accounts of the sexual production of (US) settler colonialism.[23]

As practiced by Harte, Wheeler, Norris, London, Wister, and Grey, prominent postbellum genres for narrating frontier spaces—Westerns, literary naturalism, and regional writing—registered and responded to modern sexuality's production of US settler colonialism by offering queer chronotopes. These queer chronotopes variously reproduce and reconceive the spatiotemporal production of conquest, and they all operate in a queerly settler colonial mode that does not provide an alternative to, but rather a reconfiguration of, settler hegemony. The texts that this book examines contain queer characters—namely, characters that are queer insofar as they flout or merely appear to flout the sexual, social, and economic logics that underwrite US conquest—and throughout my discussions I stress the notion that these characters, the settings that they inhabit, and the narratives through which they move condense phenomenological experience into bodily, spatial, and narrative form.

The rest of this introduction further develops a theoretical framework for understanding the mutually informing exchanges between literature and modern sexuality's production of (US) settler colonialism. It does so, first, by considering how late nineteenth and early twentieth-century white male settler authors penned characters and narratives that stand in various positions of proximity to the sexual norms that produce and sustain (US) settler colonialism. I then elaborate on the concept of the chronotope. I trace the concept's implications for conquest, nationalism, and national belonging and offer a model for reading the literary chronotope's "thickening" of orientations toward time and space within and against the sexual production of (US) settler colonialism.

This introductory chapter closes by sketching out the contours of—the competition as well as the collaboration and agreement among—the chronotopes of masculinist frontier narratives. In these chronotopes we can observe the dynamic (re)production of settler colonial subjectivities. We also witness the making of resistant alternatives in which bodies, temporalities, and spaces *appear* to exceed the forms of racialized temporal management constitutive of the temporal-biopolitical formation that this book calls settler tensing.

## The Sexual Production of Conquest

Let's return to the 1868 Frances Palmer lithograph, *Across the Continent*, with which we began this chapter. In her pictorial representation of the time and space of continual conquest, Palmer highlights connections between US settler colonialism and imperialism and discourses and institutions of sexuality that have been analyzed powerfully in the last two and a half decades by scholars working in American, Indigenous, queer, and settler colonial studies. These scholars have demonstrated the ways in which modern sexuality's construction of gender and metonymizing of ostensibly "non-sexual" attributes aids—and produces—conquest. American studies scholars have shown that nineteenth-century domesticity, long regarded in terms of separate gendered spheres and cut off from its nationalist and imperial context, was instrumental for US nationalism and imperialism in North America and abroad.[24] Queer studies scholars' critiques of "homonormativity" and "homonationalism" have traced privileged queer populations' complicity in the production and maintenance of contemporary neoliberal US Empire.[25] Scholars working at the intersections of Indigenous, queer, and settler colonial studies have demonstrated that the queering of Native Americans has aided in their dispossession and that queer settler subjects' appropriations of indigeneity in their appeals for national inclusion help to keep the structure of settler colonialism in place.[26] In limning the articulation(s) of modern sexuality with US nationalism and various forms of conquest, these scholars suggest that the (re)production of norms and the distribution of subjects and populations around these norms are key to both the (re) production and the potential destabilization of US settler colonialism.

This biopolitical sorting of subjects and populations through modern sexual norms and in the service of US conquest is dramatized in Palmer's lithograph as a form of settler tensing. In the foreground is a group of white men chopping wood. Moving to the right, we see children running around in front of a schoolhouse. As we move our gaze toward the center of the composition two small figures come into view: a white woman and, in her arms, a baby. This dyadic avatar of sentimental culture is situated at the door of a log building whose size suggests its suitability for the domestic life of a (bourgeois) nuclear family. Near the lower right-hand corner of the lithograph sit a pair of Native people on horses, situated behind US settler civilization's advance. Unlike the men chopping wood and the woman holding the baby, all of whose actions point to the gender differentiation that indicates civilization and whiteness, these imagined Natives embody a racializing lack of gender differentiation.[27] As these Native figures stand on the wrong side of US civilization's advance, opposite the white women and men who appear to be well-versed in the proper gender roles of their settler society, we as viewers are invited to understand the movement from savagery to civilization as a movement from gender-undifferentiated empty space to gender-differentiated settled space. We are invited, in other words, to assume a simultaneously temporal and spatial orientation that underwrites the sexual production of conquest. The temporalization of Native and white populations is artistically rendered as bodies, in the human subjects of the composition, and as landscape. Palmer's lithograph stamps the spatiality of these Native and white subjects and the landscape they occupy with gendered temporalities of conquest.

Bret Harte, whose California fiction is taken up in chapter 1, published a short story titled "Notes by Flood and Field" in 1862, six years before the release of Palmer's lithograph. Harte's short story tells a more complicated story about the sexual production of conquest, one that might sound more fitting for theories of the proliferation of queernesses in the twentieth and twenty-first centuries than for the pre-Wilde trials moment of the mid-nineteenth. The first-person narrator of "Notes," a US surveyor, tells of two trips to California's Sacramento Valley. The first is "to correct the exterior boundaries of township lines," with the questionable outcome of dispossessing a Spaniard named Altascar of quite a bit of land. The second trip occurs during the historic flood of 1861–62, when the narrator, "obeying some indefinite yearning," returns to the valley he had found so monotonous just three months before.[28] The implication, as Harte biographer Axel Nissen has noted, is that the narrator has returned to look for George Tryan, son of Joseph Tryan, the latter of whom benefited from the "correct[ion]" of property boundaries.[29] The surveyor-narrator seems to have more than just a friendly interest in George; rather, the narrator feels something of an erotic attraction to him, at one point going "to bed with a pleasant impression of [George's] handsome face and tranquil figure soothing me to sleep." Another character, an unnamed engineer, speaks of George's brother Wise as "a sweet one" and then proceeds to "smile at some luscious remembrance."[30] These glancing intimations of same-sex ardor allow us to see what Peter Coviello has memorably described as "something of the shape sex could take—errant, unlikely, not always legible *as* sex—before it quite became the sexuality we now know, or think we know."[31]

Harte's nineteenth-century California, full of such errancies and unlikelinesses, seems far removed from Palmer's scene of settler imperial civilization building. Harte's California, as chapter 1 will elaborate on, is instead full of queer (white) men. But there is a strange resonance between Palmer's composition and Harte's narrative. "Notes" portrays (white) men who are queer vis-à-vis what Jonathan Katz has described as "the late-nineteenth-century hypothesis of a universal male-female pleasure-sex [that] still represents to most of us a timeless, living truth."[32] Scholarship that troubles the assumption of queerness as an always-already transgressive mode of being, a mode of being that is necessarily excluded from the nation and exempt from nationalism, imperialism, and settler colonialism, has traced the ways in which privileged queer subjects and populations participate in the biopolitical production and regulation of perverse queernesses.[33] Such regulation often takes the form of death and even extermination for perverse subjects and populations such as Muslim terrorists (in neoliberal US Empire's war on terror) and Native Americans (under ongoing US settler colonialism). In

Harte's mid-nineteenth-century context, just prior to a late nineteenth and early twentieth-century period of "tense negotiations of active and contested [US] settlement,"[34] "Notes" evokes the US's biopolitical project of Native genocide and replacement in its references to the "indigeneity" of white settler George Tryan and his family. Upon encountering the Tryan house, the narrator says, "My second impression was that it had *grown out of the soil*, like some monstrous vegetable, its dreary proportions were so in keeping with the vast prospect." At the end of the story comes the epigraph to this section, the narrator's description of George Tryan's grave: "He was buried in the Indian mound,—the single spot of strange perennial greenness which the poor aborigines had raised above the dusty plain. A little slab of sandstone with the initials 'G. T.' is his monument, and one of the bearings of the initial corner of the new survey of the 'Espíritu Santo Rancho.'"[35] Such images of the Tryan house and George's grave point to the naturalization of (white) settler presence. They allegorize Wolfe's notion that "The primary object of settler-colonization is the land itself . . . settler-colonization is at base a winner-take-all project whose dominant feature is not exploitation but replacement."[36]

Yet the "replacement" allegorized in "Notes" is a bit eccentric, at least alongside Palmer's lithograph. Palmer's piece visualizes endless conquest, while Harte's narrative portrays a devastating flood that ravages Sacramento, destroys the Tryan house, and gives an ironic cast to Joseph Tryan's pronouncements of white "'Merrikins'" divinely ordained, preeminent right to the bounty of the Sacramento Valley.[37] Palmer emphasizes normative modes of (white) embodiment, while Harte fills his narrative with those oblique suggestions of same-sex desire. Palmer envisions endless development and fecundity upon the "empty" space—the "blank" page—of North America; Harte instead brings the historical Sacramento Valley flood of 1861–62 into his narrative, and it leads to George's death. Whereas Palmer works within the binary whites versus Natives paradigm that New Western historian Patricia Limerick has critiqued for its historical inaccuracy, Harte brings the Spaniard Altascar and the racial epithet "greaser" into the field of representation.[38] "Notes" offers a complicated view of white settlement that George's tombstone, situated along the border between white- and Spanish-owned settlements, complicates further. If we read George's tombstone as a symbol of settler colonial replacement, a number of questions arise about this short story's relationship to settler tensing and the biopolitics of US settler colonialism more broadly. Is George part of a prehistory that leads up to the contemporary queernesses that serve the US's biopolitical imperatives in the present? Does "Notes" dramatize the (pre)production of a privileged (white) queerness that makes the US look progressive while also maintaining settler colonial hegemony? How did these alternative queernesses impact the formation of subjects, populations, and subjectivities in the late nineteenth and early twentieth centuries, a period of contested settlement and overseas imperialism? These are the kinds of questions that this book seeks to answer in the more detailed analyses offered in subsequent chapters. In order to get to those analyses, the next section of this introduction dilates on Bakhtin's concept of the literary chronotope, the textual space in which a historical subject's apprehension of time and space is reflected *and* produced. The chronotope furnishes a basis for theorizing the formation of subjectivities around the sexual norms that produce (US) settler colonialism.

## Settler Spatiotemporal Subjectivities

> For Bakhtin, genres not only offer models of change, they are also central to how change actually happens. Literary genres are themselves special forms of speech genres, which are in turn closely linked to forms of living. We have already noted that for Bakhtin genres are neither sets of rules nor accumulations of forms and themes but are rather ways of seeing the world. In daily life, behavior is shaped by the set of values, presumed purposes, and possible actions carried by the genres we learn from our earliest days. In acquiring language, we learn genres and therefore learn ways of shaping and evaluating experience.
>
> Gary Saul Morson, "Bakhtin, Genres, and Temporality"

In their introduction to the 2017 essay collection *Critique and Postcritique*, Elizabeth Anker and Rita Felski note that we critics, scholars, and theorists are in a moment of self-examination in which "the intellectual or political payoff of interrogating, demystifying, and defamiliarizing is no longer quite so self-evident."[39] Here "interrogating" and "demystifying" point us in the direction of Marxian and psychoanalytic modes of analysis, whose elaborations in the vein of Althusser's "imaginary relationship" of ideology and Lacan's "Symbolic Order" suggest the profound difficulty of thinking and enacting any sort of meaningful political or social change.[40] The third term, "defamiliarizing," points us toward the Russian Formalists, in particular Viktor Shklovsky, and, less directly, toward Mikhail Bakhtin. Among other projects and contributions, Shklovsky and other Russian Formalists sought to develop a method for analyzing literature *qua* literature, as opposed to models of interpretation that analyze literature in relation to historical or biographical background or "everyday life" in general.[41] Such an approach, premised on what Bakhtin saw as a shared "desire" of "life and art" to remain separate from one another, seems to hold scant potential for political payoff in our contemporary world. Although he was significantly influenced by the Russian Formalists, Bakhtin did not view this tendency toward a stark life/art division as a rule of art and artistic creation; rather, this tendency toward division was something like a mutual path of least resistance for the acts of creating art and living life.[42] Accordingly, he developed theories of "life and art" that proffered a rather different understanding of the relationship between the two. "[U]ninterrupted exchange goes on between [life and art]," Bakhtin wrote in 1973, "similar to the uninterrupted exchange of matter between living organisms and the environment that surrounds them."[43] This ecological metaphor arguably captures the spirit of Marxian and psychoanalytic (and Marxian-psychoanalytic) models as well. Indeed, each of these latter models is concerned with the relation between text and some sort of context, relationships that are understood in terms of one form or another of strong or weak economic and/or psychic determination. But Bakhtin's work is where the relation between text and context, art and life, is weighted toward the kind of concrete immediacy and dynamic change that his biological imagery suggests.

Bakhtin, in "Forms of Time and of the Chronotope in the Novel" and elsewhere, furnishes understandings of literature and literary genre that emphasize forms of agency that are more or less barred from consideration from within "the diagnostic gaze of symptomatic reading."[44] In the same year that Bakhtin penned that ecological metaphor in the "Concluding Remarks" section of "Forms," Raymond Williams published a critique of Marxian theoretical development in *New Left Review*. Taking to task what he saw as the ossification and over-abstraction that later thinkers had imposed on Marx's base and superstructure model, Williams's "Base and Superstructure in Marxist Cultural Theory" sought to shift analysis toward "cultural practices" and "the specific activities of men in real social and economic relationships." By substituting dynamic "practices" and "activities" for the by then monolithic categories of base and superstructure, Williams theorized cultural practices including the production and reception of art and literature as central components in both maintaining the status quo and driving social change.[45] As Gary Saul Morson suggests in the epigraph to this section, Bakhtin held a similar view of literature; in Morson's words, "For Bakhtin, genres not only offer models of change, they are also central to how change actually happens."[46] For traditional Marxian thought, epochal changes like capitalism's succession in the wake of feudalism's demise are the only truly consequential type of transformation. Bakhtin's and Williams's models of change scale our attention down to the everyday, to the social and subjective changes that occur within epochs, without losing sight of the broader sweep of history.

In scaling our attention down to everyday practices and relations while maintaining a keen sense of diachronic change, Bakhtin and Williams connect the historical production and reception of literature to what Morgensen, citing Foucault and Judith Butler, calls the "repetition and potential destabilization" of settler colonial norms.[47] To be clear, this book does not see any significant "potential destabilization" of settler colonial norms in its archive but rather dynamic "repetition" of settler colonial norms in ways that are not always easily discernible as such. In literature, these easily missed forms of hegemony become visible chronotopically, in "thickenings" of time that imaginatively embody (literally in bodies) settler phenomenological experiences.

Bakhtin's concept of the chronotope allows us to trace ways in which literary texts are formally connected to US settler colonial imperatives and to the dynamic (re)production of settler colonial hegemony. The chronotope, Bakhtin explains, names "the intrinsic connectedness of temporal and spatial relationships that are artistically expressed in literature."[48] The chronotopes in the literature examined in this book contain historical, interconnected understandings of time and space that necessarily register and respond to settler colonialism's organization of phenomenological experience. Working within and against the phenomenological framework(s) that US settler colonialism makes available, these chronotopes articulate the possibilities and limits of human action and of historical and social reality.[49] Bakhtin very deliberately specifies, in his "Concluding Remarks" section of "Forms," that the relationship between reality and chronotopic representation is one of mutually informing exchange. The literary texts that *Settler Tenses* considers assimilate historical worldviews that bear necessary constraining and enabling relations to US settler colonialism; these texts appropriate and reflect aspects of settler colonial reality. But this appropriation and reflection of reality is not a process of one-way, mechanistic reproduction. These literary representations speak back to the settler colonial reality with which they do not fully coincide by articulating novel understandings of self and world.[50] It is in this process of subject and world (re)production that these chronotopes dynamically uphold settler colonial norms and power relations.

Insofar as these chronotopes dynamically inform phenomenological experiences of the possibilities and limits of self and world, the texts that *Settler Tenses* examines perpetuate US settler colonial subjectivity. Elaborating on Wolfe's theorization of settler colonialism as "a structure not an event," Morgensen argues that the production of US settler colonialism in the late nineteenth and early twentieth centuries "arose . . . in any promotions of sexual modernity within a settler colonial society defined by the seeming finality of Native disappearance and replacement."[51] Morgensen's formulation suggests that in this period settler colonialism was produced, not only by placing Natives in a perpetual state of exception but also by the structuring of history and social reality around "teleologies of modernity and civilization"; such teleologies were (and still are) part and parcel of the biopolitical production of settler and

Native subjects of modern sexuality within US settler colonial society.[52] Morgensen's work, in theorizing ways in which non-Native queer subjects contribute to the maintenance of settler colonialism, also suggests that settler subjectivity is not bound to one particular mode of historical heteronormative embodiment or one particular literary "thickening" of time. Instead, settler colonialism is produced by any modes of embodiment and thickenings of time that correspond to subjectivities that are defined within the parameters of biopolitically productive teleologies of modernity and civilization. To apply Jasbir Puar's description of the biopolitics of neoliberal US Empire to the production of settler subjectivities, what matters for US settler colonialism is "not the ability to *reproduce*, but the capacity to *regenerate*" the populational capacities and subjectivities that secure the ongoing process of conquest.[53] In the context of Morgensen's and Puar's work, Bakhtin's concept of the chronotope suggests that many different and even divergent chronotopes contribute to the maintenance of US settler colonialism. Again, I must stress that the theoretical framework I am developing here also opens up the possibility that some chronotopes artistically give flesh to genuinely resistant or even decolonial alternatives to settler colonial subjectivities, but my argument is that the texts in this book's archive do the work of differently and divergently maintaining US settler colonialism.

Analyzing the chronotopic perpetuation of settler colonial subjectivities also allows us to trace imaginings of queerly settler colonial forms of collectivity, or imagined communities, that cohere around reconfigurations of settler hegemony. Similar to "Forms," in "Epic and Novel" Bakhtin theorizes the novel as a genre that is "intimately interwoven" with its present; in the age of the novel's dominance, "novelization" inserts into literature "a living contact with unfinished, still-evolving contemporary reality."[54] "Living contact" also defines Benedict Anderson's and Homi Bhabha's influential theories of nationalism and national narration. Anderson conceived of the nation as an "imagined community" bound together in time and space by the representational conventions of the realist novel and the newspaper. For Anderson, nation and nationalism are reflected and produced in the act of reading these genres.[55] Against Anderson's emphasis on national synthesis, Bhabha described nationalism and national narration as sites of contestation between grand historical narratives and everything that such narratives omit or, at best, add back as Derridean supplements.[56]

Anderson's idealized national synthesis and Bhabha's model of contestation and potential resistances against national totalization are analytically useful for understanding US nationalism in the late nineteenth and early twentieth centuries and in the present. But Anderson's vision of future-oriented national synchrony and Bhabha's model of potential resistances to national forgetting need to be mobilized with a keen sense of the US's ongoing history of settler colonialism.[57] In his analysis of the "imperial dynamic" of "U.S. national policy and identity," Mark Rifkin points out that the imperial mantra of "'manifest destiny' conjures the dream of a potentially limitless projection of American power across continental, hemispheric, and even transoceanic distances . . . a vision of expansion without end."[58] If, as Anderson argued, the nation is imagined as "a solid community moving steadily down (or up) history," for US settlers that subjective experience of nationhood often has been mediated through visions of territorially and temporally limitless hegemony.[59] Morgensen's work suggests that these subjective experiences of nationhood and national belonging also have been informed by a settler colonial logic of "before" and "after": the "before" of Native Americans and sexual primitivity and the "after" of settlers and modern sexuality.[60] The chronotope of Palmer's lithograph *Across the Continent* rather unambiguously (re)produces nationalist subjectivity as settler colonial in the sense that I have just offered in my reading of Morgensen's work and imperial in the sense that Rifkin articulates in his notion of the "limitless" "dream" of manifest destiny. But what most interests me in this book are texts and chronotopes from the late nineteenth and early twentieth centuries that offer alternative reckonings of time and space that nonetheless perpetuate US settler colonial subjectivities and collectivities.

## Chapter Overview

This book's archive spans from 1868 to 1912, from Bret Harte's early postbellum regional writing to Zane Grey's Western *Riders of the Purple*

*Sage*, covering a forty-four-year period split down the middle by the 1890 "closing" of the frontier. Like the choice of an all-white male-authored archive, this 1890 midpoint presents the risk of reifying as transcendently epochal a year in US history whose status is profoundly ideological and motivated. The Superintendent of the US Census declared the frontier closed in 1890 because, as the US Census website puts it, "the western part of the country [had] so many pockets of settled area that a frontier line could no longer be said to exist."[61] But that sense of finality papers over ongoing local dynamics. The US's genocide of California Native Americans, for instance, is traditionally dated from 1846 to 1873 but is perhaps better conceptualized as part of a genocidal and assimilative project that continued into at least the early twentieth century. The so-called Indian Wars, which began in the seventeenth century and are often presented as having concluded with the 1890 Wounded Knee Massacre, also did not truly end until the early twentieth century for historical actors such as the Apaches held prisoner in Oklahoma until 1913.[62] The 1890 census's sense of finality also reduces to a matter of mere presence and number of settlers the complex, imbricated ways in which discourses, institutions, writers, and individuals produced US settlement. This book (re)reads a canon of white male settler writing for its production of settler hegemony through queerness; the 1890 closing of the frontier and Frederick Jackson Turner's 1893 historiographical coronation of the event in "The Significance of the Frontier in American History" represent sexually, socially, and temporally normative historical narratives that in certain ways contradicted, but ultimately complemented, the literary production of settler hegemony through queerness. Straight *and* queer narratives are integral to settler hegemony.

In between Harte's and Grey's writings, *Settler Tenses* takes up late 1870s and early 1880s installments of Edward L. Wheeler's Deadwood Dick dime novel series, turn-of-the-twentieth-century naturalist fiction by Frank Norris and Jack London, and Owen Wister's 1902 Western, *The Virginian*. This archive traces continuities and ruptures in the portrayal of the (national) past, present, and future and the bodies and spaces through which such conceptions of time and historical movement become artistically tangible and thinkable. Prior to the closing of the frontier, Harte's and Wheeler's fiction articulated a series of queer chronotopes that, in a seeming paradox, served US settler colonialism by imagining forms of futurity for Native American and racialized characters. Starting with Jack London's turn-of-the-twentieth-century naturalist fiction, a seeming contradiction reminiscent of Frederick Jackson Turner's elite white male-inflected drama of Americanization in the opening pages of "The Significance of the Frontier in American History"—namely, the contradiction of moving backward into primitivity to move forward into the national future—informs these later texts' projection and naturalization of present and future settler colonial hegemony.[63]

Each of the four chapters of *Settler Tenses* considers a selection of white male-authored texts—two in the final chapter, three in another, and five in each of the other two chapters—whose sustained critical attention and/or popular success suggests a certain kind of representativeness: collectively, these texts amount to a selective but nonetheless significant portion of the canon of white male settler writing in the genres of (western American) regional writing, the dime novel Western, (western American) literary naturalism, and the early twentieth-century literary Western. Chronotopic analysis, as Bakhtin's work suggests, requires that the critic focus on "representative" texts in order to arrive at chronotopic descriptions which, in turn, define those texts as instances of a genre.[64] For the present volume, I rely on the work of critics, scholars, editors, and anthologists who have given pride of place to works like Bret Harte's "The Luck of Roaring Camp" (1868), Edward L. Wheeler's *Deadwood Dick, the Prince of the Road* (1877), Frank Norris's *McTeague* (1899) and Jack London's *The Call of the Wild* (1903), and Owen Wister's *The Virginian* (1902) and Zane Grey's *Riders of the Purple Sage* (1912).[65] I also bring in texts by these authors that recapitulate or complement these texts' production of Native disappearance, racialized expendability, and white ascendance. In chronotopic analysis genres are "ways of seeing the world," to use Gary Saul Morson's formulation.[66] I pursue this mode of analysis as a way of arriving at chronotopic descriptions that specify the implications, for settler subjectivity and settler tensing, of canonical white male writing in each of the four genres with which *Settler Tenses* is concerned.

Chapter 1, "Heterochronic West: Temporal Multiplicity and Queer Futures in Bret Harte's Regional Writing," examines how regionalist narrative form challenges its genteel audience's ability to envision its own ascension alongside the decline of those who are variously queer, Native, and/or racialized. The chapter focuses on five of Harte's short stories about mining camp sociality and heterosexual marriage—"The Luck of Roaring Camp" (1868), "Tennessee's Partner" (1869), "The Idyl of Red Gulch" (1869), "The Iliad of Sandy Bar" (1870), and "An Ingénue of the Sierras" (1893)—in which California's movement from its "premodern" regional past into the "modern" national future is narrated as a process of sexual modernization. Departing from influential scholarly accounts of regional writing's ethnographic production of anachronism, I show how these five short stories use regionalist narrative form's backward glance to imagine queer and racialized futurity.[67] Full of moments that indirectly look forward to the allied dominance of white elites and bourgeois heteronormativity only to shut down the possibility, Harte's texts chronotopically gesture toward settler futures hospitable to queer socialities and racialized groups.

Chapter 2, "Settlement without Settlement: Deadwood Dick Dime Novels and the Queerness of Settler Colonialism," focuses on the working class–oriented Deadwood Dick dime novels. Building on scholarship that reads dime novel seriality as a formal means for critiquing the genteel marriage plot, this chapter considers how the Deadwood Dick dime novels valorize forms of white (working-class) queerness that engage in settler colonialism's drama of Native dispossession, genocide, and replacement by *not* settling.[68] The chapter focuses on three Deadwood Dick dime novels—the inaugural *Deadwood Dick, the Prince of the Road* (1877) as well as *Blonde Bill* (1880) and *Deadwood Dick's Doom* (1881)—in which Dick, Calamity Jane, and their band of outlaws are paradoxically positioned as figures of both queerness and whiteness. These dime novels' chronotope is defined by the abiographical stasis associated with seriality and what Bakhtin calls "adventure-time," which repeatedly keeps these characters away from full participation in bourgeois marital and domestic life, over and over again leaving them unable to transcend sexual "primitivity." In various installments in the

series these characters are rendered queer in that they do not regenerate the (hetero)normativities—what Mark Rifkin describes as "an
ensemble of imperatives that includes family formation, homemaking,
private property-holding, and the allocation of citizenship"—that produce and sustain US settler colonialism and imperialism.[69] Dick, Jane,
and the other outlaws instead perform modes of nonheteronormative
embodiment that reconceive processes of expropriation and expansion
through the negation of bourgeois domesticity and the delinking of
domesticity from the making of home on stolen land. Yet these modes
of embodiment are not demonized and consigned to death—in other
words, they are not biopolitically racialized—because they are marked as
white against the racialized bodies of Mormons and Native Americans.
Seriality and "adventure-time," which are central constituents of the
Deadwood Dick dime novels' chronotope, thus work to produce Dick
and his associates' modes of nonheteronormative white embodiment as
desirable for a (white working-class) audience invested in claiming and
inhabiting whiteness. Settler colonialism, Morgensen writes, is naturalized "whenever subjects are defined by settler desires to possess Native
land, history, or culture."[70] The Deadwood Dick dime novels analyzed
in this chapter (re)direct (reading) subjects toward modes of nonheteronormative (white) embodiment that complement US settler colonial
(hetero)normativities and teleologies.

Chapter 3, "The End(s) of Regeneration: Frank Norris's and Jack
London's Naturalist Frontier Chronotopes," reads Frank Norris's and
Jack London's naturalist portrayals of "post-frontier" frontiers for their
engagement with what Patrick Wolfe refers to as frontier representation's
"performative" role within settler colonialism.[71] Despite its 1890 "closure," the concept of the frontier remained central to the ongoing enact-
ment of US settler colonialism around the turn of the twentieth century,
and it remains so to this day. This chapter considers how Norris's and
London's naturalist aesthetics turn portrayals of white death and Native
and racialized survival on the frontier into rearticulations of the US settler state's biopolitics of white ascendance, racialized death, and Native
genocide. By once again reconsidering the critical tendency to read naturalist frontier fiction as white masculine triumphalism, I trace how five

turn-of-the-twentieth-century texts ranging from Norris's *McTeague* (1899) to Jack London's "To Build a Fire" (1908) mobilize US literary naturalism's evolutionary and typological representational idiom to imagine the survival and ascendance over generations of those marked as Indigenous or racialized. Highlighting the discursive and material importance of a simplified settler/Native binary for the founding and spread of settler colonial regimes, *McTeague*, Norris's "A Memorandum of Sudden Death" (1902), and "To Build a Fire" erase or suppress intra-settler difference in the making of narratives of white settler death that cancel the appropriation and transcendence of (Native) primitivity foundational to settler colonialism.[72] London's "In a Far Country" (1899) and *The Call of the Wild* (1903), on the contrary, call attention to intra-settler difference and ultimately channel white settler death into reconfigurations of intra-settler racial hierarchies. Taken together, these five texts re-naturalize settler temporalities and coopt racialized figures as agents of settler futurity.

Chapter 4, "'Mix with the Whole Thing': Genre Inheritances and Queerly Settler Colonial Community in Owen Wister's *The Virginian* and Zane Grey's *Riders of the Purple Sage*," concludes this book's examination of literary responses to the ambivalences of settler sexuality. The chapter offers readings of the genre inheritances of two canonical Westerns, Owen Wister's *The Virginian* (1902) and Zane Grey's *Riders of the Purple Sage* (1912). Wister's and Grey's texts draw on and reconfigure genre conventions associated with the three types of writing examined in chapters 1 through 3, drawing in particular on regional writing and romance (Harte and Wheeler, respectively), which have been theorized as genres that work to define the nature and boundaries of the social order.[73] Wister and Grey use the conventions of existing literary genres to neutralize, incorporate, and transcend sexually "primitive" threats to an imagined heteronormative future for the US settler nation. Elaborating on New Historicist–inflected readings of these Westerns' prurient containment of homoerotic desire and Mormon sexuality, this chapter examines how Wister and Grey portray the contradictory temporalities of settler sexuality as the queer center of US settler colonialism.

The analyses that this book offers across its chapters read queerness against its (ever-vanishing) associations with transgression and white male-authored frontier narratives against their connections to forms of power and privilege traditionally glossed as heteronormative.[74] *Settler Tenses* tells a story that brings to literary form and its re-presentation of time and space the incisively queer critical energy that scholars have brought to western American literary and cultural studies, work by scholars including Blake Allmendinger, Susan Lee Johnson, Axel Nissen, Nayan Shah, William Handley, Peter Boag, and Chris Packard, among others.[75] Geoffrey Bateman has written of the "queer imaginaries" of the American West, forms of collectivity that inhere in the "intimate publics of men and women organized around the circulation of desires that were distinct from identities coming into being within the emerging discourse of sexuality" in the late nineteenth century.[76] *Settler Tenses* offers a lens and a vocabulary for talking about how literary form produces the time and space of queer imaginaries and settler collectivity, and gestures toward how we might imagine and embody other imaginaries and collectivities against and beyond the settler colonial.

Before turning to chapter 1, I want to offer an additional quick note about my sense of the critical and political implications of the present volume, a volume that devotes so much space to consideration of literary articulations of settler colonial power. I take my work in this book as a starting rather than an end point for thinking about literature's enduring, world-making, and world-changing power. Literature and literary chronotopes, as this book seeks to demonstrate, do much to shape and reinforce the genocidal violence of white supremacist settler colonialism and its organization of embodiment and desire. Our capacity and responsibility to recognize and *act* on this propensity is part of the point of this book. Literature and literary chronotopes are, ultimately, sites of contestation that open up other possibilities for self, other, and world. I am compelled to repeat here an idea that I offered up just a few pages prior, and to state it more strongly: beyond this book's archive, in texts written before, during, and after the historical period centered in this book, exist chronotopes that artistically give flesh to genuinely resistant, decolonial alternatives to settler colonial subjectivities. Some of these alternatives, no doubt, are yet to take shape; I look forward to seeing them take on flesh. I hope that this book enlivens your thinking, that it gets you closer to generative ways of addressing the violences of settler colonial life, and that it impels you to denaturalize settler colonial temporalities and remake our world(s) beyond the narrow limits of time as settler colonialism has made us know it.

# CHAPTER 1

# Heterochronic West

TEMPORAL MULTIPLICITY AND
QUEER FUTURES IN BRET HARTE'S
REGIONAL WRITING

Bret Harte, born Francis Brett Hart in 1836, became the highest paid writer in the US when, in 1871, *The Atlantic Monthly* publisher James R. Osgood agreed to pay him ten thousand dollars for his next year's worth of writing. Unfortunately, the flush times were short-lived. Osgood, having agreed to publish Harte's writing sight unseen, was generally underwhelmed and refused to renew Harte's contract. Thus began for Harte a downward spiral that included financial difficulties, a disappointing lecture tour, a poorly received novel titled *Gabriel Conroy* (1876), and a public feud with co-author and friend-turned-enemy Mark Twain over the production of their play, *Ah Sin* (1877). In 1878, Harte would leave the US and never return.

*Ah Sin* was one of the final blows before Harte departed for Europe in 1878. Perhaps he should have known that the play would not go over particularly well. He had experienced a certain species of difficulty with his 1870 narrative poem, "Plain Language from Truthful James," where the play's titular Chinese character, Ah Sin, first appeared. Harte intended "Plain Language from Truthful James" as an ironic lampooning of anti-Chinese sentiment. Literal-minded readers and publishers, the latter no doubt capitalizing on the popularity of anti-Chinese sentiment in the late nineteenth century, recast Harte's poem as humorous anti-Chinese verse. "Plain Language" would be republished by the Western News Company of Chicago as a pirated, illustrated edition with the title *The Heathen Chinee* before the end of 1870.[1]

Owing to episodes like the situation with "The Heathen Chinee," Harte often comes off as a misunderstood advocate for the rights of racialized minorities and Native Americans in his historical moment and in much of the criticism up to our contemporary moment.[2] He also often comes off as a portrayer of tender homosocial relationships par excellence, an ultimately unsurprising distinction given Harte's frequent focus on spaces in or adjacent to California's mining camps, where close male bonds were for a time a defining feature.[3] How do these elements of Harte's fiction articulate with settler tensing's production of white ascendance, racialized expendability, and Native genocide? This chapter argues that Harte's Western stories actually relegate California Native Americans to extinction and, at the same time, recruit Mexican and Latinx subjects and queer white men into the project of US settlement. Audiences' misconstruing of Harte's anti-racist intent prompts urgent questions about the unintended consequences of this white male author's attempts to speak for and in favor of targeted groups such as the Chinese. That Harte often injected seemingly sympathetic portrayals of targeted groups into stories that were mostly about white characters, and often about sentimental relationships between white men, suggests that any unintended consequences must be understood in intimate relation to these queer white male characters.

One of Bret Harte's best-known short stories, "The Luck of Roaring Camp" (1868), was first published in the second issue of the *Overland Monthly*, a genteel periodical for which Harte served as inaugural editor. Like a number of Harte's other stories from the 1860s and 1870s, "The Luck of Roaring Camp" narrates nineteenth-century rural California as a scene of profound male intimacy. Perhaps less obvious, the story also figures regional time as cyclical, making the path to futurity a relatively circuitous route. The story begins by placing its narrative squarely in the historical moment of the California gold rush: "There was commotion in Roaring Camp. It could not have been a fight, for *in 1850* that was not novel enough to have called together the entire settlement."[4] The text then proceeds to detail the numerous and, by the narrator's reckoning, beneficial changes occasioned by the introduction into Roaring Camp of mixed-blood baby Tommy Luck (to whom Roaring Camp's miners affectionately refer as "The Luck"). At the end of the story, a destructive flood rips through the mining camp, obliquely recalling the Book of Genesis while also killing Tommy and bringing Roaring Camp's narrative of "regeneration" to a rather different end than readers might have been led to expect (22). Thus, while the opening sentence of "The Luck of Roaring Camp" anchors the story to a specific historical moment eighteen years prior to the text's initial publication and audience reception, the text's ending points to a biblical past and to a foreclosed future of continuing "regeneration"; when translated into social and economic terms, this future also would have been one of continuing "progress" and "development."[5] In other words, "The Luck of Roaring Camp" conjoins disparate historical moments—namely, the deep biblical past and more recent events in California—while also disrupting the fulfillment of the future that, the narrator suggests, time's inexorable passing would have effected. As the narrator notes, "three months" simply needed to pass and then the hotel signifying economic development and greater translocal connectivity would have been built (25).

Harte's readers' textually mediated understanding of time—their understanding of the nation's and its citizens' movement through it[6]—therefore diverges significantly from conceptions of time as medium of linear progress and agent of Manifest Destiny. For one, the year 1850 and the deep past narrated in the Bible come together in such a way that this deep past finds itself repeated, with a few differences, in Gold Rush California. Time, in this sense, operates as a recursive loop or cycle, the very view of time that already had begun to be displaced in the Anglo-American context as early as the mid to late eighteenth century. As John Demos writes, in this period, conceptions of history as "cyclical movement" began to be abandoned in favor of "fresher, more linear, channels."[7] And in place of what Lloyd Pratt calls the "uniform national destiny" and "determinate future" put forth by John L. O'Sullivan and a host of other nineteenth-century writers,[8] Harte offers readers a vision of an uncertain future in the far West: will the future of social progress and economic development forecasted in Roaring Camp's increasing civility and the proposed building of a hotel eventually come to pass? Or will the Western "wilderness" continually intervene and throw Roaring Camp into an endless cycle of rise and decline that locks the locale into a permanently "primitive" state relative to parts of the North American continent further east?

Scholars have for a long time linked the texts that this chapter examines—"The Luck of Roaring Camp" as well as Harte's "Tennessee's Partner" (1869), "The Idyl of Red Gulch" (1869), "The Iliad of Sandy Bar" (1870), and "An Ingénue of the Sierras" (1893)—to the genesis of the literatures variously referred to as regional writing, literary regionalism, and local color.[9] As June Howard puts it, "Literary histories of local color often begin with the publication, in the new California magazine *Overland Monthly* during the summer of 1868, of an anonymous story entitled 'The Luck of Roaring Camp.'" Readers would subsequently find out, as Howard notes, that Bret Harte was the author of the tale, and Howard writes as well that we could easily start with other authors—for example, English writer Mary Russell Mitford or Harte's compatriot from earlier in the nineteenth century, Washington Irving—as we look for the beginning of the genre to which Harte is so intimately connected.[10] Regardless of whether we accord Harte little or much distinction for his contributions to this body of writing, twentieth-century critics and writers were apt to view Harte as an important, if not originary, figure in postbellum regional writing, even if they loathed his writing, as did Cleanth Brooks and Robert Penn Warren.[11]

I would like to suggest that Harte's importance in US literary history, and in the history of US settler colonialism, also lies in his imag(in)ing the course of US national history through tropes of queer and racialized futurity. To say that writings such as Harte's are in fundamental ways about (settler) national history and futurity is to rehearse a claim that has centered much of the critical history of local color and regional writing, as this chapter will flesh out just below. While much literary critical debate, as June Howard observes, has focused, often unhelpfully, on whether local color and regionalism are distinct, I use the terms interchangeably in this chapter and in chapter 4, where the genre terms resurface.[12] To say that writings such as Harte's are in fundamental ways about queerness in relation to histories and futurities national and otherwise is to rehearse another, albeit more recent, central claim (this, too, I'll flesh out just below). In implicit as well as explicit ways, I agree with both of these centering claims in my discussion in this chapter. This chapter shows that Harte's writings, in looking back, narrated US national history and futurity as scenes of queer and racialized regional difference. The queer and racialized regional difference of Harte's American West is neither a holdout against modernity nor a soon-to-be or already eclipsed victim of modernity. It is instead part of late nineteenth-century American literature's discursive wedding of queerness and racialized difference to the project of settlement, the recruitment of the nation's nominal others—region, queerness, racialized other—as key, enduring players in the making of settler futurity.

Thinking about Harte's writings in terms of queer and racialized regional difference entails a reconsideration of the critical tendency to view regional writing as a genre that narrates the inevitable demise of local particularity at the hands of a nationalizing and homogenizing modernity.[13] "The new consensus view," wrote Pratt in 2010, "is that nineteenth-century literary regionalism participates in the disappearance of the local in the face of modernity rather than working to preserve the local or to function as its advocate."[14] The local, in this account, functions as a signifier of anachronistic regional isolation in the social, political, and economic spheres. Moreover, the local is the soon-to-be or already historically superseded; the local is being, or already has been, dissolved into the national. Pratt shows how this generally accepted account assumes a national(ist) teleology in which readers and regions are on an inexorable march in the direction of expanding networks of affiliation and increasing national homogeneity. One of regional writing's ostensible purposes, he further argues, is to produce the temporal simultaneity upon which an imagined community rests. But Pratt demonstrates that this writing actually functioned, at least in one of its forms (antebellum Southwestern humor) in a rather opposite fashion: it denied the temporal simultaneity that binds an imagined community together. It achieved this effect in part by showing that "there is no such thing as a universal and contingency-transcending measure of time," and by severing the link between narrative discourse and "linear progressive time."[15]

A different kind of challenge to "the new consensus view" of regional writing emerges from this chapter's discussion of the work of Bret Harte. This challenge emerges out of this chapter's consideration of sexuality, which, to use Michael Warner's words, "figures only peripherally or not at all"[16] in the work of the social theorists (such as Anthony Giddens) whose work is integral to Pratt's analysis. In foregrounding sexuality in this chapter's discussion of regional writing and temporality, I'm engaging the queer readings of regional writing and Harte's fiction that began to appear in the late 1990s and run through more recent work by Valerie Rohy, Sarah Ensor, Peter Coviello, and J. Samaine Lockwood.[17] Judith Fetterley and Marjorie Pryse's work on regional writing and Axel Nissen's work on Harte has shown that Harte's writing and regional writing more broadly often portray characters and plots that "do not participate actively in the reproduction of heterosexuality."[18] But whereas queer readings of regional writing that focus on questions about temporality and history, such as Peter Coviello's *Tomorrow's Parties* and Valerie Rohy's *Anachronism and Its Others*, argue that postbellum New England regionalist Sarah Orne Jewett effectively concedes the demise of queer socialities in the face of "the homogenizing drive of modernity"[19] and national(ist) futurity, this chapter suggests that Harte's writing offers no such concession. Like the queer women of Ensor's and Lockwood's analyses, Harte's fiction aligns queerness and futurity, although not necessarily in ways that we might expect. If conceptions of time as a linear, progressive, and ultimately impartial force naturalize "historically specific regimes of asymmetrical power" between dominant and marginalized groups,[20] then Harte uses literary narrative's power to shape readers' conceptions of time to restore power and vitality to those otherwise made to lose out and disappear in the course of time and history's movement.

There is a key qualification here, though: Harte's restoration of power and vitality to marginalized groups reorganizes power within the settler polity, reinstating settlement as a process that is heterogeneous and proliferative rather than homogenizing and unifying. This reorganization and reinstatement is the crux of Harte's contribution to settler tensing. Settlement becomes an inclusionary vision: Harte's regionalist narrative form includes, rather than leaves behind, sexual and racial others. For Coviello, and to a lesser extent for Rohy as well, regional writing's importance for queer theory lies largely in Jewett's tender representations of social forms and affective ties that lie outside the forms of social life and attachment imposed by the (heterosexual) marriage plot and the late nineteenth-century crystallization of hetero- and homosexuality. These alternative social forms and affective ties are encapsulated profitably in the notion of queer socialities and exemplified in stories about women and men whose affective and erotic energies are not captivated by a singular, heterosexual mate and a nuclear family. Yet because Coviello's and Rohy's projects do not share Pratt's concern with how literary texts produce readers' conceptions of how time moves and what time's passage will accomplish, both scholars stay away from any extended consideration of how regional writing's production of readers' temporal consciousness interacts with the genre's portrayals of queer socialities.

This interaction between the production of readers' temporal consciousness and the portrayal of queer socialities in Harte's fiction takes center stage in the following two sections of this chapter, which focus on "The Luck of Roaring Camp," "Tennessee's Partner," and "The Iliad of Sandy Bar." In light of the historical analogy between sexual and racial otherness that anachronizes these forms of otherness by equating them with one another, the final section of this chapter considers how "The Idyl of Red Gulch" and "An Ingénue of the Sierras" mark the future as a site of racial heterogeneity and thereby bolster the other three stories' articulations of the futurity of queer socialities. This approach to Harte's fiction allows for a rethinking of two related and influential notions about postbellum regional writing: that it narrates the disappearance of local cultures and ways of life in the face of postbellum national incorporation, and that it serves narrow racial and class interests, namely the interests of those who are white and of the middle and upper classes.[21] In testing these two notions about postbellum regional writing via a consideration of Harte's Western version of the genre, this chapter also examines the relationship between some of Harte's most well-known texts and the unifying, nationalizing, and "Americanizing" functions that Frederick Jackson Turner would locate in the frontier and the American West in the post-frontier moment of the last decade of the nineteenth century.

Harte's short stories about California mining camp sociality and heterosexual marriage articulate temporalities (in the sense of both expressing *and* joining temporalities) in ways that militate against the linear, progressive logics that enable equations of regional writing and Western space with the consolidation of certain forms of national identity, unity, and futurity. Harte's West emerges as a space where time's multiplicity and variable effects open up a number of possible futures and disrupt (hetero)normative narratives of progress, unity, and identity formation associated with the region and regional writing; in other words, Harte carves out space for the historical persistence of abjected racial, sexual, and economic identities that these narratives otherwise would consign to a safely sealed past. Whereas Turner would later elegiacally characterize the frontier as the site where heterogeneous elements are forged into a unified "American" type, the temporalities embedded in Harte's texts characterize the frontier and the American West as sites that maintain and even create heterogeneity and fluidity within the settler polity. Harte therefore figures national identity and futurity in ways that resist the dialectical and unifying impulses that would otherwise erase abjected sexual and racial identities so as to narrate a singular national identity and future. In place of neat synthesis, Harte's writings figure settler futurity as a proliferation of sexualities and socialities.

## A Mixed-Blood Baby, a Queer Sociality, and National (Dis)unity: "The Luck of Roaring Camp"

The close reading of "The Luck of Roaring Camp" ("Luck") offered earlier in this chapter provides a starting point for thinking about how the temporalities articulated in Harte's fiction disrupt the narratives of reductive nationalization associated with postbellum regional writing and the nineteenth-century American West. But what that close reading fails to disclose are the intimate and complex links between race, sexuality, nationalization, and temporality in Harte's tale of mixed-blood Tommy Luck and the miners who come together to care for him. Those links elucidate the contours of the story's participation in settler tensing's production of white ascendance, racialized expendability, and Native genocide: the story narrates the futurity of queer white male sociality and of imagined Native figures, the latter perched, in a peculiarly settler colonial paradox, on the precipice of assimilation and death.

The flood at the end of "Luck" figures, significantly, as an impediment to the introduction of heterosexual domesticity via the "decent families" that would have been invited to reside in the hotel.[22] In the short story's narrative logic, the forward movements of "progress" and "development" are essentially inseparable from a movement from perverse sexuality and masculine individualism to all-male domesticity to ultimately unrealized heterosexual domesticity. In linking these movements to one another, heterosexual domesticity takes on the status of a more "advanced" mode of social organization toward which Roaring Camp's social and economic changes were tending. In a strange move for a writer noted for his sympathetic representations of racialized groups and celebratory portrayals of intimacy between men, it would seem as though the racial others and the homosociality of Roaring Camp are relegated to a place of anteriority; they are but an evolutionary prelude to the (white) heterosexual domesticity that would have found its way into the camp absent the flood.[23]

The story's portrayal of Native American sex worker Cherokee Sal foregrounds the racialized sexuality that is traditionally counterposed to the modern nation-state. As Elizabeth Freeman notes, "bourgeois-liberal entities from nations to individuals are defined within a narrow chronopolitics of development at once racialized, gendered, and sexualized. Western 'modernity,' for instance, has represented its own forward movement against a slower premodernity figured as brown-skinned, feminine, and erotically perverse."[24] Consistent with a number of arguments about regional writing, within the premodernity/modernity binary, the physical space of Roaring Camp, the miners, Tommy Luck, and nearly everything else that the narrator presents to us fit rather neatly into the category of the premodern—a premodernity poised to give way to an impending modernity. Cherokee Sal, who is also Tommy's mother, is essentially a perfect match for the "brown-skinned, feminine, and erotically perverse" premodernity that Freeman describes. Not just a Native American woman, Sal also is a sex worker whose labor is presented as sexual perversity: "She was a coarse, and, it is to be feared, a very sinful woman. . . . It was, perhaps, part of the expiation of her sin, that, at a moment when she most lacked her sex's intuitive tenderness and care, she met only the half-contemptuous faces of her masculine associates."[25] Although irony undeniably suffuses the narrator's tone, the story also illustrates some of the associations that Freeman notes. Sal dies shortly after this description of her "sinfulness" and suffering in childbirth, and her death relegates her to the past and secures her characterization as the premodern other against whom progress can be made and measured. Given the 1850 historical moment in which "Luck" is set, this representation of Sal as premodern other unfit for modernity also gestures toward the particularly violent 1846 to 1910 period in the history of the US's genocide of California Native Americans. As Benjamin Madley has pointed out, since Theodora Kroeber and Robert F. Heizer's 1968 articulation of "the genocide of Californians," a number of scholars have convincingly described as genocide the US's treatment of California Native Americans across the second half of the nineteenth century and beyond.[26] Sal's giving birth to Tommy and her death function as plot points that enable and emphasize the subsequent forward movement of the text's fairly linear narrative of social and material progress. In between the description of Sal's suffering and her death, we are told of Tommy's birth in both auditory and temporal terms: "Above the [sounds of the wilderness and the camp] rose a sharp, querulous cry,—a cry unlike anything heard before in the camp. The pines stopped moaning, the river ceased to rush, and the fire to crackle. It seemed as if Nature had stopped to listen too." The text figures Tommy's birth as a pause that marks the point that separates the cyclical, repetitive period of gambling and violence registered in the story's first paragraph from the relatively linear, progressive time of "change" and "improvement" that Tommy's introduction ultimately inaugurates.[27]

This change in temporalities corresponds to fundamental changes in the camp whereby the formerly violent "assemblage" of Roaring Camp is transformed socially and affectively, remade into willing participants in the capacious, all-male domestic space that Roaring Camp becomes.[28] Axel Nissen insightfully has read "Luck" as an importation of "the cult of domesticity" to the Sierra Nevada foothills, which allows Harte to show readers that men can be just as good as, if not better than, women in fulfilling the duties of the home.[29] Nissen's analysis suggests that if we read the domestic arrangements of Roaring Camp in terms of Michael Warner's understanding of "queer" as "resistance to regimes of the normal" and as that which "gets a critical edge by defining itself against the normal rather than the heterosexual," Roaring Camp's domesticity is unmistakably queer vis-à-vis dominant forms of white, Christian, middle-class domesticity in the nineteenth-century US.[30] None of Roaring Camp's miners—not even the two most feminized miners, Kentuck and Stumpy—can be identified as homosexual or queer on the basis of sexual object choice, the behavior that would become central to the making of modern sexual categories less than twenty years after the publication of "Luck." On the other hand, in terms of gender expression, which Mark Rifkin identifies as the other centerpiece of modern sexual categories, many of the members of Roaring Camp fall within the orbit of the queer.[31] Kentuck, we are told, "had the weaknesses of the nobler sex" and becomes very interested in being around and caring for Tommy. The entire male-only camp actually becomes active, to one degree or another, in the care of Tommy, keeping his cabin "scrupulously clean and white-washed [and subsequently] boarded, clothed, and papered." Moreover, the miners begin to practice "stricter habits of personal cleanliness."[32] But Roaring Camp's queerness also is legible in the ways that the miners (fail to) perform the "ensemble of imperatives" that would come to be bundled together into the hegemonic force of compulsory heterosexuality. From a Foucauldian perspective and in the context of the US's treatment of Native American kinship formations, Rifkin writes that "compulsory heterosexuality can be conceptualized as an ensemble of imperatives that includes family formation, homemaking, private propertyholding, and the allocation of citizenship, a series of potential 'detachable parts' fused to each other through discourses of sexuality."[33] In a certain formal sense, Roaring Camp achieves some of the "heterosexual" characteristics that Rifkin identifies: Tommy occasions the formation of a trans-species nuclear family composed of himself, Stumpy, and the donkey "Jinny," and homemaking becomes something of a preoccupation in the all-male camp. Even in these descriptions of the camp's "heterosexual" characteristics, though, variance from "regimes of the normal" is the reigning dynamic. In short, Roaring Camp's alternative to "the normal" amounts to what Coviello identifies as a queer sociality, for the camp contains a form of social life and a set of affective ties that revolve around an all-male collectivity and the mixed-blood baby that brought all these men together, rather than around the heteronormative nuclear family.

Subsequently, the camp's desire for the presence of "decent families"[34] highlights Roaring Camp's variance from "regimes of the normal," giving the camp's queer sociality the status of an intermediate stage between the perverse sexuality embodied in Cherokee Sal and the normative heterosexuality symbolized by the "decency" of these families. The story translates into sexual terms the Turnerian historiographical dynamic that Neil Campbell criticizes for its "displacing [of] the uncertainty and fluidity of migration and movement" on the frontier so as to service a vision of the inevitability of "one destination (nationhood, union, a fixed identity)."[35] In this way, "Luck" forecasts the displacement of the perverse sexuality and sociality of the miners so as to narrate the supposed inevitability of the "one destination" of heterosexual domesticity. Linking this sexual-social "progress" to Roaring Camp's insertion into an ostensibly transregional tourism and hospitality economy, the narrator notes, "With the prosperity of the camp came a desire for further improvement. It was proposed to build a hotel in the following spring, and to invite one or two decent families to reside there for the sake of 'The Luck,'—who might perhaps profit by female companionship."[36] This "hotel" and these "decent families" point to "the regimen of the upper-class vacation" that was developed in the postbellum period and whose participants composed the primary readership of the highbrow East Coast magazines that the original publication venue of "Luck," the *Overland Monthly*, sought to imitate.[37] "Evolved *at* this time," writes Richard Brodhead, "elite vacation habits also took on a heavily symbolic function *in* this time in dramatizing this group's social superiority."[38] Crucially, the "social superiority" of this newly formed "translocally incorporated social elite" was one part of the larger processes of post-bellum (re)unification and incorporation that Brodhead, Amy Kaplan, and others have described.[39] The proposed hotel and the families that were to inhabit it thus serve as metonymic representations of the (re) unification and incorporation that some scholars have regarded as central characteristics of the present and near future of the moment in which "Luck" was published. From this perspective, the normative hetero-sexuality and domesticity implicit in those "decent families" become linked to notions of progress and national unity, and to readers' present and future. On the other hand, the perversity of Cherokee Sal and the queerness of the miners become remnants of the past and signs of the supposed regional backwardness and isolation that have no place and no future in the contemporary world; Sal and the miners are, to use Rohy's words, "what must be summoned into national consciousness in order to be disavowed in favor of progress, fertility, and futurity."[40] Obliquely looking forward to Freud's narrative of the individual's psychosexual maturation, Harte positions normative heterosexuality as the desired endpoint of Roaring Camp's narrative of development.[41]

Of course, the desired and actual endpoints of Roaring Camp's nar-rative are not identical due to the flood at the end of the story, and much about the movement toward normative heterosexuality and domesticity in "Luck" relies on counterfactually denying the flood's occurrence. But this counterfactual consideration helps us to see the ways the story invokes and troubles hegemonic temporalities of the sexual, racial, national, and epochal sorts. The outlines of this temporal reconfigura-tion emerge when the text suggests that Tommy's death is synonymous with the death of Roaring Camp's plan to build a hotel. The narrator tells us that this plan "can only be accounted for by [the miners'] affec-tion for Tommy," and so we are left to assume that the desire to build the hotel will leave Roaring Camp along with Tommy.[42] If the hotel symbolizes Roaring Camp's forecasted insertion into the postbellum United States's increasingly nationalized economy, then the unlikelihood of its construction spells the improbability of Roaring Camp's entrance into this economy. This failed economic insertion might seem at first to support processes of national consolidation by narrating the historical supersession of Roaring Camp's regional peculiarities. In other words, we might read "Luck" as a text that hermetically seals off and relegates to the past those regional particularities that may come off as threats to the smooth homogenization of the nation. But reading "Luck" in this fashion would amount to our own capitulation, as readers, to the linear conceptions of time and narratives of national consolidation that inform "the new consensus view" of regional writing and expansionist discourse's reduction of Western space to "destiny."[43] And capitulating to these conceptions of time would run counter to the alternative temporalities that "Luck" presents to readers, temporalities that ask us to regard the American West and regional writing as vectors of enduring locality and heterogeneity at the heart of the settler colonial project.

Indeed, the aspects of "Luck" that connote different conceptions of time—linear on the one hand, as in the part of the story between Tommy's birth and death; cyclical and repetitive on the other, as in the invocation of a deep biblical past at the story's close—capture with particular elegance part of what Harte's fiction does when it *articulates* temporalities in the sense of articulation as "joining together": "Luck" joins together, in one narrative, a temporality of linear progress and a temporality of cyclical repetition. In Harte's version of the frontier West, time is at least double, like time in the account of the (postcolonial) nation offered by Homi Bhabha and other postcolonial thinkers.[44] Crucially, the text also endows this temporality of linear progress with a distinctively Christian character in associating it with "regeneration."[45] This temporality, then, is similar to the simultaneously religiously inflected and linear temporality that undergirds John L. O'Sullivan's version of Manifest Destiny. This temporality of Manifest Destiny turns the physical space of the American West into a temporal abstraction ("destiny") divested of any place-based contingency, promising the fulfillment of O'Sullivan's prophecy that "we [US Americans] are not merely to possess and occupy an unequalled extent of territory, or to extend our laws and institutions over a countless population, for the territory, though vast, will be compact, and what is of still greater value, the population will be *homogeneous*."[46] O'Sullivan is certain that time's passage will effect sameness among the US population, and "Luck," similarly, spends much of its narrative suggesting that time will make Roaring Camp economically, socially, and sexually harmonious with the middle- and upper-class values of Harte's historical moment. Yet at the end of the text, this vision of time's passage as that which promises to effect a transcendence of the contingencies of place and homogenize the nation turns into a fantasy that the Sierra Nevada foothills will not support.

Right before the flood sweeps through Roaring Camp, "Luck" invokes a place-based and cyclical conception of time that works against the future envisioned by O'Sullivan and by the story itself up to that point. As Pratt has pointed out, influential theories of how individuals become phenomenologically and materially connected to large aggregates such as the nation have posited a close connection between "universal metrics" of timekeeping, linear conceptions of time, and the process of transcending place-based contingency so as to unite geographically diverse peoples into a collectivity.[47] Linear time therefore stands as a figure for the transcendence of place-based contingency, and "Luck" and O'Sullivan's versions of linear time are figured as such in that they promise to turn contingency and difference into national homogeneity. But scholars also have drawn a connection between cyclical conceptions of time, in which the comprehension of time is inseparable from the distinctive features of place, and an experience of deep locality antithetical to such transcendence of the contingencies of place.[48] Significantly, the narrator of "Luck" links the comprehension of time to the particularities of place right before telling readers of the flood that wipes out part of Roaring Camp and kills Tommy. "The winter of 1851," the narrator observes, "will long be remembered in the foothills. The snow lay deep on the Sierras, and every mountain creek became a river, and every river a lake. Each gorge and gulch was transformed into a tumultuous watercourse that descended the hillsides, tearing down giant trees and scattering its drift and debris along the plain."[49] Rather than looking to "universal metrics" (such as the mechanical clock or the calendar) to orient readers—for surely the flood happened on a specific day and at a specific time—the narrator suggests that we only know that the flood occurred in the winter of 1851 because that was the year that the particularities of local topography were especially peculiar (namely, the large amount of snowfall). Moreover, the narrator continues, "Red Dog had been twice under water, and Roaring Camp had been forewarned. 'Water put the gold into them gulches,' said Stumpy. —t's been here once and will be here again!' And that night the North Fork suddenly leaped over its banks, and swept up the triangular valley of Roaring Camp."[50] Not only is time's comprehension linked to place, it also is presented as cyclical movement, as something that entails the recurrence of phenomena that have occurred before. The temporality that dominates the narrative in this moment *theoretically and literally* denies the possibility of transcending the contingencies of place, and it links this denial to the negation of Roaring Camp's entrance into "more advanced" social, sexual, and economic arrangements.

The religio-linear time of both Manifest Destiny and the portion of "Luck" that narrates Tommy's short life therefore is overlain by a cyclical temporality whose assertion of the ascendance of local contingency is synonymous with a logic of *enduring* regional difference. It is not simply that the queer arrangements of Roaring Camp have been given a bit more time to reign before the normalizing forces of the postbellum United States take over. Rather, these normalizing forces have been rendered inert by a cyclical conception of time that pushes Roaring Camp's queer arrangements into the future: if time's passage entails an experience of repetition, then the future holds more queer socialities that resemble the one portrayed in "Luck." Moreover, the racial mixing and Native American assimilation symbolized by Tommy, when the narrator tells of his "mottled legs" and reminds readers that he is an "Ingin [*sic*] baby," and the Native presence embodied in Sal are wrested away from death and the past and pushed into the future as well; "Luck" places California Native American futurity on the precipice of the assimilation and death symbolized by Tommy and Sal.[51] Of course, one implication of this reading is the notion that Western locales will remain perennially frontier-like, with all of the connotations of primitivity and violence that this would imply. Yet we ultimately would be wrong to proclaim that "Luck" associates Western American locales with only this cyclical temporality, given that the short story also associates Western American space with the religio-linear temporality that features in O'Sullivan's conception of the US's Manifest Destiny. This temporal heterogeneity offers an incipient vision of the American West as a space that is amenable to "progress," but only if this progress allows for the difference and social heterogeneity that advocates of Manifest Destiny such as O'Sullivan strove to expunge. In future stories, Harte suggests that difference and heterogeneity can be incorporated into the nation without disappearing or being relegated to the past or the status of the "primitive."

## Living Beyond the Demands of Heterosexuality: Male Intimacies in "Tennessee's Partner" and "The Iliad of Sandy Bar"

In the years directly following the 1868 publication of "Luck," Harte would continue to use regional writing in its genteel periodical genre form to explore queer socialities, turning in "Tennessee's Partner" (1869) and "The Iliad of Sandy Bar" (1870) to portrayals of white male "partners" who carry on complex affective and economic relationships with one another. Whereas "Luck" narrates an ultimately thwarted movement toward heterosexual domesticity, "Tennessee" and "Iliad" tell of men whose lives have moved in something of an opposite direction: Tennessee's Partner and Scott of "Iliad" at one point had wives to whom they were legally married—Scott and his wife even may have lived in a home, just the two of them, as husband and wife—but subsequently moved on to queerer arrangements. In this section, I examine the significance of this queer movement vis-à-vis the modernization and nationalization (the "progress") of the American West registered in "Tennessee" and "Iliad" (the same processes upon which the flood in "Luck" intervenes). I also focus closely on the racialized bodily dispositions toward time that take hold in some of these queer white men, embodied relationships to time that Dana Luciano has theorized in the context of nineteenth-century grief culture.[52] These stories do the work of settler tensing by (re)articulating biopolitical distinctions between queer white bodies that must be protected and queer racialized and Indigenous bodies that can or must be sacrificed.

There are striking differences between how "Luck" describes the world to which Roaring Camp belongs and how "Tennessee" and "Iliad" do so. "Luck" presents a world of local isolation that minimizes interaction with those outside of one's immediate surroundings. Miners from the camp make a trip to Sacramento to procure "articles" for Tommy, and the narrator does mention another camp, Red Dog, located at "a distance of forty miles," but he also tells us of an "expressman" who is Roaring Camp's "only connecting link with the surrounding world."[53] For the most part, Roaring Camp is a hermetic world unto itself. In contrast, the worlds of "Tennessee" and "Iliad" call attention to travel and translocal connections. In other words, they feature phenomena that Brodhead associates with the emergent postbellum "modern order"[54] and that social theorists including Anthony Giddens associate with modernity. Tennessee's Partner finds his wife by traveling outside of Sandy Bar, meeting her in Stockton while on his way to San Francisco. If, as Giddens claims, modernity is a condition in which "personal ties are continually forged with others with whom one was previously unacquainted,"[55] then the conditions of life in "Tennessee" seem more in line with a modern order than do the conditions of life in "Luck." Moreover—and importantly—Tennessee's Partner meets his wife at a hotel, the very sign of nationalization and sexual "progress" in "Luck." In "Iliad" two lawyers travel to Sandy Bar from San Francisco, and the story's main characters, Scott and York, leave Sandy Bar for Sacramento and Paris, respectively, both eventually returning to Sandy Bar. When York returns to Sandy Bar, at which point it has been supplanted by the new town of Riverside, his demeanor and dress make him sound like a member of the apt-to-travel postbellum middle and upper classes described by Brodhead. "Among [the coach's] passengers," the narrator notes, "was one [York], apparently a stranger, in the local distinction of well-fitting clothes and closely shaven face, who demanded a private room and retired early to rest."[56]

The seclusion that York desires points to changes in travel in the American West during the 1850s through 1890s. According to Stephanie Palmer, "for the first time in US history, travel hindered rather than fostered interactions between travelers of different classes and between travelers and people outside the travel-service industry."[57] Crucially, Palmer suggests that in the context of the American West, the changes in travel that York's desire for privacy registers were inseparable from modernization. As she writes, "modernization happened unevenly across the country, but as soon as luxury accommodations or transportation choices were available in a specific location, travelers who could afford to use them did so. Thus on a local level modernization was swift and seemingly irrevocable."[58] In addition to the modernizing effect of such travel, these later texts are also careful to note the presence of newspapers, the print form that Benedict Anderson has called an exemplary and "vivid figure for the secular, historically clocked, imagined community" of the modern nation.[59] These two stories suggest that the inhabitants of Sandy Bar and the locales that surround it, including Red Dog, the establishment that seems so cut off from Roaring Camp in "Luck," are at least connected to one another, if not to the larger nation, through print. This connection, if we follow Anderson, is synonymous with a nationally unifying, contingency-transcending experience of time as the linear unfolding of "'homogeneous, empty time.'"[60] In short, "Tennessee" and "Iliad" narrate the more modern, more nationalized American West that Roaring Camp was primed to enter but did not quite reach.

It is within this version of the American West that Harte portrays men whose lives are not structured around the heterosexual, reproductive logic of the marriage plot but, rather, around their attachments to their male "partners." Peter Stoneley notes the difficulties involved in classifying Harte's representations of same-sex relationships in gold rush California. As he observes, these relationships "cannot be translated into an approximation of modern homosexuality, or of nineteenth-century heterosexual marriage," and Harte offers little help in classifying them.[61] The relationships between Tennessee and his Partner and between York and Scott of "Iliad" are among those that resist being "translated." Giving names to these attachments is beside the point; rather, I wish to delineate the relationships to linear progress and the (national) future that, these two texts suggest, proceed out of the queer, untranslatable sociality of the frontier West and do not disappear as the American West becomes modernized and nationalized. Clarifying these attachments, Matthew Watson historicizes them within the context of the "business partnership," which was the "'dominant form of commercial enterprise' in the United States for much of the nineteenth century" and a "common figure for a network that exacted parallel economic and personal obligations." Despite parallels between mining and business partnerships, Watson writes that "the discourse of the mining partnership also suggested an extraordinary loyalty and affection between partners," which "images of the fraternal and even the marital" emphasized.[62]

Both "Tennessee" and "Iliad" foreground these qualities and images in the mining partnerships that they portray. In "Tennessee," the loyalty that the Partner shows toward Tennessee is so unshakeable that he welcomes back Tennessee "with affection" after Tennessee returns from having run off with his wife.[63] While loyalty is perhaps less in evidence in York and Scott's relationship, "Iliad" opens with a description of dissension between the two men that is cast in strongly marital-domestic terms: "There was no trace of disorder or confusion in the neat cabin. The rude table was arranged as if for breakfast; the pan of yellow biscuit still sat upon that hearth whose dead embers might have typified the evil passions that had raged there but an hour before."[64] The list of elements that qualify these two relationships as "mining partnerships" extends further, but the point is that "Tennessee" and "Iliad" tie the affective intensity of these homosocial relationships to the socioeconomic conditions of gold rush California. Lest we think of these relationships as precursors to "civilization" in the West, Watson persuasively argues that "rather than reading the civilizing of the West through the nineteenth-century sentimental notion of marriage's power to subordinate husbands to the moral sway of wives, Harte imagined a West civilized by a sentimentality separate from the gendered hierarchy of the traditional nineteenth-century marriage."[65] This equation of a "civilized" West with the horizontal sentimentality of the mining partnership becomes even more legible when we consider the signs of modernization and nationalization in "Tennessee" and "Iliad" noted above: modernization and nationalization in the region do not come after these (queer) mining partnerships have run their course and given way evolutionarily to normative domestic arrangements; rather, modernization and nationalization are propelled by the performance of these partnerships.

If affection and loyalty between men are the basis for "civilization," modernization, and nationalization in the West, then "Tennessee" and "Iliad" show us that the embodied experiences of extralinear time that Luciano has described work in distinctive ways in the region. In *Arranging Grief: Sacred Time and the Body in Nineteenth-Century America*, Luciano elaborates on the temporal implications of Foucault's conception of biopolitics to trace the nineteenth-century development of "the deployment of the feeling body as the index of a temporality apart from the linear paradigm of 'progress.'"[66] As a central expression of "the feeling body," grief was associated with an extralinear (monumental and repetitive) temporality linked to the domestic, the maternal, and the heterosexual family. In particular, grief was linked to human origins and the reproduction of bonds and values that found the sociality of the family and the nation. Grief and its temporality thus possessed a potentially double-edged role vis-à-vis the linear time of progress: the act of lingering in grief furnished an affective continuity with the past that was necessary for the cohesion and the very existence of the family and the nation; yet one potentially could linger too long in the extralinear time of grief, thus "allowing [affective ties] to overtake the future-directedness of the present."[67] The affectively charged mining partnerships that Harte portrays amount to distinctively Western American, queer analogues of the sociality-founding bonds and values that Luciano associates with the domestic, the maternal, and the heterosexual family. Thus, the grief that might proceed out of Harte's mining partnerships could be productive for the project of settlement if his miners do not indulge for too long in the extralinear time that grief occasions. And if the discipline requisite not to linger too long in this extralinear time could be displayed to readers, then these partnerships could be presented as consonant with the genteel values of Harte's predominantly middle- and upper-class readership. Put another way, Harte's Western, queer partnerships represent something radically different from normative heterosexual arrangements, but they are also, in terms of temporality, fundamentally similar to these normative arrangements and therefore not necessarily a threat to national progress and cohesion in linear time. However, if these partnerships were presented as lacking in the discipline that allows one to dwell in grief without letting it detract from a primary orientation toward the future, then they could signify as asynchronous threats to national progress, progress which, in the postbellum US, was synonymous with social, political, and economic changes that served the interests of the emergent middle and upper classes. As I will elaborate, "Tennessee" and "Iliad" demonstrate how the distinctively Western queerness of the mining partnership might be made to register as both consistent with and resistant to the synchronization of bodies with the priority of linear progress.

Critics have tended to view Tennessee's Partner as either "a cunning and hard-boiled avenger" or as Tennessee's "homosexual lover,"[68] but if we resist such stark binaries and instead view the relationship between these two men as a form of queer sociality, we can see how "Tennessee" figures the American West as a space that is not conducive to the cultivation of "proper" temporal orientations. "Tennessee" points to such "improper" orientations early on, when the narrator implies that Tennessee and his Partner both had un-reproductive sexual relationships with the Partner's wife. In 1853, the year before the main narrative action of "Tennessee" unfolds, the Partner sets out to "procure a wife" in San Francisco, getting no further than Stockton before he finds a suitable mate, marries her, and returns with her to the Sierra Nevada community of Poker Flat. "Of their married felicity but little is known," the narrator relates to readers, a subtly comic and ironic suggestion that their hastily contracted marriage had little chance of success. Perhaps equally destructive to the union is Tennessee's residence in the same habitation as the Partner and the Partner's wife; regardless, Tennessee takes it upon himself "to say something to the [Partner's wife] on his own account," these words as mysterious to readers as the contours of the (un)happiness of the Partner and his wife, and soon Tennessee and the Partner's wife have run off to live together. The story expends only a couple more sentences to tell—or, rather, tell almost nothing about—the time that Tennessee and the Partner's wife spend doing some unmarried "housekeeping" in Marysville before she runs off with a third "somebody."[69] As Lee Edelman trenchantly claims, "the Child [is] the emblem of futurity's unquestioned value,"[70] a value to which Tennessee, his Partner, and (ostensibly) the Partner's wife do not pay obeisance.

Yet it is not until the end of the text that a link is drawn between the queer sociality of the American West and (over)indulgence in the extralinear time of grief. After Tennessee is hanged in the wake of an unsuccessful highway robbery attempt, the narrator tells us, "from that day [the Partner's] rude health and great strength seemed visibly to decline; and when the rainy season fairly set in, and the tiny grass-blades were beginning to peep from the rocky mound above Tennessee's grave, he took to his bed." We should note here the emphasis on the body, on the decline of the Partner's "rude health" and "great strength," for the text proceeds to link this embodied decline to what looks like grief over Tennessee's death. Lying on the deathbed that he enters shortly after Tennessee's death, the Partner rehearses an oft-repeated scenario in which he would fetch a drunken Tennessee and bring him home safely. Once the Partner's narration of this scenario is complete (it ends with an impassioned cry of "Tennessee! Pardner!"), the text ends with the narrator telling us, "and so they met," signaling the Partner's death and suggesting a reunion of the two men in the afterlife.[71] According to Luciano, the promise of future reunion with a lost loved one worked to turn the grieving subject away from "the memory of past connection" and toward the future, and those who could be redirected in this way "understood themselves as the leaders and guardians of the nation's steady progress toward a spiritual and social future." The capacity for such redirection was keyed to Christian spirituality as well as race: the "ordering of the middle-class white interior" relied in part on the contrast between "proper, Christian mourning" and "disorderly modes of bereavement . . . associated with the Indian and the [B]lack slave."[72] The important point here is that regardless of whether we read (or are encouraged to read) characters like Tennessee's Partner and York as middle-class or of some other class status, as devoutly Christian or relatively godless, their whiteness already orients them toward a form of futurity that gains shape and coherence through contrast with the abjected temporalities of Native Americans and enslaved Blacks.

Although "Tennessee" suggests, as noted just above, that the Partner achieves a desired reunion with Tennessee, the means by which he reaches this reunion places the Partner somewhat apart from those whose relationship to time helps to ensure national progress. In the text's relatively languid movement from Tennessee's hanging to the Partner's bodily-legible grief to the Partner's death, the implication is that Tennessee's Partner dwells inappropriately in the extralinear time of grief, never returning to linear time before his own death. Rather than lingering in grief's temporality for an appropriately limited duration, he allows the pull of past connection to supplant what should be his primary orientation toward the future and linear progress. Because this perverse temporal orientation is tied to regional socioeconomic particularities that do not die out in the face of modernizing and nationalizing currents, the American West emerges from "Tennessee" as a space that draws queer socialities into the nation yet reserves for these socialities a kind of anti-futurity inhospitable to the religio-linear temporality of nineteenth-century US nationalism and the rhetoric of Manifest Destiny. But this queer anti-futurity becomes something other than a negation: it is instead a reconfiguration of the temporality of US settler nationalism, a folding of queer anti-futurity into the nation so that queer bodies and subjectivities do the work of (re)articulating biopolitical distinctions between queer white bodies that must be protected and queer racialized and Indigenous bodies that can or must be sacrificed.

Although less obvious, "The Iliad of Sandy Bar" similarly focuses on the temporal orientations that proceed out of the queer mining partnerships of the American West. The story is structured around a more than three-year feud between mining partners York and Scott. As is the case in "Tennessee," the community of Sandy Bar in "Iliad" takes a keen interest in a conflict between two of its members, and the Sandy Bar community and readers alike are offered little in the way of definite knowledge about why and how the feud has progressed: "Among the various conjectures, that which ascribed some occult feminine influence as the cause [of the feud between York and Scott] was naturally popular, in a camp given to dubious compliment of the sex," but no one—reader included—is ever given anything approaching a clear picture of the reasons for their feud. Ultimately, though, "Iliad" affirms Watson's account of the "extraordinary loyalty and affection between [mining] partners": antagonists throughout most of the text, the partners are, by the end, "reunited."[73] Unlike the reunion in the afterlife that "Tennessee" portrays, this reunion is an earthly one that ends within a day, with the death of Scott. And unlike Tennessee's Partner, the man left to grieve in "Iliad," York, is distinctly similar, if not the same as, Harte's primary readers. Even though Watson suggests that Tennessee's Partner "accrues both monetary capital and social capital in the form of class-marked respectability,"[74] it is the much more cosmopolitan York who might have struck Harte's middle- and upper-class readers as their social and economic equal (or superior). For example, in a detail evocative of the fabulously wealthy and powerful "Big Four" (Collis P. Huntington, Leland Stanford, Mark Hopkins Jr., and Charles Crocker) of the Central Pacific Railroad, which relied heavily on Chinese labor to complete its leg of the first transcontinental railroad, York's "Mongolian laborers" are driven off when Scott organizes "active opposition to the Chinamen."[75] York, then, is the character whom we might expect to conform most closely to a temporal orientation that is "properly" future-directed. As Luciano points out, "proper" temporal orientation was thought to be most strongly developed in white, middle-class Christians.[76] From one perspective, "Iliad" follows this equation of racial and class identity with one's mode of inhabiting time. Scott's death occurs in the very last paragraph of the text and signals that "the feud of Sandy Bar was at an end."[77] Achieving an apparently neat narrative closure, this ending might be read as suggesting that the affective relationship between York and Scott has reached an equally neat and contained conclusion. York perhaps will grieve for a period of time appropriate to a white, middle-class Christian, and then he will return to life in future-directed, linear time. One of the implications of this reading of the end of "Iliad" is the notion that the queer sociality of which York and Scott are a part is just as effective in cultivating "proper" temporal orientations as a sociality founded on the heterosexual family.

Yet we can also read "Iliad" as another queer retemporalization of US settler nationalism that, like "Tennessee," (re)articulates biopolitical distinctions between queer white bodies that must be protected and queer racialized and Indigenous bodies that can or must be sacrificed. Indeed, the narrative's conclusion might not be as neat as it seems at first, and the affective dynamic that this conclusion portrays can be read as unamenable to the nineteenth-century injunction that one must not grant priority to past connections over future-directedness. The end of "Iliad" narrates rising affection between York and Scott; after years of discord, the two men finally seem to be reconciling their differences and regarding each other with an affection that continues to grow through to the end of the story. The narrator offers us the image of York "holding the convulsed frame of his former partner on his knee, and wiping the foam from his inarticulate lips." We also are given an affectionate and eventually jesting verbal exchange in which Scott cries out "'Old man!'" to York, to which the latter responds in kind with "'Old chap.'" And in the penultimate clause of the text's closing sentence, we are told that "the sun" "saw the hand of Scott fall cold and irresponsive from the *yearning* clasp of his former partner."[78] In this last detail's articulation of intense longing for a lost partner ("yearning"), the text leaves readers with an image of York oriented squarely toward the past, and it is unclear whether he will proceed to grieve appropriately and then return to life in linear time, or if he will act like Tennessee's Partner and linger inappropriately in grief.

Regardless of which reading we choose and whether we see neat closure or messy ambiguity at the end of "Iliad," the homosocial intimacy that founds Western American sociality and persists as the region becomes modern and nationalized occasions unexpected outcomes for US expansion and settlement in the region. If we find neat closure in "Iliad," the region becomes a site where queer sociality is compatible with a "proper" orientation toward the complementary hegemonic temporalities of (heterosexual) human bondedness and linear-progressive US national time. Queer sociality becomes a part of the nation's linear-progressive march into the future. And insofar as a "proper" orientation to the temporalities of (heterosexual) human bondedness and US nationalism indexes fidelity to a hegemonic figuration of national identity (white, middle- or upper-class, Christian), those who participate in queer social forms also become unproblematically aligned with the "recognizable 'American' type" supposedly forged by the Anglo-American encounter with and development of the American West.[79] On the other hand, if we find messy ambiguity in the end of "Iliad," the region becomes, as in

"Tennessee," a site of queer anti-futurity that retemporalizes US settler nationalism as a formation in which what might look like queer negation is actually queer reconfiguration, a simultaneously inclusionary and exclusionary dynamic that solidifies the biopolitical distinction between white subjects and racialized and Indigenous subjects. Regardless of whether we read the conclusion of "Iliad" as a straightening of queerness or a queering of settler national time, the sexual production of settlement continues apace.

## Imagining the (Interracial) Community: Marriage Plots, Assimilation, and Inclusion in "The Idyl of Red Gulch" and "An Ingénue of the Sierras"

Whereas the three texts that this chapter has examined thus far revolve around queer socialities, "The Idyl of Red Gulch" (1869) and "An Ingénue of the Sierras" (1893) center on heterosexual courtship and marriage plots. Opposed to the negation of futurity traditionally associated with queerness, the temporality of the marriage plot is all about the future: as Valerie Rohy has argued, "the formal closure of the marriage plot . . . offers the glimpse of futurity that assures readers of generations to come."[80] "Idyl" invokes the future-oriented temporality of the marriage plot by "juxtapos[ing] a wanton westerner, the dissolute Sandy Morton, with a genteel easterner, the chaste schoolmarm Miss Mary."[81] Taking a different approach to the marriage plot, "Ingénue" narrates the tense and treacherous events leading up to the marriage between a not-so-ingenuous "ingénue" and Mexican bandit Ramon Martinez. "Idyl" and "Ingénue" participate in settler tensing by manipulating the proleptic, heteronormative temporality of the marriage plot in ways that serve the genocidal, inclusionary, normatively white vision of settler futurity contained in "Luck," "Tennessee," and "Iliad." In service of that vision's genocidal impulses, "Idyl" turns a failure of (white) heteronormative consummation into a story of Native American assimilation. In service of that vision's inclusionary impulses, "Ingénue" turns marriage into a scene of Mexican and Anglo-Saxon racial union.

The overall vision that emerges from Harte's short stories about California mining camp sociality and heterosexual marriage, then, can be described as a vision of settlement without heteronormativity and nationalism without racial purity—an alternative to the phantasmic contours of John L. O'Sullivan's vision of endless and homogeneous fecundity. As Amy Kaplan has noted, around the middle of the nineteenth century, in the midst of debates about the potential benefits and pitfalls of the US's westward expansion, O'Sullivan and a number of politicians articulated "visions of imperial expansion as marital union [which] carried within them the prospect of marriage as racial amalgamation."[82] O'Sullivan attempted to defuse rhetorically the prospect of racial mixing by prophesizing that "the [US's] population will be homogeneous."[83] The homogeneity that O'Sullivan looks forward to registers primarily as political-ideological sameness, and Pratt chillingly suggests that "O'Sullivan seeks to clear the future—our present—of intralocal democratic contest and to conjure in its stead a homogeneous population."[84] But it also undeniably registers as a prophesized racial sameness: we should remind ourselves here that O'Sullivan claimed in 1845 that it is the "manifest destiny" of the "Anglo-Saxon" "to overspread the continent allotted by Providence for the free development of our yearly multiplying millions."[85] O'Sullivan's language of procreation—"our yearly multiplying millions"—joins with the Anglo-Saxonism and future orientation of his rhetoric to foretell a very specific future for the American West: it will be a space populated by a politically and racially homogeneous people who will give birth to generations of equally homogeneous people.

Published roughly twenty-five years after O'Sullivan's comments, "Idyl" seems to work toward this future of racial homogeneity forecasted by O'Sullivan and later recapitulated by figures including Frederick Jackson Turner and Owen Wister, the latter figure a focus of chapter 4 of this volume. In this story of the love that blossoms between dissipated Alexander "Sandy" Morton and virginal Miss Mary, the narrator's descriptions of the two characters specify phenotypical characteristics suggestive of the "Anglo-Saxon," a term that "was often used by the 1840s to describe the white people of the United States in contrast to [B]lacks, Indians, Mexicans, Spaniards, or Asiatics [sic], although it was frequently acknowledged that the United States already contained a variety of European strains."[86] The narrator describes Sandy as "a kind of *blond* Samson, whose *corn-colored*, silken beard apparently had never yet known the touch of barber's razor or Delilah's shears," and in similarly racially redolent terms, Miss Mary is described as a "*gray-eyed* schoolmistress."[87] Yet the seemingly imminent union of these mutually smitten Anglo-Saxons is prevented when the mother of Tommy, a pupil of Miss Mary's whose name recalls the mixed-blood Tommy Luck of "Luck," approaches Miss Mary wearing her "'war paint'" of inebriation. In the course of asking Miss Mary to take Tommy away from Red Gulch, this racially ambiguous mother—it is unclear whether the "facetiously" described "war paint" refers solely to her drunkenness or, alternatively, to her intoxication as well as Native American ancestry—also reveals that Sandy is Tommy's father. The "rosy tints" of Miss Mary's infatuation with Sandy quickly fade away in the wake of this revelation, and she leaves Red Gulch with Tommy the following morning.[88] In Gary Scharnhorst's estimation, "Harte problematizes the settlement of the West by failing to consummate the marriage of the Eastern schoolmarm and Sandy."[89] But the narrative's overall movement does not problematize a key logic of settlement—on the contrary, it symbolizes that logic in Tommy's fate. Tommy's departure under the care of the pedagogical figure Miss Mary evokes the logic of Native American assimilation through education that took shape as early as the Indian Civilization Act of 1819, which led to the establishment of residential Native American boarding schools.[90] In 1860, nine years before the publication of "Idyl," the Bureau of Indian Affairs opened the first on-reservation Native American boarding school on the Yakima Indian Reservation in Washington state.[91] In this context, Tommy's "departure for Boston on the Slumgullion stage"[92] with Miss Mary dramatizes the genocidal logic of Native assimilation through education that had been legally and institutionally sanctioned by the time of the publication of "Idyl."

Unlike the four short stories that this chapter has considered thus far, all of which Harte originally published in the *Overland Monthly* between August 1868 and November 1870, Harte published "An Ingénue of the Sierras" in May 1893 in the New York *Sun*, a "penny press" newspaper whose low price allowed it to reach a wide audience that included readers from the working and middle classes.[93] Thus, while the original audience of "Ingénue" may have been qualitatively different from the audiences of Harte's earlier texts, this 1893 audience was ostensibly also considerably larger. Adding an inclusionary wrinkle to the genocidal logic of his earlier portrayal of Tommy's imminent assimilation in "The Idyl of Red Gulch," Harte offered readers of "Ingénue" a depiction of the future-oriented marriage plot as engine of racial mixture. In this narrative of Yuba Bill's attempt to spare his coach and passengers the misfortune of being robbed by "the Ramon Martinez gang of 'road agents,'" an "ingénue" traveling under the alias of Polly Mullins tricks Bill and all of the coach's passengers into believing that she has run away from her miserly and usurious father to marry a poor man named "Charley Byng," of whom her father does not approve. Telling Bill and the others that "'dad didn't like [Charley] just because he was poor, and dad's got money,'" "Polly" garners their sympathy and, arguably, the sympathy of the less wealthy readership of the *Sun*. Softened by the "ingénue's" plight, Bill and the passengers—a group that includes a judge, Judge Thompson—overlook potential signs that she is in league with the Ramon Martinez gang and unwittingly allow her to orchestrate with "Charley" the theft of "a lot o' woman's wedding things from [a] rich couple who got married the other day out at Marysville." "Polly" and "Charley" secure their escape when Judge Thompson marries the two of them and they ride off into what looks to be a happy and socially productive marriage: Bill suspects that "Charley" is part of the Ramon Martinez gang and that this marriage will domesticate the young man, ridding the Sierra Nevada foothills of at least one bandit and bringing "Charley" "among white men and civilization again." A supposed counter to this assumed movement toward whiteness and "civilization," the end of the text reveals that "Charley" was in fact the outlaw Ramon Martinez himself, "a dark, stylish chap, with shifty black eyes and a curled-up merstache [*sic*]."[94]

Famous nineteenth-century California outlaw Joaquín Murrieta provides a compelling historical and literary reference point for Harte's Ramon Martinez. The wide reach of Murrieta's story, disseminated in multiple genres from the 1850s to the 1880s, suggests that Murrieta may have provided some of the inspiration for Harte's character.[95] Ambiguities around Californio racialization, along with the nature of the US's treatment of California Native Americans in the wake of the Mexican-American War, suggest that a figure like Joaquín Murrieta/Ramon Martinez provided a convenient vehicle for imag(in)ing settler futurity as the incorporation of Mexican and Latinx people alongside the genocide of Native Americans. As Shelley Streeby puts it, in California and Texas in the second half of the nineteenth century, "the attribution of whiteness to people of Mexican origin was connected to land ownership and class."[96] This racial indeterminacy would explain how, Harte's comic purposes aside, Ramon Martinez could easily trick a group of Anglo Americans into thinking that he too is an Anglo American by the name of Charley Byng.

In discussing the historical Murrieta family, Susan Lee Johnson notes that Joaquín and his relatives experienced a common fate for settlers in Sonora: "Indian resistance often frustrated settlers' efforts to eke out a livelihood from the land—Apaches, Yaquis, Seris, and Mayos all challenged the Murrietas and related families in the hinterlands." Johnson suggests that as Sonorans "accustomed to Spanish and Mexican styles of conquest that stressed incorporation and exploitation of native peoples over elimination," the Murrietas "may have known they were headed to a country where an aggressive Indian policy touted removal of Indians from areas settled by whites as an ultimate goal." Regardless of whether Joaquín Murrieta and his relatives thought of the US's genocide of California Native Americans as conditions under which they "could finally make their fortune," figures like the historical and literary Joaquín Mur(r)ieta and Harte's Ramon Martinez should be read as figures who do more to normalize than contest US settlement.[97] To be clear, I am not suggesting that Joaquín Mur(r)ieta/Ramon Martinez should be read as stand-ins for white supremacist US settler colonialism—to imply as much would be to erase the asymmetrical relationship between Anglo Americans and Californios in the mid-nineteenth century. Rather, I am suggesting that Joaquín Mur(r)ieta, as historical personage and subject of literary representation, and the character Ramon Martinez should be understood, in part, as figures who reorganize intra-settler racial power dynamics. Such reorganization is fundamentally different than addressing the (il)legitimacy of settlement. Indeed, "Ingénue" is careful to align Ramon Martinez with the long history of European—in particular, Spanish—exploration and colonization in California: midway through the story, Polly Mullins tells her fellow travelers that, so far as she can tell, Charley Byng/Ramon Martinez works as a bill collector for "a Spanish firm." When Ramon Martinez rides off with the "ingénue," who "appeared to be a well-matured country girl [with] frank gray eyes"[98] not unlike those of Miss Mary of "Idyl," the "generations to come" implied in the marriage plot's "glimpse of futurity" will be (in readers' present, already are) the offspring of the imbrication of Mexican and Latinx racialization and California Native American genocide.

In "Ingénue" and the four other Bret Harte short stories discussed in this chapter, literary representation of the American West furnishes an occasion for (re)orienting readers' apprehensions of time in ways that turn the queer socialities and racial heterogeneity of the California frontier into enduring and integral components of the US, its national identity, and its settler colonial logics of genocide and settlement. In other words, the queerness and heterogeneity characteristic of settler life in the opening decades of California statehood are transformed from momentary ephemera to constituents of the national community. In the middle and at the end of the nineteenth century, John L. O'Sullivan and Frederick Jackson Turner encouraged US Americans to think of the American West as the stage where time, figured as a linear and progressive force, would turn the continent's difference and heterogeneity into the nation's unity and homogeneity. Harte, on the other hand, prompts his readers to imagine that the queerness, heterogeneity, and difference encountered on the frontier and in the American West not only will survive in the course of time and history's movement(s) but also compose some of the very stuff out of which the larger nation and its settler national identity are made. In doing so, he prompts us as critics to recognize that the genteel periodical genre form of regional writing, whose beginnings are often tied to the California geography of "Luck," did not work only or even principally in the service of elite condescension or ethnographic preservation. Rather, it worked to give a vital place in the settler colonial project to those who are often conceived as white settler heteronormativity's nonvital others.

# CHAPTER 2

# Settlement Without Settlement

DEADWOOD DICK DIME NOVELS
AND THE QUEERNESS OF SETTLER
COLONIALISM

B ret Harte's short stories were often published in fancy and expensive magazines. Dime novels, the subject of this chapter, were usually published in the cheapest format possible.[1] Dime novels had a great many eager readers during their late nineteenth and early twentieth-century heyday. Frank Norris, whose writing is examined in chapter 3, apparently was not one of those readers. In an essay titled "The Literature of the West," published in January 1902 in the *Boston Evening Transcript*, Norris complained of the lack of an epic bard, a Homer, to tell the story of the American West. "[T]he conquerors of the West," Norris wrote, "have gone to their graves unsung, save in the traducing, falsifying dime-novels."[2] Toward the end of that same year, in an essay titled "A Neglected Epic" published posthumously in New York–based magazine *World's Work*, Norris reiterated, in evident exasperation, "What has [the conquest of the American West] produced in the way of literature? The dime novel! The dime novel and nothing else. The dime novel and nothing better."[3] Two of his last critical statements about the region and its literature before his death at the age of thirty-two, these essays suggest that for Norris the dime novel's problems are of focus, scale, and *temporality*: to dilate on the escapades of small-time outlaws is to scale attention down to a decidedly non-epic scale; to scale attention down to this decidedly non-epic scale is to miss the historical movement culminating in the American West, where Norris believes "Civilization has circled the globe and has come back to its starting point, the vague and mysterious East" across the Pacific Ocean.[4] In other words, Norris regarded the dime novel as an utterly insufficient form for the task of narrating and memorializing conquest.

This chapter argues, contra Norris, that the dime novel narrated conquest in its own unique, important way. Settler tensing is about the temporal management of individuals and populations according to the imbricated imperatives of Native genocide, racialized expendability, and white ascendance. In the serial outlaw adventures of the Deadwood Dick dime novel series of the late nineteenth century, the dime novel form delineates the contours of settler citizenship to include queer white lives in the face of Mormon and Indigenous challenges to the legitimacy of US settler colonialism. The temporality and thematics of the dime novel bring together seriality, "adventure-time," and white working-class utopianism, a conjunction that I will clarify and elaborate on as this chapter unfolds. This conjunction in the dime novel accomplishes two things at once: it recognizes and includes some queer white lives as part of settler colonial futurity, and it excludes from that future Mormons and their particular modes of queerness by aligning them with excludable Indigenous and racialized others.

While early twentieth-century iterations of the Western such as Owen Wister's *The Virginian* (1902) and Zane Grey's *Riders of the Purple Sage* (1912), which I analyze in chapter 4, were immensely popular in the years following their publication, the serialized dime novel Westerns that preceded them were arguably more influential, reaching a mass audience of diverse class backgrounds in an affordable and relatively short format.[5] Critical statements and studies on the dime novel accordingly conceive of the form and its ideological as well as literary historical significance in terms that suggest these texts' expression or reconfiguration of the US's internal dynamics at levels including class and gender. In the mid-twentieth century, for example, Henry Nash Smith wrote of the "presumably close fidelity of the Beadle [one of the major dime novel publishers] stories to the dream life of a vast inarticulate public."[6] Closer to the end of the twentieth century, Michael Denning's class-centered analysis read the stock characters of dime novels, including the outlaw figure instantiated in Deadwood Dick, as embodiments of working-class values and interests and, hence, as avatars of working-class identity.[7] Skip forward to 2011 and Daniel Worden's *Masculine Style* reframed the dime novel in terms of masculinity and gender performativity, reading dime novel protagonists as heroes of masculine self-fashioning who address (and imaginatively redress) industrial and patriarchal oppression by bucking any stable identity, class or otherwise. Yet, whether the focus is an undifferentiated American "dream life," or working-class identity and interests, or masculine performance, questions about how and why the dime novels fit into late nineteenth and early twentieth-century processes of US settler colonial consolidation tend to be treated with a light touch. The tendency to emphasize class antagonism in the critical history of the dime novel form has left quite a bit of room for consideration of the form's parallel and significant interest in the intersections of masculinity, sexuality, and settlement.

Worden's work actually highlights at least one of the ways the dime novels' formal and narrative qualities seem to make them hard to read in terms of late nineteenth and early twentieth-century processes of settler colonial consolidation. Reading dime novel protagonist Deadwood Dick's performance of (white) masculine embodiment as a destabilization of the imperialist, patriarchal culture that masculinity often is thought to enforce, Worden ultimately concludes that these dime novel narratives are "inextricably bound to the racial and national consolidation inherent to manifest destiny."[8] In my estimation, Worden is correct in regarding this "subversive" form of masculinity as one part of the period's discursive production of settler colonial hegemony. But I think that Worden's implication that Deadwood Dick's masculine performance supports settler nationalism in spite of, rather than because of, its "subversiveness" forecloses some needed consideration of the precise ways in which nonnormative gender and sexuality in these texts fits into the (re) production of US settler colonialism. I'm going to suggest that the dime novel's preoccupation with class and masculinity is also a preoccupation with defining settler citizenship so as to include queer white subjects in the settler national community.

Scholars including Peter Boag, Nayan Shah, and George Chauncey have demonstrated the complex links between race, class, and sexuality in and around urban centers from New York to San Francisco and Portland in the late nineteenth century. This work demonstrates that for racialized and working-class subjects, sexualities and domesticities were quite fluid in comparison to the middle-class development of a relatively rigid, heterosexual/homosexual binary and the middle-class nuclear family norm.[9] Scholars such as Worden and Denise Cruz suggest that late nineteenth-century literary articulations of racialized and working-class sexualities and domesticities complicate the facile assumption of turn-of-the-twentieth-century white hypermasculinity as necessarily tied to or striving toward rigid middle-class norms regarding heterosexual desire and familial and social life. In other words, the often aggressive and frequently violent masculinity of a character like Deadwood Dick need not be uncomplicatedly heterosexual to further the settler colonial project, and it need not participate in forms of familial and social life predicated on the nuclear family to serve settlement.[10] Lacking the stability of marriage, family, and home, and barred from embodying the developmental and linear temporalities associated with individual bourgeois maturation and nationalism alike, Deadwood Dick and dime novel narrative do the complementary work of folding queer masculinities and queer sociality into the project of US settler colonialism.

## Mormons and Outlaws

Before proceeding further, a brief consideration of the history of Mormon persecution in the nineteenth century is in order, and not just because Mormons feature as villains in *Deadwood Dick's Doom*, which I discuss at the end of this chapter. From the perspective of the closing years of the first quarter of the twenty-first century—roughly six decades after the end of the 1924 to 1965 period that Matthew Frye Jacobson associates with the "consolidation of a unified whiteness"[11]—the persecution of Mormons represents a curious but not altogether surprising moment in the history of sexuality and racialization in the US. Roderick Ferguson, for example, connects the subjection of racialized groups in the US to their queered status vis-à-vis white heteropatriarchal norms.[12] In a related but distinct way, Mormons in the period before their official disavowal of polygamy in 1890 were queered in relation to US norms of white, Christian, monogamous, heterosexual marriage. William Handley gestures toward this history when he writes that "the end of polygamy . . . allowed the Mormons to become identifiably 'white,' in the period's moral and ethnic senses, and thus American."[13] Handley's reading of Mormon racialization through sexuality and queerness also points to the ways in which institutions and discourses of sexuality have been central to European and US hegemonies, from the imposition of colonial heteropatriarchy in the Americas, to the subjection of queered racialized groups and Mormons in the US, to contemporary homonationalism in the US and Western Europe. Institutions and discourses of sexuality—in particular, US and European heteronorms regarding marriage, kinship, labor, consumption, and ownership—have at every turn been instrumental in processes of settler colonialism and imperialism.[14]

The Mormon case represents an instance in which the US's biopolitical deployment of sexuality functioned in the service of defeating a domestic "empire," the Mormon "empire," as Zane Grey's narrator, as well as Grey's gunslinger hero Lassiter, put it in *Riders of the Purple Sage*.[15] The concerns about Mormon empire that Grey and many others articulated in the second half of the nineteenth and early twentieth century identify this queered and racialized population as perpetrators of imperialism and, implicitly, settler colonialism. Roughly a century after Grey's fictional commentary on Mormon empire, scholars including Amy Kaplan and Jasbir Puar noted an early twenty-first century willingness to name the US an empire in public discourse as the US simultaneously went about a biopolitical project of anti-terrorism that relies on the queering and racialization—the marking for death—of terrorist bodies, or "perverse populations."[16] This queering and racialization of perverse populations, as Puar argues, operates through the valorization of queer subjects who participate in heteronormative patterns of kinship, consumption, and ownership. In the post-1965 era of "inclusion," US imperialism has relied on the production of "regulatory" queer, or "homonational," subjects who embody an ensemble of heteronormative social and economic attributes.[17] Perhaps unsurprisingly, the work of a number of scholars of US settler colonialism and imperialism points to a set of historically specific but strikingly similar connections between (hetero)normativity and US hegemony in North America and beyond. Kaplan's work on the links between domesticity and US Empire suggests that nineteenth-century middle-class culture (re)produced US imperialism and settler subjectivity by linking middle-class, heteronormative domesticity to the fraught making of "home" in previously foreign spaces and the dissemination of US values abroad.[18] Mark Rifkin traces how the US mobilized heteronormative logics of kinship, private property, domesticity, and citizenship to dispossess Native peoples. Writing of the historical moment of the Deadwood Dick dime novels' publication, Rifkin suggests that both state institutions and "allied nongovernmental discourses, like late-nineteenth-century and early-twentieth-century anthropology," were key to the modes of Native queering and racialization that dispossessed Native Americans and legitimized the continuing existence of the US settler state.[19] This is all to say that theorizations of US settler colonialism and imperialism have tended to locate a crucial portion of these formations' effectivity in institutional and discursive mobilizations—one is tempted to say enforcements—of heteronormative social and economic logics that serve the interests of the state and capital.

The Mormon case certainly supports these theorizations of the heteronormative heart of US settler colonialism and imperialism. In the nineteenth century, the Mormons' own versions of imperialism and settler colonialism operated through nonheteronormative (polygamous), communalist social and economic arrangements. Thus, Mormonism needed to be quashed, because Mormons threatened the universality of US settler colonialism's social and economic logics. The polygamous Mormons constituted a convenient group through which US institutions and discourses could articulate and enact a (rhetorically) anti-imperialist position and biopolitics in the service of its own settler colonialism and imperialism, using the threat of racialized perversity and "theocratic empire"[20] as an ideological cover. There is simply nothing like the invocation of a potential threat to the (white) nuclear family when it comes to justifying US settlement and imperialism. But a wrinkle introduces itself when we take into account scholarship by historians including George Chauncey and Peter Boag that demonstrates that white and white-adjacent working-class US Americans in the late nineteenth century did not or could not live out the middle-class nuclear family ideal and the stricter heteronormative requirements of middle-class culture.[21] If, as Michael Denning has argued, the dime novel's stock characters embody working-class values and interests, then these stock dime novel characters need to be read as embodiments of values and interests defined by both class and settler colonialism. In other words, these characters and the stories they populate need to be read in terms of the work of accommodating at once the relatively fluid sexual and social worlds of white and white-adjacent working-class US Americans in the period and the settler colonial imperatives of Native disappearance, racialized expendability, and white ascendance.

In this context, the dime novels discussed in this chapter—*Deadwood Dick, the Prince of the Road* (1877), *Blonde Bill* (1880), and *Deadwood Dick's Doom* (1881)—refract working-class lives and interests insofar as these dime novel narratives often focus on the adventure and pleasures offered by refusal of middle-class, heteronormative social and economic logics. Crucially, this refusal simultaneously serves US settlement in the American West. How is it that while the US was working to settle the American West and developing its anti-Mormon rhetoric and policies, dime novel heroes like Deadwood Dick became massively popular? The answer, in brief, is that Deadwood Dick and the dime novels that bore his name separated the imperative to endlessly reiterate the legitimacy and naturalness of US settlement in the American West from the imperative to endlessly reiterate the legitimacy and naturalness of the middle-class white nuclear family. Heteronormativity and the nuclear family are helpful, but other, distinctly non-Native forms of social, sexual, and economic life had important roles to play in the project of settlement.

The miner and outlaw characters of the Deadwood Dick dime novels, in particular Deadwood Dick and Calamity Jane, are queer vis-à-vis a number of the social and economic heteronorms associated with US settler colonialism and imperialism, and Dick and Jane's queerness is inseparable from the imbricated seriality, "adventure-time," and (working-class) utopianism of the novels. Serialization and the conventions of popular literary form—in particular, the convention of an "adventure-time" of narrative that tends away from historical and biographical development[22]—were instrumental, if not requisite, for these novels' utopian imaginings. Serialization and abiographical narrative time affected the representation of the Deadwood Dick series' miner and outlaw characters along the axis of sexual norms, the same axis along which Mormons were demonized for their racialized "perversion" of polygamy. But, in ways important to a (white) readership invested in its whiteness, characters including Dick and Jane tend to be portrayed as moral opposites of Mormon characters. Mormon queerness, a queerness in specific social and economic senses that matter for the regeneration of US settler colonialism and imperialism, led to their racialization, charges of perversity, and their subjection to US state violence. In contrast, the miner and outlaw queerness of characters including Dick and Jane, characters who also are queer in important social and economic senses, is one of the principal constituents of their (white) preindustrial utopias. These miner and outlaw modes of embodiment are not demonized and consigned to death—in other words, they are not racialized—because they are marked as white against the racialized bodies of Mormons. Seriality and "adventure-time," which are central constituents of the Deadwood Dick dime novels' literary form, produce and sustain modes of nonheteronormative white embodiment that are desirable for a (white) audience that is invested in claiming and inhabiting whiteness.[23] Scott Morgensen writes that settler colonialism is naturalized "whenever subjects are defined by settler desires to possess Native land, history, or culture."[24] In the Deadwood Dick dime novels analyzed in this chapter, (reading) subjects are (re)directed toward modes of queer white embodiment that, in a seeming paradox, support

US settler colonialism despite their refusals of the interlocking logics of heteronormativity, whiteness, and settler colonial possession.

In the remainder of this chapter, I trace this desire for and orientation toward modes of queer white embodiment in three Deadwood Dick dime novels: the inaugural installment, *Deadwood Dick, the Prince of the Road* (1877); *Blonde Bill* (1880), which, like the inaugural installment, offers a vision of (white working-class) preindustrial utopia; and *Deadwood Dick's Doom* (1881), in which Dick and Jane get married on the heels of Native American repossession of the fictional town of Sequoy / Death Notch.

## Establishing the Parameters of Settler Sociality in the Deadwood Dick Dime Novel West: From *Malaeska* to *Deadwood Dick, the Prince of the Road*

The very first of the Deadwood Dick dime novels, *Deadwood Dick, the Prince of the Road* (1877), establishes tropes that feature throughout the series: characters who take on visual and nominal disguise; threatened and violated white women; caricatured and often grotesque depictions of Native Americans and racialized groups; and extreme and often absurd plot twists. This first Deadwood Dick novel also evokes the tortuous paths that heterosexual love and domesticity traverse in the very first dime novel, Ann S. Stephens's 1860 *Malaeska, the Indian Wife of the White Hunter*. Originally serialized in *Ladies Home Companion* in 1839, *Malaeska* was chosen by pioneering dime novel publisher Erastus Beadle to appear as number one of Beadle's Dime Novels in June of 1860. "Not only did Erastus Beadle begin with a proven bestseller," writes Christine Bold, "but he grafted an example of sentimental or women's fiction— the most popular genre of the mid-nineteenth century—onto a new format and new publicity that exploited public interest in the westward movement."[25] A brief foray into *Malaeska* will help to highlight how the figuring of queerness as negation of sociality gives way to the futurity of queer settler sociality in the Deadwood Dick dime novels discussed later in this chapter. In Stephens's seminal text, a bygone historical moment in New York's Hudson Valley and Manhattan provides the scene for two tragic interracial couplings. The opening chapters of *Malaeska* introduce two couples, one couple composed of the white Martha Fellows and the similarly white Arthur Jones, and the other comprised of the titular Malaeska, a Native American woman, and a white man named William Danforth. Fellows and Jones end up happily married, replete with happy domestic lives and high social standing. Danforth, on the other hand, meets a considerably less sanguine fate when he is killed in a skirmish involving Malaeska's tribe. Danforth's death leaves Malaeska and their baby son, also named William, to seek out Danforth's parents in Manhattan. The parents welcome baby William and begrudgingly take in Malaeska on the condition that she serve as William's nursemaid and not divulge that she is his mother. William is raised as a well-to-do white man, all the while unaware of his mixed blood, and the bulk of the middle of the novel focuses on the white–Native American conflict literally embodied in William: Malaeska attempts but fails to steal William away and make him the chief of her alienated tribe, and William instead ends up being "refined" under the auspices of his white grandparents into an upper-class, Indian-hating "gentleman." In the novel's final chapter, Malaeska informs William of his Native lineage, upon which he promptly takes his own life. Importantly, William's death precludes his upcoming marriage to Sarah Jones, the white daughter of Martha Fellows and Arthur Jones. The closing paragraphs of *Malaeska* present a pathetic picture of Sarah many years after William's death, as she watches the demolition of the Danforth home in Manhattan as an older, lonely, and unmarried person.

*Malaeska* does, however, carve out a future for Sarah, bleak as that future may be: at the end of the novel, we are left with the image of her walking away from the ruins of the Danforth home, "stilling the wave of anguish that surged over her heart from the past, and going back to her useful life," a life whose contours readers are left to guess.[26] The emphasis on Sarah's pain suggests that her queerness, her falling aslant of the normative trajectory of middle-class heterosexuality, does not function as the basis of a wider queer sociality. Instead, Sarah's exclusion from the bourgeois heterosexual economy of marriage, reproduction, and domesticity allows *Malaeska* to portray white–Native American union as a tragedy for all involved, or, more precisely, as a tragedy for white women and those "tainted" by Native blood. The destruction of the Danforth home, symbolic of the end of the Danforth family, articulates the novel's sense of the ruin that awaits whites who admit Native Americans into their homes and Native blood into their lineage. A different kind of ruin, or at least the logic of a different kind of ruin, awaits Native Americans in this situation: as Harry J. Brown discusses in *Injun Joe's Ghost: The Indian Mixed-Blood in American Writing*, in the years leading up to and following the Indian Removal Act of 1830 a number of voices, including those of Thomas Jefferson and the pages of the *North American Review*, entertained the idea that Native American and white intermarriage could eventually "eradicate any trace" of Native American presence.[27] Even before he takes his own life, mixed-blood William Danforth symbolizes Native American genocide simply by living his life under the assumption that he is a white man, an upper-class, Indian-hating "gentleman" with no biological or cultural ties to his mother's tribe. *Malaeska* engages in the work of settler tensing via the language of bourgeois, heteronormative generational transmission, or, rather, via the evocation of that logic in order to turn mixed-blood William Danforth's death into a symbol for the supposedly inevitable disappearance of indigeneity within a social world captivated by bourgeois heteronormativity. But once the dime novel moves from the sentimental idiom of *Malaeska* to the adventure fiction form of the Deadwood Dick series, the production of Indigenous genocide begins to operate via other, queerer logics.

In the move from the sentimentalism of *Malaeska* to the adventure fiction form of the Deadwood Dick series, imperiled or "corrupted" white womanhood becomes a catalyst for imag(in)ing queerness as part of settler futurity, as a corrective for the divisive and destabilizing effects of bourgeois, heteronormative generational transmission. The opening chapter of the inaugural novel in the Deadwood Dick series, *Deadwood Dick, the Prince of the Road* (1877), identifies a character named Fearless Frank as one of the narrative's heroes when he pursues the far-off screams of an unknown woman and saves her from a fiendish Native American character named Sitting Bull, ostensibly a fictionalization of the Lakota leader Tatanka Iyotake, and his "score of hideously painted savages."[28] This opening conflict, articulated via the damsel in distress trope, aligns

*Prince* with a literary tradition of patriarchal heroism that stretches back to antiquity and the Sanskrit epic (such as in the *Ramayana,* where Rama saves Sita by slaying her abductor, Ravana) and Greek mythology (such as the story of Perseus saving Andromeda from Poseidon's sea monster). It also speaks to what Brian Klopotek, Lisa Tatonetti, and Ty P. Kāwika Tengan describe as distorted settler imaginings that associate Indigenous masculinity with hypermasculinity, misogyny, and violence, "negative stereotypes," as Tengan puts it, "associated with the ills of colonization."[29] When Frank locates the source of the screams, which come from a character named Alice Terry, he finds that "She was stripped to the waist, and upon her snow-white back were numerous welts from which trickled diminutive rivulets of crimson." While the novel marks Sitting Bull and his warriors as violent threats to white women, the opening portrayal of Frank presents white settler masculinity as chivalric, an extension of the knight errant of Arthurian romance, and as a check to violent Indigenous men. This portrayal of Indigenous masculinity transmogrifies the by-then contained threat to settler sovereignty once posed by Tatanka Iyotake and his followers, the same historical actors who defeated General Custer and the 7th Cavalry Regiment of the United State Army in June 1876, into a threat to white settler men's protection and control of white settler women. Historical conflicts over territory between the US Army and the Lakota, Northern Cheyenne, and Arapaho are sublimated in this popular fiction into conflict between violent Indigenous men and a chivalrous white settler with competing claims to a white woman. Yet this conflict, like the Great Sioux War of 1876 / Black Hills War that ended in US annexation of Sioux land in the Black Hills in February 1877, already has a victor: when readers are finally returned in chapter 5 to the conclusion of the scene of Frank's rescue of Alice, we find that Sitting Bull regards Frank as a "brother" and "friend" because Frank once nursed him back to health when his own warriors had no idea how to revive him. Consequently, Sitting Bull promptly agrees to hand Alice over to Frank. (*Prince*'s condescension toward what it regards as Lakota ways, or at least its parroting of a condescending attitude, is evident when Sitting Bull describes his warriors as running "hither and thither in affright, calling on the Manitou to preserve their chief" when what was actually needed were the "simple remedies" that Frank knew to administer.)[30] Having translated territory into a white female body, *Prince* establishes gender and sexuality as central terrains on which white settlers enact sovereignty.

As this book has noted before, work by scholars including Scott Morgensen and Mark Rifkin has demonstrated the multiple historical moments and discourses and institutions where settler gender and sexuality have furnished the grammar for Indigenous genocide and settler authority.[31] *Prince* participates in a long-standing conjunction of settler gender, sexuality, and authority, and this section demonstrates that the novel bases settler authority in queer sexualities and socialities defined in opposition to Indigenous and upper-class settler foes. As the novel's white heroes fight off enemies that include Sitting Bull and his "painted savages" and Dick's own upper-class relatives, the novel participates in settler tensing by linking queer settler sociality to (white) working-class utopianism. *Prince* figures marriage and the heteropatriarchal family's logic of inheritance as corrupting influences to be avoided. As a preferable alternative to these corrupting influences, Dick, Jane, and a host of other characters build economic justice for white workers on the foundation of a wider, queer sociality. In *Prince*, the (re)production of a settler society worth living in (for settlers, that is) requires refusal of social and economic forms that have historically secured the legitimacy and continuity of the settler colonial project.

In *Deadwood Dick, the Prince of the Road*, the "corruptibility" of white womanhood furnishes a narrative element through which different modes of sociality can be contrasted with one another. The unknown woman whom Fearless Frank saves, Alice Terry, has come from the Eastern US to find her father, and her Eastern origin and refined speech mark her as a genteel figure among the "rough" Western characters who populate the novel. While Frank is initially the most logical romantic possibility for Alice, narrative complications intervene, in the form of another suitor, Harry Redburn, and Frank's already being married to another woman, Anita Harris. Unlike Frank, who is portrayed as an analogue of the titular outlaw Deadwood Dick, Redburn is a "pilgrim" from the East whose refinement is evident in the narrator's notion that grooming has made his appearance "almost perfection itself."[32] Couple Alice's and Redburn's appearance and association with the East with the fact that they do not possess pseudonyms or alliterative names, which are hallmarks of the more firmly Western characters in the novel and the series, and it is easy to see that the two represent a rigidity and refinement associated with a genteel Eastern social world. Thus, it is not surprising that of the romantic couplings in the novel, theirs resembles most closely the normative trajectory of the genteel marriage plot, replete with a slightly rocky courtship and a felicitous marriage at the end. In relatively slight contrast to Alice and Redburn's coupling, Anita Harris and Fearless Frank are remarried at the same time that the former couple are joined in matrimony. Anita and Frank's remarriage rectifies a long-running misunderstanding between the two that had left Anita believing that Frank had married and then divorced her. Their reunion, like the union of Alice and Redburn, offers readers a glimpse of the generational futurity that consummated marriage plots promise.[33]

Alongside the heteronormative settler futurity offered by these two romantic plots, the fates of Deadwood Dick and Calamity Jane, another major character who recurs in the series, might appear to be dead ends. But in Dick and Jane's fates lie the roots of a queerly settler colonial sociality. Jane, the novel is careful to point out, has been subjected to forms of social and sexual violence, as Dick tells Redburn in a pained yet triumphant tone: "'She was *ruined*'—and here a shade dark as a thunder-cloud passed over [Dick's] face—'and set adrift upon the world, homeless and friendless; . . . but her character has not suffered blemish since the day a foul wretch stole away her honor!'" Despite—or perhaps as a consequence of—being "ruined," Calamity Jane is the most powerful female character in the world of *Deadwood Dick, the Prince of the Road*, possessing an appearance and mannerisms that are marked as signs of masculinity located in a female body. The narrator's introductory description of Jane notes her "trim boyish figure," and when she saves Dick and Redburn from a deadly situation shortly after, Redburn mistakes her for a "chap." During a subsequent altercation with a card sharp, Jane speaks with the distinctive accents of a Deadwood Dick or any number of other gunslinger types, confidently exclaiming, "'Come on,

you black-hearted ace-thief! . . . come on! slide in if you are after squar'
up-an'-down fun. We'll greet you best we know how, an' not charge you
anything, either. See! I've got a couple full hands o' sixes [six-shooters];
every one's a trump! Ain't ye got no aces hid up yer sleeves?'" Like Alice
and Anita, Calamity Jane has her chance to get married at the end of the
narrative, when Dick asks her to marry him. But she "haughtily, sternly"
replies in the negative and tells him, "I have had all the *man* I care for. We
can be friends, Dick; more we can never be!" Dick goes one step further
than simply accepting friendship, although he desired marriage: offering
up a statement that remains more or less true throughout his exploits
in future dime novels, he says in response to Jane's refusal, "I rec'on it is
destined that I shall live single."[34] The novel thus ends by flirting with
neat closure only to pull back and send Dick and Jane onto an alternate
path and into a temporality that exceeds the bourgeois heteronormative
logic of the marriage plot. Rather than getting married and "settling
down," Dick and Jane continue lives in which their principal allegiances
and intimacies are with "friends" who occupy the same social world of
fluid identities and relatively non-hierarchical relationships that they do.

Viewed in terms of the market and the dictates of serialization,
Dick and Jane's failure to fulfill (or success in escaping) the logic of the
marriage plot might look like little more than a narrative contrivance
necessary for the Deadwood Dick dime novel series to continue. But
in exceeding this bourgeois heteronormative logic, Dick and Jane also
become central figures in the making and maintenance of novel social,
political, and economic relationships to self and others. More precisely,
they become key components in the continuation of a more communal
and egalitarian settler social world free of many of the ills occasioned by
class divisions.

These destructive class divisions are figured in terms of patriarchal
generational transmission. Logically enough, in a text that working-class
people read, two of the villains are an "aristocratic" father and son,
Alexander and Clarence Fillmore. At the end of the novel, the scope of
these men's depravity is revealed: we find out that Alexander is Dick and
Anita's uncle and former guardian; that he was appointed guardian after
Dick and Anita's parents died in a car accident when the siblings were

children; and that Alexander mistreated Dick and Anita and stole their inherited wealth. Alexander and Clarence feature in *Prince* because they wish to complete their long-thwarted plot to kill Dick and Anita. Their presence also allows the text to contrast Dick and Clarence, two young men from the same family and of the same generation. Obviously one of the crucial differences between Dick and Clarence is their upbringing. Whereas Dick escaped his tyrannical uncle and grew into adulthood among fur traders, gamblers, and outlaws, Clarence's upper-class upbringing turned him into "a counterpart of [his father] in every particular. . . . The same faultless elegance in dress, the same elaborate display of jewels, and the same haughty, aristocratic bearing produced in one was mirrored in the other."[35] The transmission of behavior and outward signs of class status across generations is figured as the product of profound patriarchal influence and maturation under conditions that more closely resemble those that obtain when the nuclear family is the organizing principle of social life. For reasons that are never divulged, Clarence has never met his mother; rather than a sign of a failure to achieve heteronormativity, this aspect of Clarence's history seems designed to emphasize the influence of economically powerful men in the Eastern US of the late nineteenth century, where "civilization" and its heteronormative organization are more firmly entrenched than in the American West of *Prince*.

The implications of class conflict and capitalist avarice that Alexander and Clarence Fillmore introduce into the narrative thus are tied most closely to oppositions between East and West and between a logic of rigid (heteronormative) inheritance and the more capacious sociality of the dime novel's version of the settler colonial American West. The more purely economic opposition between those who control capital and those who have no choice but to sell their labor to survive ultimately fails as an explanation for why Alexander and Clarence are the "bad guys." For the world of the novel is one in which selling one's labor for a wage is merely one of many ways of surviving, and by the narrative's conclusion most of the "good guys" mentioned above have become capitalist types through mining or, in the case of Dick and Anita, the restoration of inherited wealth when crooked Alexander and Clarence Fillmore are hanged. In a general sense, *Prince* condemns capitalist relations and the greedy, morally objectionable behavior that they engender. But this critical take on capitalism operates through a more specific censuring of the workings of class and cultural inheritance (figured in the mirroring of Alexander and Clarence Fillmore), an inheritance that is predicated on the nuclear family and heteropatriarchy.

Freed from the influence of the social world that produced Clarence, Deadwood Dick embodies a form of settler legitimacy that derives, not from the logic of heteropatriarchal inheritance that centers Alexander and Clarence's (economic) power, but from an escape from this logic into a capacious sociality in which differences of class and region are imaginatively resolved. In this way, *Prince* (as well as later Deadwood Dick dime novels) figures heteropatriarchal generational transmission as a source of division and injustice, social ills that are rectified through the leadership of those who live outside the timelines and imperatives of this generational logic. A "just" settler sociality—"just" in the sense of a leveling of (class) difference between white settler subjects—becomes synonymous with freedom from heteronormative generational transmission. Although Dick's legitimacy is based in violence and extralegal actions, which would seem to point to an antisocial ethic, he is actually a figure around which heterogeneous individuals cohere. As Daniel Worden writes, "As leader of his band of rebels, Deadwood Dick forms a community free of social hierarchy. This 'dauntless band' is described as a group of singing males, exquisitely dressed and on sleek horses, yet containing a diverse assemblage of voices. . . . Deadwood Dick's band blends the cultivated with the uncultivated. While [dime novel hero] Seth Jones ultimately gives way to the imperative of the marriage plot, Deadwood Dick persists in using masculinity to produce new forms of social belonging."[36] In other words, Dick's escape from the marriage plot allows him to persist in bringing diverse people together, a feat he accomplishes by bridging the regional and class differences whose potential for harm is embodied in Alexander and Clarence Fillmore. For example, the Eastern and relatively genteel "pilgrim" Redburn enters *Prince*'s narrative by way of an alliance with Dick founded in an act of outlaw justice meted out to a cheating card sharp. Tellingly, in the moments leading up to Redburn and Dick's alliance, Dick is introduced under his alternate name, Ned

Harris, and we are told that he "commenced to pare his finger-nails. The fingers were as white and soft as any girl's." This description emphasizes similarity between the well-groomed Redburn and Dick, two men whose differences are highlighted at other points in the novel. The description also contrasts sharply with an earlier one, where the narrator notes that Deadwood Dick's hands are "large and knotted."[37] Dick's body, like his history of dispossession and outlawry, figures the mutable, bridgeable difference between the working-class identity symbolized by "large and knotted" hands and the middle- or upper-class status signified by "white and soft" fingers. As the alliance with Redburn suggests, Dick is able to do with others what he does within his own body and identity, bringing together the outlaw and the gentleman, the uncouth and the genteel, the Western and the Eastern in ways that work to rectify the social ills that these differences would otherwise exacerbate. If nothing else, Deadwood Dick is a figure for settler society freed from any internal divisions that threaten ideological coherence and legitimacy.

Moreover, rather than the hyper-patriarchal dominance suggested by the absence of Clarence Fillmore's mother, the social world of Dick and his heterogeneous allies is one in which agency and power bear no necessary connection to male bodies.[38] It is a social world in which settler colonial power does not depend on heteropatriarchy. In particular, Calamity Jane represents the agency that a settler subject assigned female at birth can wield once freed from the marriage plot. As noted above, in the novel's logic, Jane wields the most power and agency of the three main female characters by virtue of dress and behavior that resemble those of a masculine gunslinger such as Deadwood Dick. This resemblance proceeds in part out of the contrasts that the novel draws between Jane on the one hand and Alice and Anita on the other. Alice, as we know, enters the narrative as a captive of Sitting Bull and only escapes because Fearless Frank saves her. Subsequently, her role in the narrative entails little more than falling in love with Redburn and marrying him. Similarly, Anita spends her time looking after the home that she and Dick inhabit before her reunion with Fearless Frank, all the while sad because of the supposed "dishonor" that she and Dick think Frank has brought upon her. Her happy ending of a reunion and remarriage with

Frank only comes about because of Dick's exploits. As mentioned above, Jane also has been "dishonored," but instead of cloistering herself and letting sadness take over, she takes on the kind of active and vengeful role that Dick performs. At the end of the novel, Dick and Jane mirror one another as they continue on as mobile members of the outlaw social world to which they have long belonged: Jane, the narrator notes, "is still in the Hills," and Dick similarly "roams through the country of gold."[39] Their membership in this world is enabled and forged by their living outside the heteronormative roles and intimacies that cause so much pain for Anita and Frank and, to a lesser extent, for Alice and Redburn as well.

While Mormons were denigrated in popular discourse and media and disenfranchised through two 1880s US acts and an 1890 Supreme Court ruling, Jane, Dick, and Dick's band of outlaws are ethical heroes within the world of cheating and immorality that stretches from East to West, from the avarice of Alexander and Clarence Fillmore to the cards hidden up the sleeve of the Black Hills card sharp who tries to hustle Redburn. As figures of settler justice in an unjust settler society, Dick, Jane, and the outlaws with whom they are allied embody a version of whiteness and queer sociality that furthers the settler colonial project by loosening the connections between heteropatriarchy, capitalist development, and the dispossession of Native Americans. The Mormons, who represented a contemporaneous historical example of (almost) white people who stood in the way of US settler colonial empire's advance, were denigrated and excluded from the ranks of fully white US Americans. Conversely, the outlaws of *Prince* are portrayed in celebratory terms in large part because they live lives that escape the heteronormative logic built into commonplace notions of manifest destiny, a logic that the text also implicates in the class dissension and gender inequalities that structure life outside the outlaws' social world. In championing the outlaw sociality to which Dick and Jane belong, the novel forwards a version of (normatively male) settler whiteness that is distinguished from the outset from Indigenous masculinity. But this settler whiteness and the sociality that it anchors bear a striking resemblance to the "threatening" Mormon others against whom whiteness and US "civilization" found key parts of their shape and coherence. In subsequent Deadwood Dick dime novels, the distinctions between outlaws and Mormons would harden.

## "friends to whom I am deeply indebted": Queerness, Whiteness, and Settler Citizenship in *Blonde Bill; Or, Deadwood Dick's Home Base*

Originally published three years and many entries in Beadle's Half-Dime Library after *Deadwood Dick, the Prince of the Road*, *Blonde Bill*'s narrative is propelled (as are the narratives of many other Deadwood Dick dime novels) by the death of Dick's wife.[40] The novel commences with a stagecoach attack, carried out by an outlaw gang called the Silent Tongues, in which the wife of a man named Blonde Bill is killed. Readers later find out that Blonde Bill is actually Deadwood Dick, and the death of his wife Edith sets in motion the revenge plot that runs throughout the novel. Dick gets a restrained kind of revenge by the end, but the closure of this revenge plot is accompanied by a social open-endedness made possible by the death of Dick's wife. Freed from the demands of marriage, Dick finds a "home base" in the resource-rich valley formerly controlled by the Silent Tongues, a valley that provides wealth and happiness to Dick and "his little band of friends . . . among whom are Calamity Jane, Old Avalanche, Beautiful Bill and Raphael."[41]

Mormonism again provides an apt historical referent for consideration of this portrayal of life outside the circuits of heteronormativity. In *Deadwood Dick, the Prince of the Road*, Dick and Jane embody a departure from bourgeois heteronormativity that is emphasized by the contrast between them and the two couples who get married. In *Blonde Bill*, on the other hand, Dick and Jane's ending in a social world where their closest ties are to "friends" is counterposed to the sexual and social practices of the Silent Tongues, a group whose actions resemble the supposed threat that the Mormons posed. *Blonde Bill* normalizes US settlement in its narrative of Deadwood Dick and his band's victory over the Silent Tongues, the novel's proxy for Mormonism. The novel's narrative trajectory does the work of settler tensing by pulling Deadwood Dick out of marriage and into the making of a settler community that legitimates its queer sociality and sutures itself to the imagined space of the nation by defeating the threat of Mormonism.

Anti-polygamists considered Mormon polygamy and the broader sexual and social arrangements of Mormon life a form of slavery for white women.[42] *Blonde Bill* aligns one of its principal villains, the Ohio congressman Ray Vernon (who happens to secretly be one of the leaders of the Silent Tongues) with woman-"enslaving" Mormons. After portraying the stagecoach attack that leaves Dick's wife dead, the novel's opening chapters proceed to offer a lengthy, drawn-out account of, in the words of the second chapter's title, "a queer street auction." In this auction, a "slave-trader" by the name of Salamander Sam attempts to sell his daughter, Dashing Dolly, and the narrator gives this auction specifically sexual and reproductive stakes in noting that she "was a young woman or maiden of perhaps eighteen years of age." A bidding war ensues between Dick and Vernon. While Dick is bidding to "'give her her freedom,'" Vernon, in Dick's estimation, has "'base designs'" in attempting to win Dashing Dolly.[43] The implication here is that Vernon wishes to own Dolly as a sexual slave, which would render her place similar to the status that anti-polygamists attached to Mormon women under polygamy.

Dick wins the auction and gives Dolly her freedom, actions that constitute part of the novel's efforts to define and valorize Dick and his associates in opposition to the Mormon-like threat that Vernon represents. As one of the three "chief members" of the Silent Tongues—the other two are a minister named Van Syckel and a deputy named Garwood—Vernon's characterization portrays the Silent Tongues as a secretive (or "Silent") society headed by a man eager to "enslave" women.[44] The Silent Tongues' secrecy moves past nominal suggestion when the narrative offers an account of a secret Silent Tongues meeting in which Vernon, Van Syckel, and Garwood are revealed as the men who lead the Silent Tongues while maintaining their public identities as a congressman, minister, and deputy. The composition of the Silent Tongues' leadership, which fuses religious and political authority, evokes the "'theocratic' rule" that, along with polygamy, accounted in large part for the US's fear and distrust of Mormons.[45] Without actually being (named as) Mormons, the Silent Tongues and their secret society are eerily similar to those denigrated others in their "perverse" sexuality and "un-American" combination of church and state. Conversely, the sexual mores of Dick and his band are defined, in part, as an effort to rectify the perversity and excesses of Vernon and his accomplices. One of the more curious aspects of this ameliorative role is its reliance, within the narrative's logic, on Dick's loss of his wife and subsequent seeking of revenge. In other words, it is through Dick's (forced) movement outside the structures (strictures) of the marriage plot that he comes to head efforts to combat the deviant sexuality and sociality of the Silent Tongues. His removal from the roles and responsibilities of bourgeois heteronormativity ends up being one of the keys to ensuring the defeat of a group whose threat to white womanhood is figured as deadly right from the beginning of the novel, when the Silent Tongues kill Dick's wife.

In constructing a sexually and socially deviant other in the form of Vernon, Van Syckel, Garwood, and their band of Silent Tongues, the novel carves out a space of legitimacy for—indeed attaches great value to—the queer arrangements that Dick and his band proceed to forge. Like nearly all the Deadwood Dick dime novels, *Blonde Bill* ends with Dick and his comrades victorious, as Vernon and his accomplices are defeated and graciously granted their lives and freedom provided that they "leave the mining country forever." With the Silent Tongues' leadership and other "ruffianly" members banished, Dick assumes control of the more upstanding contingent within the Silent Tongues, and everyone seems to live harmoniously and happily in Golden Pocket, the rich mining valley that the Silent Tongues formerly held. Similar to *Deadwood Dick, the Prince of the Road*, one of Dick's associates in *Blonde Bill*, Rosebud Rob, is on the verge of getting married at the end of the novel (to a woman named Cinnamon Chip, who does not feature in *Blonde Bill*). The narrator offers no opinions, let alone excitement, regarding Rosebud Rob's decision to leave Golden Pocket and his "friends." Instead, the narrator quickly proceeds to skip ahead in time to "to-day," when Golden Pocket has proven to be a "bonanza" and "Peaceful and undisturbed, the band is mining the days away, out of the reach of the strong, stern arm of the law."[46] This outcome for Dick and his unmarried comrades is portrayed in utopian terms, in distinct contrast to the narrator's flat description of Rob's marriage plans.

Gesturing toward a future moment of social closure through marriage, the last sentence of the novel reads, "and in the *dim* future, it is not improbable that Dick and Calamity will enter into a loving partnership for life, which long delayed consummation, we believe, our readers will welcome with— Three cheers for Deadwood Dick!"[47] The vagueness of this presumed future marriage calls into question whether it will even happen. The pain that Dick experiences when he loses his wife Edith calls into question whether his and Jane's marriage would be a desirable development or just another instance where his wife must be killed off so as to open up the possibility of further adventures, all at the cost of further grief.[48] Indeed, killing off Calamity Jane would most likely prove bothersome for the writers and disappointing for readers, given Jane's recurrent and central role in the series. Moreover, romantic feelings and the prospect of marriage between Dick and Jane often figure (as they do in chapter 5 of *Blonde Bill*, which details Jane's unrequited love for Dick and the pain it has caused her) as a source of suffering and disappointment, in contrast to the happiness occasioned by the wider sociality of an arrangement such as the one they enjoy in Golden Pocket at the end of the novel. Ultimately, the prospect of Dick and Jane's marriage reads as lip service to the presumed naturalness and inevitability of heterosexual coupling.

As we have seen, *Blonde Bill*'s narrator suggests that Dick and his "friends" are living outside the boundaries, or "strong, stern arm," of the law. Yet Dick's insistence a couple of pages earlier that he will only take command in Golden Pocket if everyone understands "that we are miners, and *citizens*, and not outlaws" suggests otherwise, and it separates the possession of settler citizenship and capitalist prosperity from any necessary connections to heteronormativity.[49] As Cathy J. Cohen has argued, the state's regulation of sexuality, "in particular through the institution of heterosexual marriage," historically has been used to distinguish those "'fit' for full rights and privileges of citizenship" from those who are not.[50] Nonnormative behaviors vis-à-vis biological reproduction and family formation have served as the pretext for excluding certain individuals and populations or coercing them into following normative patterns—again, the treatment of Mormons as well as Native Americans and racialized groups is illuminating in this regard. Despite the fact that *Blonde Bill* does not detail whether Dick and his associates are in fact accorded the full rights and privileges of citizenship, Dick's proclamation that he and his fellow Golden Pocket denizens are citizens subtly works to sever heteronormative conformity from (state-sanctioned) privilege. Rather than being a state technology of sexual regulation, settler citizenship is figured as something that the individual performatively enacts and subsequently lives in her or his own modality. In this (re)configuration of citizenship, Deadwood Dick and his associates' potential (white working-class) threat to normatively bourgeois settler hegemony is (re)cast as but another way of belonging in the settler nation. In *Mythohistorical Interventions*, Lee Bebout theorizes "the *mythohistorical*, [composed of] an integrated network of myths and histories," as the materials out of which shared narrative, identity, and community are forged. Hegemonic as well as subordinated groups use manipulations of the mythohistorical to "imagine new communities and new boundaries as well as fashion new citizenships."[51] Alongside and in contrast to Richard Slotkin's argument that the working-class press identified with the plight of the victims of US settler expansion, *Blonde Bill* demonstrates that the dime novel imagined new communities, boundaries, and citizenships that sutured white working-class queerness to the settler national community.[52] *Blonde Bill*'s form and content, or, more precisely, the ways in which the narrative is informed by its serial publication format, "adventure-time" narration, and mythohistorical manipulations, hails white working-class queerness as a constituent component of a settler hegemony that transcends class.

In case readers have any concerns about the racial character of the forms of settler citizenship and community that Dick and his associates forge in *Blonde Bill*, the novel is careful to mark Dick as white. More precisely, the novel early on associates Dick with whiteness in its phenotypical sense as well as its late nineteenth and early twentieth-century moral sense, in the visual whiteness of his Blonde Bill disguise and the moral "whiteness" of his act of saving Dashing Dolly from sexual slavery.

Right after Dick frees Dolly from the lascivious designs of her father, Salamander Sam, and Vernon, he reveals that Blonde Bill is merely an alias, and we as readers of a Deadwood Dick dime novel are confirmed in our suspicions that Blonde Bill is in fact Deadwood Dick. The name Blonde Bill refers to Dick's appearance while in disguise, as he is "attired in a stylish suit of light cloth, with a shirt front of spotless white . . . [and] his white complexion harmoniz[es] well with his long blonde hair, and sweeping mustache of the same hue."[53] This visual description of Blonde Bill contrasts sharply with Deadwood Dick's "undisguised" appearance, which is marked by dark clothing and features.[54] It also casts Blonde Bill as a possessor of a valorized form of (Anglo-Saxon) whiteness within the US's hierarchy of white "races" in the second half of the nineteenth and first quarter of the twentieth century.[55] Not only does the text call to mind the hierarchy of white races that was promulgated in various discourses, it also unsurprisingly links privileged racial and class identity to sexual propriety.[56] Indeed, Blonde Bill is not only blonde but also possesses outward signs of high socioeconomic status, wearing "a blazing diamond pin" on his spotless shirt.[57] And yet Blonde Bill is actually Deadwood Dick, the man who normally wears black and has "raven curls and mustache," like a member of the supposedly morally and politically inferior "swarthy" white "races" of late nineteenth and early twentieth-century US racial thought and classification.[58] But within the logic of the "adventure-time" of dime novel narrative, a narrative temporality that tends toward biographical stasis rather than development, Dick is the same person he was at the beginning of *Blonde Bill*; regardless of costume or marital status, he's the same person who protects white women from Mormonesque villains. Deadwood Dick serves as a central figure in *Blonde Bill*'s fashioning of a version of settler whiteness that protects white womanhood yet does not accede to the sexual and social norms traditionally associated with settler sovereignty. While Dick and his associates emerge from *Deadwood Dick, the Prince of the Road* in a position of potentially unsettling proximity to the Mormon threat, *Blonde Bill* normalizes their alternative mode of sexual and social life by organizing its narrative around their differences from and opposition to the Mormonesque Silent Tongues.

## Settling: Social Reproduction in *Deadwood Dick's Doom; Or, Calamity Jane's Last Adventure*

In *Blonde Bill*, the bad guys resemble Mormons; in *Deadwood Dick's Doom*, one of the bad guys actually is a Mormon. Rather than have Deadwood Dick and his comrades fashion a queer settler sociality as an answer to the Mormon threat, *Deadwood Dick's Doom* is about the dissolution of settler sociality as a form of (limited) punishment for Native American dispossession along the route from Pioche, Nevada to Helena, Montana. Connected to this dissolution is the very form of intimacy that the Deadwood Dick series often works so hard to avoid: *Deadwood Dick's Doom* more or less rectifies Dick and Jane's sexual and social errancy by having them get married at the narrative's conclusion. This conclusion follows on the heels of a violent maelstrom in the narrative's principal setting, "an imagined, out-of-the-way stage stop and supposed mining town" called Sequoy / Death Notch where Deadwood Dick and his associates defeat Mormonism alongside a Pawnee-Apache coalition's murderous expulsion of the town's white denizens.[59] Indigenous repossession in this text can be read as a half-hearted settler "move to innocence"; in other words, the very limited restoration of Indigenous land and control that occurs near the end of the novel can be read as an (likely unwitting) attempt to assuage settler feelings of guilt and complicity in historical and ongoing dispossession, which ultimately helps to secure settler futurity.[60] But the narrative's ordering of events toward its end—from Mormon defeat and the dissolution of queer settler sociality, to Indigenous repossession, to Dick and Jane's marriage—shows us that settler futurity is also secured by the complementarity of queer and heteronormative modes of reproduction.

From early in *Deadwood Dick's Doom*, the vibrancy of Sequoy / Death Notch as a space of settler control is underwritten by the camp's white inhabitants' capacity to imagine and forge intimacy in the absence of heteronormative objects and legally legible forms of connection and affection. Indeed, the eventual rectification of Dick and Jane's sexual errancy via marriage takes place after the novel has whisked readers through scenes of a wider, queer sociality. For example, the first pieces of dialogue involving Vergie Verner, one of the women endangered by male

Mormon character Carrol Carner's sexual appetite, characterize Death Notch as an all-male space where the lack of proper (female) objects of affection and sexual desire has forced these men to redirect their affection and desires toward one another. As resident "poet" Hank Shakespeare declares after asking Vergie if she intends to settle down in Death Notch, "We're just needin' a woman, in this hyar camp, 'ca'se how, ye see, when ther b'yees wanter go courtin' they've got ter court one another."[61] Vergie does not intend to stay in Death Notch, but even if she did, the arrangement that Hank proposes transposes the social and affective dynamics of normative heterosexuality ("courtin'") onto a situation that sounds more like sex work. Hank claims that the men need *a* woman, not women in the plural, calling to mind the arrangements that obtain at the beginning of Bret Harte's "The Luck of Roaring Camp," where sex worker Cherokee Sal is the only woman in the otherwise all-male camp. Soon after this exchange between Vergie and Hank, Carrol Carner forcefully attempts to kiss a half-Pawnee, half-white girl named Siska, but Dick swoops in at the last moment to foil Carner's attempt. Just one page later, a "human wild beast" named Devil Dwarf strikes an agreement with Siska's father, Red Hatchet, to kill the white inhabitants of Death Notch if Red Hatchet allows him to "possess" Siska. Throughout the novel, narrative impetus is provided in large part by the fact that Carner, "Villain that he was," "had set his heart on capturing [Vergie] and making her his wife."[62] Vergie, of course, would be one among the numerous wives that Carner holds in sexual slavery.

In contrast, Dick and Jane's marriage at the end of the novel represents an escape from captivity for Jane. Jane is captured (rather than simply killed) by the Pawnee-Apache coalition that takes control of Sequoy / Death Notch, and she is subsequently freed through Siska and Dick's negotiations with her captors. The opposition between captivity/ perversity and freedom/propriety—figured, in part, as the opposition between Mormon polygamy and monogamous marriage—that the novel articulates through Vergie's Mormon endangerment and Jane's salvation bestows a measure of legitimacy on the Pawnee-Apache repossession of Sequoy / Death Notch. Paradoxically, Native control is linked to Native respect for settler sexual propriety. In the novel's last chapter, Apache and Pawnee warriors retake Sequoy / Death Notch in a siege that results in the deaths of the "bad guys," a group composed of Carner and nearly all the white men of the camp. The siege acts as a sort of purification, for the "good guys"—Dick, Jane, and Vergie among them—either escape or, in Jane's case, are spared death and soon freed. Although the Mormon threat that Carner signifies has been wiped out by the end of the narrative, the result of this is Native American repossession, rather than the consolidation of settler sovereignty. Dick and Jane's marriage, not to mention the sexual saving of Vergie, would not have been possible absent the actions of the Pawnee-Apache coalition. Siska saves Dick from sure death by quicksand (the "doom" of the title), and Vergie escapes from Carner and the other lascivious men of Death Notch in the chaos of the siege. Rather than being an imperative of US settler colonial empire, the defeat of Mormonism and of the more general sexual impropriety and queer sociality of Sequoy / Death Notch are instrumental in Native American repossession.

Carner's defeat sets the stage for Dick and Jane's marriage and the heteronormative domesticity that assumedly follows, but the novel locates this portrayal of normative family life in Pioche, Nevada, rather than the principal setting of Sequoy. The novel performs two crucial moves in this closing contortion. As in *Deadwood Dick, the Prince of the Road* and *Blonde Bill, Deadwood Dick's Doom* loosens the connections between (white) heteronormativity, white settlement, and Native dispossession. The narrative trajectory of *Deadwood Dick's Doom* also suggests the complementarity of queer sociality and heteronormativity in the settler colony. Absent the continuing reproduction of Sequoy's queer settler sociality, the novel turns to marriage and its promise of biological and social reproduction to secure settler futurity.

## The Heterogeneity of Settlement

Michael Denning's argument, in *Mechanic Accents*, that the working class read dime novels as "a set of stories one tells oneself to situate oneself in the world, to name the characters and map the terrain of the social world,"[63] represents an important moment in the critical history of the dime novel, a moment when the form was linked intimately to readers' perception of social reality. This chapter has sought to flesh out a part of this social map that settler colonialism renders natural and difficult to perceive: the queer and heteronormative formations of settler sexuality and sociality in the dime novel and their contributions to the project of settlement. Similar to Bret Harte's practice of local color writing analyzed in chapter 1, the very form of the dime novel, with its narrative temporality of "adventure-time," serves the settler tensing of white ascendance, racialized death, and Native genocide.

The dime novels analyzed in this chapter generally valorize the queer and heteronormative formations of settler sexuality and sociality that they portray. The novels' valorization of queerness looks backward to Bret Harte's writings of the 1860s and 1870s; their valorization of queerness *and* heteronormativity, which only emerges once we consider *Deadwood Dick's Doom*, looks forward to the early twentieth-century Westerns analyzed in chapter 4. The Deadwood Dick dime novels, and dime novel form more broadly, begin to trace the contours of a settler queerness that confounds the difference between queer and heteronormative, hegemonic and marginalized: these novels' heroes occupy both sides of these binaries. The working class–oriented dime novels served as prime sites for doing the work of (re)producing settler colonialism's queer protagonists.

# CHAPTER 3

# The End(s) of Regeneration

FRANK NORRIS'S AND JACK
LONDON'S NATURALIST FRONTIER
CHRONOTOPES

What do dentists and frontiersmen have to do with one another? Around the turn of the twentieth century, quite a bit more than one might assume. Zane Grey, whose work is taken up in the next chapter, practiced dentistry in New York City before turning full-time to writing. For Grey, the writing of fiction entailed a whole lot of stories about one iteration of the frontiersman, the cowboy, whom Grey no doubt took as a romantic and exciting figure against the example of his former life as a dentist: Grey biographer Thomas H. Pauly regards Grey's first novel, *Betty Zane* (1903), as "an exercise of compensation by an unhappy dentist hoping to overcome his despondency by writing about ancestors whose lives were more eventful and more satisfying than his own."[1] Frank Norris's novel *McTeague* (1899), one of the subjects of this chapter, draws a different kind of relationship between dentistry and frontier life, connecting titular character McTeague's dentistry to his earlier work of resource extraction in the California mines; gold and teeth are parallel objects of extractive work in the life of the miner-turned-dentist. By the end of *McTeague*, McTeague has returned to the mines as part of a pattern in the novel where undomesticated frontier life and its seeming opposite, urban middle-class life, bleed into one another in strange and unsettling ways. Walter Benn Michaels and Colleen Lye have discussed how naturalist writing of the late nineteenth and early twentieth centuries has a tendency to collapse the distinctions between seeming opposites: human and nonhuman animal, human and machine, Anglo-Saxon and racial other easily slide into relations of indistinguish-ability.[2] Fear of becoming one's opposite—fear of being reduced from rational human to unreflective animal, from free white worker to coo-lie, from daring frontiersman to bourgeois dentist—lurks and surfaces repeatedly in naturalist writing. Another version of this fear, the fear of being displaced from one's position of cultural power and prestige by one's supposed inferiors, animated elite white male culture at the turn of the twentieth century. In her study of the "frontier club," an exclusive group composed of men including Theodore Roosevelt, Owen Wister (whom I discuss in the next chapter), Henry Cabot Lodge, and S. Weir Mitchell, Christine Bold observes that these men "felt threatened by rapid industrial, urban, and demographic change ... and ... feared the rise of new financial power brokers and non-Anglo groups."[3]

This chapter considers how white male-authored literary natural-ism refracted similar fears and, in particular, how some of this writing staged white male settler power on the frontier in rather queer ways. The readings of naturalist texts in this chapter initially depart from the previous two chapters' focus on literature's (re)presentation of queer sociality and suturing of queerness to the settler national community. By its concluding sections, this chapter returns to texts that mesh queerness and nation, texts that produce, as did the California fiction of Bret Harte discussed in chapter 1, a vision of settlement without heteronormativity and nationalism without racial purity. In what follows, I argue that Frank Norris and fellow naturalist author Jack London (paradoxically) turn the representation of white settler death into a source of white settler futurity. In other words, naturalist narrative (re)produces white settler futurity even when it seems to say otherwise.

The lives of the fictional McTeague and historical personages such as Zane Grey and Theodore Roosevelt ask versions of the same ques-tion: what happens when the frontier has been declared "closed" and no longer can provide the imaginative and physical geography upon which romanticized national regeneration can unfold? Frederick Jackson Turner, intellectual mouthpiece for just these kinds of elite white male concerns, also posed this question, if only implicitly, in "The Significance of the Frontier in American History" (1893), an address that in one fell swoop proclaimed American national identity to be the product of European encounter with the frontier West and asserted that such encounters were no longer possible. Turner's positioning of the frontier's supposedly transformative work in a recent yet irretrievable past is ultimately unsurprising: within his historiography circulates an anxiety about the American West's and the entire nation's historical situation that seems all too fitting for the middle- and upper-class milieux of the 1890s, where assumptions about historical and social progress gave way to concerns over "degeneration."[4]

Elite white men and literary culture mounted responses to this perception of loss. Roosevelt turned to hunting in the American West and military exploits in the Caribbean—what he would term "the strenuous life" in an 1899 speech of the same name—to (re)find the frontier and its possibilities.[5] Fiction writers of the *fin de siècle* also turned to the frontier, particularly white male writers associated with the movement that came to be known as American literary naturalism: Stephen Crane, Richard Harding Davis, Jack London, and Frank Norris, among others. In the decades since, critics and scholars have made naturalist writing into a corpus with a history of being conceived in terms of an oscillation between triumph and decline. Indeed, naturalist authors—including the subjects of this chapter, Frank Norris and Jack London—often turned the possibility of degeneration and atavism into a formative premise for narration and plot construction. In his 1985 study *Hard Facts: Setting and Form in the American Novel*, Philip Fisher wrote about the naturalist novel as a form that often embodies "the plot of decline."[6] In *Women, Compulsion, Modernity* (2004), Jennifer Fleissner demonstrated that readings such as Fisher's rely on a "fatalistic" reading of life in the 1890s, a fatalism that represents but one response to conditions in the (urbanized) US at the turn of the twentieth century.[7] Another major response, a "nostalgic" one, finds "plots of triumph" in the genre; as Fleissner observes, in this latter reading naturalism "goes along with a renewal of what Roosevelt called 'the strenuous life,' returning masculine power and adventure to a vitiated modernity by rediscovering the freedoms and struggles associated with a still wide-open, untarnished natural landscape."[8] This "nostalgic" response contains many of the same key elements as Turner's elegiac account of the American West and national development, minus Turner's sense of the frontier's pastness: pessimistic and fearful in the face of modernity's advance, the nostalgic response locates the potential for (white settler) redemption in a return to a "natural landscape" that allows for—in fact requires—a momentary return to "primitive" modes of thought and action.[9]

But the triumphalists' (e.g., Roosevelt's and Turner's) and the naturalists' understandings and rhetorical uses of "nature" and cognate terms such as the "primitive" do not map neatly onto one another, as I will discuss shortly. This difference turns naturalist aesthetics into a representational mode that often replicates, but also sometimes stages critiques of, triumphalist frontier representation's fiction of unfettered (white, male) freedom. Crucially, these critiques uniquely help to consolidate the phenomenological orientations that underwrite US settler colonialism's ongoing biopolitical (re)production of white ascendance, racialized death, and Native genocide, the formation that I have described throughout this book as settler tensing. If works like Stephen Crane's *The Open Boat* (1897) and Richard Harding Davis's *Soldiers of Fortune* (1897) are about the struggles and ultimate triumphs of what Roosevelt would later term "the strenuous life," contemporaneous naturalist frontier texts by Frank Norris and Jack London are often about the ambivalence, messiness, and unexpected temporalities of frontier adventure.

Frontier logics and frontier representation are central to the discursive production of US settler colonialism as something other than its genocidal, appropriative self: as Jodi Byrd points out, "the first iterations of American studies that naturalized U.S. exceptionalism . . . as anything but colonization and empire" were "formed within the frontier logics of Frederick Jackson Turner and Theodore Roosevelt." In order to foreground the genocidal and appropriative nature of US settler colonialism as it fashions and forms settler subjectivity, we can turn to frontier representations from settler authors like Norris and London. As in the works by Bret Harte and Edward L. Wheeler analyzed in chapters 1 and 2 of this volume, Norris's and London's frontier representations dramatize the spatiotemporal site that serves as the final scene of Native appearance, and therefore the final scene before Native disappearance, in much of settler literature and settler critical theory.[10] In his oft-cited 1999 book *Settler Colonialism and the Transformation of Anthropology*, the late Patrick Wolfe argued that in settler colonial contexts, the frontier "was a performative representation—it helped the invasion to occur."[11] Such performativity, he stressed, owed to the frontier's capacity to bind an otherwise heterogeneous group of settlers together in opposition to Natives, so that what matters about the idea of the frontier is not its veracity but its capacity to forge a new shared identity for settlers. As we will see, the forging of a shared settler identity and subjectivity in Norris's and London's narratives of white settler death operates in part through a symbolic recognition and inclusion of racialized settler subjects.

Turner's account of US settler subject formation in "Significance" gives dramatic historiographical form to Wolfe's notion of frontier performativity and emphasizes the importance of settlers' adoption of an imagined Native primitivity: one well-known passage involves a nameless European colonist who appropriates indigeneity by trading his "garments of civilization" for the Native American's supposed agricultural practices and supposed proclivity to "shout[] the war cry and take[] the scalp in orthodox Indian fashion."[12] Turner also offers a historiographical account of the formation of the "settler subjectivity" that Scott Morgensen critiques. This subjectivity is defined by a seemingly contradictory incorporation and erasure of indigeneity, including the adoption and transcendence of primitivity; as Morgensen puts it, white settlers are "nostalgic for an indigeneity that modern people must transcend, even while incorporating [that indigeneity] as part of their history."[13] Naturalist aesthetics, whose idiosyncratic representation of character development and narrative temporality has been remarked upon by critics from Georg Lukacs to Jennifer Fleissner, bear an ambivalent relationship to the linear, progressive models of "settler subjectivity" formation that Turner dramatizes and Morgensen critiques, as naturalism's social Darwinist, evolutionary underpinnings at once promised white racial dominance and held out the possibility of widespread degeneration and decline.[14]

If frontier representation is crucial to the settler colonial project of appropriation and replacement, Norris's and London's naturalist frontier representations complicate the imbricated frontier and evolutionary teleologies that underlie the representational grammar of the US settler state's biopolitics of Native genocide, racialized death, and white settler ascendance. Yet, as the following discussion demonstrates, the New Historicist "expressive" conception of the literary, where literature only appears to resist the dominant cultural logics of its historical moment while instead actually embodying those logics, is particularly apt for reframing US literary naturalism as a settler colonial literary genre par excellence.[15] I must note here that, like many other scholars, I find the "expressive" understanding of the literary, as exemplified in the work of Walter Benn Michaels, to have meaningful theoretical and methodological shortcomings, in particular its view of history and culture as relatively static and monolithic domains.[16] But combined with the chronotopic reading method laid out in the introduction to this volume, this expressive conception of literature becomes a means for elucidating the ways in which naturalist aesthetics participated in settler tensing. In the frontier narratives of white settler death examined in this chapter, Norris's and London's naturalism stages "resistance" to settler colonialism's imperatives of Native genocide and racial hierarchy while simultaneously (re) affirming the governing logic of a US settler culture that takes individualist, masculinist struggle as a central, orienting horizon of action and meaning. In other words, by reframing literary naturalism as, specifically, a settler colonial literary genre, we can trace the supple, seemingly contradictory ways in which naturalist literary aesthetics supported (white) settler colonial power at the turn of the twentieth century.

In his influential essay "The Reorientation of American Culture in the 1890s," John Higham writes that in the 1890s (white) middle-class US Americans conceived of "untamed nature" as a space of "tonic freshness and openness" that was intimately linked to notions of health and virility.[17] This view represents a health-oriented version of Turner's understandings of "wilderness" and "nature," two abstractions that Turner located on and beyond the Western frontier and made central to his idea of an "American" identity. For Turner, wilderness was something to be won and "inanimate nature" something over which to hold dominion.[18] Similarly, for (middle- and upper-class) US Americans in the 1890s, the "openness" of nature provided a salutary blank space for masculinized self-aggrandizement. If Turner carved out a crucial role for a feminized, passive nature vis-à-vis national identity, he also helped to create, along with numerous other writers of the late nineteenth and early twentieth centuries, a lasting association between nature and the American West, as Nicolas Witschi has argued in *Traces of Gold*.[19] Teddy Roosevelt, in particular, endowed this association between West and nature with deep connections to notions of masculine, racial, and national revitalization.[20] But this connection to revitalization depended in large part on a romanticized conception of nature as a metonym for national and white racial agency and vitality, both of which were in question at the turn of the century. In the post-Darwinian moment of the late nineteenth and early twentieth centuries, evolutionary thinking had turned nature into "an ever-changing part of history's story"; nature was newly imbricated in, rather than just the passive background for, the unfolding of history.[21] Roosevelt was well aware of this newfound agency. Evolutionary thinking formed part of the foundation for his belief in the US's capacity for imperial hegemony in the Caribbean and the Pacific.[22] In matters closer to home, a paranoid evolutionary logic underlay Roosevelt's exhortation to (white middle-class) women to bear and raise children rather than work for a wage.[23] Evolutionary thinking's penetration into and interweaving of the categories of nature and history promised dominance but also threatened utter enfeeblement.

While Roosevelt apportioned evolutionary dominance to the masculine realm of geopolitics and enfeeblement to the feminine sphere of the home, this chapter argues that Norris and London offer a more supple view in which white and US dominance in masculinized frontier spaces becomes a genuine, rather than rhetorical, question. Such questioning, such coexistence of US and white dominance and enfeeblement in frontier spaces, bears on Norris and London's *fin-de-siècle* present as well as on their evolutionary and biopolitical future. In naturalism's generally typological mode of representation, it is not individual characters but instantiations of a group or population that win out or perish. From the population-focused perspective of biopolitics and evolutionary science alike, individual death can be interpreted as part of a process of optimization, in this case the optimization and maximization of the life of the white US population. But from the standpoint of US naturalist literature, which formally registers and responds to phenomenologies of time and space within the context of US settler colonialism and imperialism, individual instances of (white) death take on a different significance. Such instances (re)cast the spatiotemporal frontier zone in ways that associate masculine vigor and evolutionary dominance, two prized qualities within turn-of-the-twentieth-century middle- and upper-class (white) culture, with the racialized and Indigenous populations whom the US settler state has consigned to death and extermination.

In the following section, this chapter introduces the notions of naturalist "regenerative frontier" and "degenerative frontier" chronotopes in order to develop a theoretical context for understanding US literary naturalism's chronotopic rendering of spatiotemporal subjectivity. I then turn to Norris's *McTeague* (1899) and "A Memorandum of Sudden Death" (1902) and London's "To Build a Fire" (1908) and read these texts as articulations of a "degenerative frontier" chronotope that "resists" (in the Foucauldian and New Historicist sense of resistance as immanent in power) the settler state's biopolitics by situating the deaths of typologized white characters within the context of evolutionary and generational timescales.[24] The preoccupation with human–canine difference in "To Build a Fire" leads to a discussion of London's "In a Far Country" (1899) and *The Call of the Wild* (1903) in the final section of this chapter. I consider these last two texts alongside contemporaneous racial and species hierarchies that underwrote US settler colonial and imperial violence. Complementing the "resistance" staged in the "degenerative frontier" chronotope of naturalist narratives of white settler death, the racial and species comparisons drawn in "In a Far Country" and *Call* relocate masculine vigor and evolutionary dominance in racialized characters who participate in settler colonial logics of appropriation and Native disappearance.

## Regeneration and Degeneration on the Frontier

Let's turn to three novels that are *not* foci of this chapter: Frank Norris's *Moran of the Lady Letty* (1898), Theodore Dreiser's *Sister Carrie* (1900), and Edith Wharton's *The House of Mirth* (1905). Bear with me here; the reasons for turning to these novels should become clear shortly. The narrative of *Moran of the Lady Letty* tells of the events leading up to and following Anglo-Saxon protagonist Ross Wilbur's transformation from a relatively effete Yale graduate into a "moral and physical" superman after physical fights on the Pacific frontier with a "Chinaman" and a Nordic woman named Moran.[25] *Sister Carrie* delineates at least two tragedies: George Hurstwood's death by suicide after he is reduced to begging on the streets of New York City, and Carrie's eventual loneliness and unhappiness in spite of her attainment of fame and wealth. *The House of Mirth* traces the events leading to the death of protagonist Lily Bart, a New York socialite whose fortunes seesaw and ultimately plummet, until she dies by overdosing on the sedative chloral hydrate. Viewed within the binary scheme of US literary naturalism's critical history, which Jennifer Fleissner has elegantly laid out as the oscillation between the "plots of decline" and "plots of triumph" readings of the genre, *Moran of the Lady Letty* tells a tale of triumph while *Sister Carrie* and *The House of Mirth* dwell in a trajectory of decline. The settings of these three novels rather neatly map onto the story that we critics and scholars have been telling ourselves about US literary naturalism: as the story goes, in this genre, frontier spaces are where triumph takes place, and life among the denizens of the city is where decline commences and completes. But the actual experience of reading naturalist texts, especially those by Frank Norris and Jack London, suggests that this story about naturalism that we critics and scholars have been telling ourselves is only part of a larger picture.

What if we bring chronotopic analysis and a consideration of settler tensing into the frame? Mikhail Bakhtin's taxonomy of generic chronotopes in the rather compendious essay "Forms of Time and of the Chronotope in the Novel" does not include an entry for (US) literary naturalism, but if it did, this would likely be one of its major statements about the temporality of naturalism: (US) literary naturalism often presents character history as a collection of relatively detailed individual experiences and so-called racial characteristics that, over the course of narrative time, lead to a metamorphosis, often a metamorphosis of a degenerative or revitalizing nature.[26] Using *Moran of the Lady Letty*, *Sister Carrie*, and *The House of Mirth* as literary test cases, we would end up with the same binary scheme familiar from US literary naturalism's critical history, with a revitalizing metamorphosis (triumph) in the frontier setting of *Moran* and degenerative metamorphoses (decline) in the urban settings of *Carrie* and *Mirth*. But if we shift to texts including Norris's *McTeague* and "A Memorandum of Sudden Death" and London's "To Build a Fire," frontier settings become the stage for a different binary, one that consists of a *regenerative frontier chronotope* and a *degenerative frontier chronotope*.

The regenerative frontier chronotope governs literary representation in naturalist frontier texts like *Moran of the Lady Letty*, where a thematic emphasis on "intense struggle"[27] away from the constraints of "civilization" accompanies a transformative narrative temporality of white regeneration and remasculinization, forms of revitalization that are achieved through a return to a valorized past state supposedly free of modernity's ills. This regenerative frontier chronotope does important biopolitical work insofar as it induces readers to cognitively and bodily orient themselves toward their world(s)—in other words, it induces readers to phenomenologically orient themselves—in ways that support the hegemony and expansion of the US settler imperial state within the parameters of the optimization and maximization of white life. Biopolitics, as Foucault's theorization of the concept and other scholars' subsequent elaborations demonstrate, works through the differentiation and distribution of bodies and populations.[28] The regenerative frontier chronotope supports the state's biopolitics by prompting readers to understand and direct their own raced and sexed bodies in accordance with a politics and a worldview organized around the notion that white triumph on the frontier is more or less a foregone conclusion and is part of the "natural" order of reality. By inducing readers to organize their cognition and direct their bodily forces according to this "natural" order, finding alternatives to the cognitive and bodily orientations that support the US settler state's biopolitics becomes an ever taller order, as the death of racialized and Indigenous bodies and populations in North America and beyond is normalized as part of the "natural" course of history. Moreover, such death is normalized as a process of optimization over evolutionary time.

But chronotopic representations can participate in less obvious ways in this normalization of white ascendance, racialized death, and Indigenous genocide, even in texts where racialized and Indigenous characters are not literally dying or are actually "thriving" according to the phenomenological orientations enforced by settler anatomo- and biopolitics. One important way in which US literary naturalism almost imperceptibly works to normalize the phenomenological orientations that underwrite white ascendance and racialized and Indigenous death is by articulating, to play off of Colleen Lye's reading of the "snapshot possibility of American degeneration" in naturalist writing, a degenerative frontier chronotope.[29] My formulation is intended to highlight the coming together of a degenerative narrative time and an alternately materialist and mythicized frontier space, a combination that governs literary representation in Norris's *McTeague* and "A Memorandum of Sudden Death" and in London's "To Build a Fire." This degenerative frontier chronotope is crucial for understanding the significance of literary naturalism's staging of its critiques of US settler colonialism from within settler logics: the degenerative frontier chronotope portrays white settler death as the foreclosure of a process of coming into settler subjectivity, which (re)installs the achievement and continuation of settler subjectivity as the normative goal of human action.

## White Death

Published over the span of roughly a decade, Frank Norris's *McTeague* (1899) and "A Memorandum of Sudden Death" (1902) and Jack London's second published version of "To Build a Fire" (1908) constitute a set of naturalist frontier representations that builds toward increasingly unqualified portrayals of white enfeeblement on the frontier. Each of these representations, as I just noted, is an example of the degenerative frontier chronotope. Exactly how each of these representations is an example of the degenerative frontier chronotope, and why that matters for settler tensing, is the subject of the rest of this section.

*McTeague* is about a California miner-turned-dentist who lives and works in San Francisco, loses his practice, murders his wife, flees to the Mojave Desert in southeastern California, kills again, and finally ends up handcuffed to the corpse of his former "pal" Marcus Schouler, left to await his own death at the hands of the Mojave. In "Memorandum," a frame story leads to an episodic narrative of a young man named Arthur Karslake's last hours before his death in a skirmish in Western Arizona. London's "To Build a Fire" follows an unnamed male protagonist who freezes to death as he travels solo and unsuccessfully to a prospectors' camp in the Klondike. While *McTeague*'s killing off of its titular Irish character can be read as an erasure of the lower-class ethnic other, the later "Memorandum" and "To Build a Fire" do not invoke supposed ethnic deficiencies as explanations for their white protagonists' deaths. If anything, protagonist Arthur Karslake of "Memorandum" and the unnamed protagonist of "To Build a Fire" die because they possess "civilized" and "refined" qualities that the lower-class Irish McTeague and other racialized subjects of US settler imperial rule allegedly lack.[30] Read against Norris's *Moran*, which Joseph McElrath describes as a fledgling Frank Norris's attempt to write a potboiler "according to the popular tastes of his time," Karslake and the unnamed man's deaths look less like anti-modernist nostalgia and more like meditations on the assumptions about civilizational and white superiority that made trajectories like Ross Wilbur's consonant with popular thought.[31] This section demonstrates that Norris and London bring together naturalist-evolutionary and settler-frontier versions of primitivity in narratives of stalled settler subject formation. These narratives cancel the appropriation and transcendence of primitivity that underwrite settler histories and futures, and thus "resist" the settler imperatives of Indigenous appropriation and transcendence while also positing the attainment and persistence of settler subjectivity as the normative basis for success or failure.

From its opening pages, *McTeague* invites readers to think about the titular character in terms of repetition: "McTeague looked forward to [his] Sunday afternoons. . . . He invariably spent them in the same fashion," first consuming the same meal as always, then drifting off to sleep, and finally waking to play the "six lugubrious airs that he knew" on his concertina.[32] As the narrative unfolds, repetitive behaviors and phrases become integral to the representation of the characters who populate the novel, from Mexican housemaid Maria Macapa's repetition of the same odd phrase ("Had a flying squirrel an' let him go") after reciting her name, to McTeague's frequent recourse, in situations that baffle him, to the notion that no one can "make small of [him]," to the narrator's repetitive mention of the "dot of Chinese White" for the eyes of the wooden animals that McTeague's wife Trina makes.[33] Toward the end of the novel, McTeague's return to the California mining country where he spent his youth underscores the novel's vision of its characters as creatures of repetition while also linking this vision to the amalgamating process of settler identity formation.

McTeague's return to the Placer County mines where he spent his youth initially is cast as an escape from the supposedly enervating effects of urban spaces and feminine influences. Crucially, this return becomes an occasion to articulate a settler identity for McTeague, as the narrator transforms his brutal crudeness, which was so often a hindrance in his life in San Francisco, into a sign of his essential connection to the land and to primitivity. Around the middle of the novel, McTeague is barred from the dental profession around which he had built his life when his erstwhile "pal" Marcus Schouler alerts the authorities that McTeague is practicing dentistry without a diploma from a dental college. Left to search, mostly unsuccessfully, for a new job, McTeague becomes increasingly dependent upon his "economical" wife Trina, who "had become especially penurious" after winning five thousand dollars in the lottery. McTeague eventually takes to stealing from Trina, first carrying off four hundred dollars and subsequently killing her so as to get his hands on the five thousand. Fleeing San Francisco to escape punishment, McTeague returns to the mines of Eastern California. His flight represents not simply an evasion of the law but also a moment in which the text ties the urban and the feminine together as forces that must be destroyed or left behind in order for the novel's masculine (anti)hero to survive. At first, the Eastern California landscape proves familiar, comforting, and welcoming, particularly in contrast to McTeague's prior situation with Trina in the often confusing urbanity of San Francisco: "The life [of the miner] pleased the dentist beyond words. The still, colossal mountains took him back again like a returning prodigal, and vaguely, without knowing why, he yielded to their influence—their immensity, their enormous power, crude and blind, reflecting themselves in his own nature, huge, strong, brutal in its simplicity."[34]

While the large, hulking, and dim-witted McTeague is physically and mentally out of place in San Francisco, in Placer County he sees himself reflected in the natural world. This identity between McTeague and the landscape comes on the heels of his finding work as a miner, so that he reads as a settler revision of Hegel's bondsman, who sees himself salubriously reflected and objectified in the products of his labor.[35] Folded into this settler revision of Hegel is McTeague's first and only claim that he is an "American." McTeague's self-identification, which is voiced during a conversation with a mine foreman whose "strong German accent" calls attention to McTeague's linguistic erasure of his own ethnic particularity, turns McTeague's essential connections to the land and primitivity into key ingredients in a US settler identity alchemy.[36] Norris's imputation of naturalist-evolutionary primitivity to McTeague during his days in San Francisco marked McTeague's essential foreignness; in Placer County such primitivity blurs into a settler-frontier primitivity that indigenizes him.

When McTeague claims that he is an "American," Norris's novel shifts from an Anglo-Saxonist frame that emphasizes differences within the settler polity to an Anglo-Saxonist settler colonial frame that highlights the binary division between settler and Native. Sara Quay suggests that McTeague and the other members of his San Francisco milieu "exist [] in a liminal state of identity, one which is tied to [their] ethnic background[s] but is simultaneously in the process of becoming fully 'American'" through the gradual shedding of ethnic particularity and movement from the working to the middle class.[37] In the setting of San Francisco, the novel registers this transitional state in McTeague and Trina's class aspirations (their movement toward middle-class identity through McTeague's professional work and Trina's consumerism) and in frequent references to characters' ethnic backgrounds (for example, Maria Macapa is referred to as Spanish-American by McTeague and as Mexican by other characters and the narrator; Trina's ancestors, we are told, were all German-Swiss; and junk shop owner Zerkow is identified as a Polish Jew). Although not explicitly labeled as such, McTeague's name, among other characteristics, marks him as Irish-American.[38] Yet with McTeague the text resists the kind of clear-cut racial-ethnic classification afforded other "ethnic" characters, with the narrator at one point noting that the dentist has "the great blonde mustache of a viking."[39] If the identities of the characters that surround McTeague in his life in San Francisco are in flux, then McTeague's identity is even less stable, thrown into ambiguity by his being "physically an Anglo-Saxon superman"[40] but nominally an Irishman and mentally rather dull. When the ethnically marked Trina, Maria, and Zerkow all perish within San Francisco—both women murdered and Zerkow mysteriously drowned in San Francisco Bay—the novel issues a serious blow to the generations-long process of "Americanization" of which these characters are a part.[41] (The contrast that the novel draws between Trina's essentially flawless English and the thickly accented English of her parents represents the most obvious instance of the novel's articulation of how outward signs of ethnic particularity diminish over the course of generations.) But two of the novel's major characters, McTeague and Marcus, survive their experiences in the city, with Marcus escaping to live "a cowboy's life" filled with moments of "intense satisfaction" on a cattle ranch in southeastern California's Panamint Valley.[42] Like McTeague, who returns to the mines to do the kind of work associated with Turner's valorized "miner's frontier," Marcus turns to a lifestyle associated with the "rancher's frontier"; and like McTeague, Marcus does not just survive the city but takes on a role associated with what Denise Cruz calls, in a reference to spokesman of white, imperial hypermasculinity Teddy Roosevelt, "'the strenuous life' of the westward-moving cowboy."[43] In other words, McTeague's and Marcus's stories appear to confirm both the Turnerian and "plots of triumph" accounts of Western "nature": McTeague and Marcus are "Americanized" by their frontier experiences, and for a while they are revitalized by a "natural landscape" that the novel associates with both a deep geological past and a more recent frontier history. If McTeague and Marcus were ethnic "types" in San Francisco, in rural California each of them embodies an ethnically departicularized settler type.

But the two characters' frontier experiences rehearse these settler identity outcomes, not to project a settler future predicated on the selective erasure of ethnic difference but to stage "resistance" in the form of a narrative cancelation of the frontier teleology that representationally complements the ongoing historical and political realities of conquest. By the end of *McTeague*, McTeague's and Marcus's experiences on their respective frontiers have led them to death, as McTeague kills Marcus in Death Valley and is left handcuffed to his former friend's body, waiting for the desert to kill him. Some scholars have read the novel as an example of Norris's Anglo-Saxonism, and from this perspective McTeague's and Marcus's deaths, as well as those of Trina, Maria, and Zerkow, look like moments in which Norris expels ethnic others from the US.[44] This reading has its merits, seeing as the expulsion of ethnic characters is the ultimate outcome of the novel. But it restricts us to reading *McTeague* in terms of Norris's racism and classism, rather than through the prism of his concerns about the matter of representing the American West as well.

In the years following the publication of *McTeague*, Norris published the essays "The Literature of the West" (1902) and "The Frontier Gone at Last" (1902), in which he articulated his concerns and ideas regarding literary representation of the American West and the status of the frontier in the post-frontier US. In the former essay, he stressed that the literature of the American West should represent characters who embody what is "typical" of (that is, unique to) the region in the contemporary moment, figures who share essential qualities with the revolver-wielding, chaps-wearing "red shirt fellow" of an older, wilder version of the West but who do not necessarily share their forefathers' uncouth mannerisms and appearance. "[T]he product of the West," Norris wrote, "from the very first and up to this very hour of writing has always been, through every varying condition, occupation or calling, the adventurer."[45] In the latter essay, Norris reformulated the trope of the Americanizing frontier for a post-frontier moment, envisioning a nominally postnational future in which US trade and commerce play a leading role in Americanizing the globe, making "the whole world [] our nation and simple humanity our countrymen."[46] Together, these essays suggest Norris's commitment to the notion that "frontier" names a space where difference is transformed into sameness, and that representations of the American West should strive to capture, with a sensitivity to historical change, what is unique about the region and its settler inhabitants.

In the context of these two essays, McTeague and Marcus read like caricatures of Norris's "adventurer" type who are caught between Norris's contradictory commitments to both the Turnerian view of the Westerner as an embodiment of American uniqueness and the Anglo-Saxonist view of the Westerner as an iteration of the inexorable Anglo-Saxon.[47] McTeague and Marcus are able to take on their settler identities because, as Westerners, they partake of a western American uniqueness that is regional rather than ethnic; yet they are also ethnic others to Norris's valorized Anglo-Saxon. Norris protects his vision of Anglo-Saxon supremacy in killing off McTeague and Marcus, but it comes at the "cost" of canceling the frontier teleology that underwrites US settler colonial conquest. Futurity, in *McTeague*'s narrative logic, is only conceivable as the continuation of Anglo-Saxon(ist) settler identities and subjectivities in linear and evolutionary time. In other words, the novel may displace the frontier teleology that representationally complements US settler colonialism, but it leaves in place the linear and evolutionary conceptions of time and space that have displaced other, non-settler ontologies of time.[48] The degenerative frontier chronotope as it manifests and governs representation in *McTeague* traces transformations in the novel's ethnic characters that ultimately (re)articulate the notion of Anglo-Saxon settlers' exclusive right to futurity on North American land.

Three years after the publication of *McTeague*, Norris published a short story titled "A Memorandum of Sudden Death" in *Collier's Weekly*, on January 11, 1902. "Memorandum" colonizes not just futurity, but temporality itself. "Memorandum" focuses on a young man named Arthur Karslake whose personal history as a lawyer, fiction writer, and ethnologist suggests an affinity with patrician figures like Roosevelt, Turner, and Owen Wister. Karslake's proximity to such figures, Roosevelt in particular, is further suggested by the regiment that he joins when he decides to become a US cavalryman: Karslake becomes "a member of B troop of the Sixth Regiment of United States Cavalry," the

regiment some of whose members fought alongside Roosevelt's Rough
Riders during the 1898 Battle of San Juan Hill in the Spanish-American
War.[49] Karslake's story would have been simultaneously familiar and
foreign to men like Roosevelt, fitting into the mold of an aristocratic
"regeneration through violence" but ending in a gruesome death that
Roosevelt, Turner, and Wister did not endure.[50] While *McTeague* waits
until its final three chapters to efface McTeague and Marcus's ethnic
particularity in favor of settler identities, "Memorandum" quickly pits
Karslake and his multiethnic troop against a group of Native American
fighters[51] in a fictional 1896 skirmish in Western Arizona that calls to
mind historical fights between Native American rebels and US and
Mexican soldiers in and around that year. Particularly resonant here is
the continuing resistance to and independence from the US and Mexico
that Haskay-bay-nay-ntayl (the "Apache Kid") and his associates put up
in 1896, which, according to some historians, they continued to exercise
into the twentieth century.[52] Although the story does not explicitly identify the group of fighters as Haskay-bay-nay-ntayl and his associates or
another group of Native American fighters, details from the story are suggestive. Karslake and his fellow troops refer to one of the fighters as "the
Red One," which calls to mind the historical figure Kan-da-zis-tlishishen,
of the Bedonkohe band of Chiricahua Apache, born in 1790 and known
by Mexicans as Mangas Coloradas ("Red Sleeves"), a reference to either
the red shirt he wore or the blood of slain Mexicans soaking his sleeves,
or perhaps both. Another of the fighters is referred to as "the One with
the Feather," this latter name evocative of the Aravaipa Apache practice
of adorning warriors' caps with different kinds of feathers according to
their status as novice or more experienced.[53]

As Patrick Wolfe's work suggests, contemporary multiculturalism
can occlude the differences between, on the one hand, racial divides
within settler society and, on the other, the binary division between settler and Native.[54] "Memorandum" highlights the fundamental difference
between intra-settler and settler versus Native distinctions by grouping
Karslake with both Mexican-identified and white-identified US soldiers
in a fight against a group of Native American fighters. Karslake's and
his other troop members' deaths, situated in a narrative driven by the

frontier binary between settler and Native, turns frontier violence into a source of narrative incoherence and settler death.

"Memorandum" begins with a frame narrative that draws attention to Karslake's interest in the anthropological study of "primitive" peoples and cultures, ironically pointing to his perception of the pastness of Indigenous peoples. The frame narrator tells us that one of Karslake's pen names, Anson Qualtraugh, "recalls at once to thousands of the readers of a certain world-famous monthly magazine of New York [which "Memorandum" does not name] articles and stories he wrote for it while he was alive," such as "his admirable descriptive work called 'Traces of the Aztecs on the Mogolon Mesa,' in the October number of 1890." More tellingly, just a few sentences later, such "descriptive" ethnography is characterized as a way of recording the "traces" of past civilizations as well as the supposedly "primitive" ways of extant Indigenous peoples, in this case the Hopi (Moki): an 1892 issue of the same magazine includes Qualtraugh's "much shortened transcript of a monograph on 'Primitive Methods of Moki Irrigation,' which are now in the archives of the Smithsonian."[55] Consonant with Johannes Fabian's account of anthropology's "denial of coevalness," Karslake's anthropological writing figures the Hopi, who continue to live in Arizona to this day, as lagging behind.[56] For twenty-first century readers, the irony is compounded by the more than two-thousand-year history of Hopi agricultural ingenuity in dryland farming, which the US-based nonprofit Environmental Defense Fund described in a 2019 article as a way to "inspire other farmers seeking to become more resilient to climate change and increasingly finite water supplies."[57] These aspects of Karslake's ethnographic writing are nestled in an opening paragraph that distinguishes between the various kinds of writing that he published by noting the quality of his novel and anthropological writing and the mediocrity of one of his pieces of popular fiction. Such distinctions, in tandem with the attention that the frame narrator pays to the notion of Indigenous pastness encoded in Karslake's anthropological writing, invite questions about how Karslake's other writings handle the issue of representing Native temporality, for, as we soon find out, his travels to Western Arizona are presumed to be motivated by a desire to gather firsthand materials for "a novel of military life in the Southwest" (154).

Native temporality looks rather different in Karslake's notes for his novel than in the titles of his ethnographic writing, shifting from a relegation to pastness to an inescapable co-presentness that grants Native Americans a necessarily limited form of agency insofar as Euroamerican temporalities provide the orienting frames of reference for Norris's critique of the "denial of coevalness." While those ethnographic titles define Native temporality, in Karslake's notes Native American characters dictate when and how he writes. In a telling example, these notes, which are re-presented in the short story with occasional bracketed comments from the frame narrator, proceed as follows: "Monday, about eleven o'clock.—No change. The heat is appalling. There is just a—Later.—I was on the point of saying that there was just a mouthful of water left for each of us in our canteens when Estorijo and Idaho both at the same time cried out that they [the Natives] were moving in" (158–59). The notes figure this very literal Native American presentness, spatial and temporal, as temporal control over the act of written narration, registering Native co-presentness as a form of agency over when and how representation occurs. The form of Karslake's notes—what he at one point describes as its "'incoherence'"—marks not simply Native American co-participation in the present of Karslake's writing, but decisive control over his narration of events and sensations.[58] In this light, the short story's resonances with historical skirmishes, those events that traditionally mark significant moments in national history, draws Indigenous people into the act of narrating (national) history as agents rather than observers. If, as Mark Rifkin suggests, countering Native anachronization through the assertion of Native co-presentness carries the problem of leaving settler temporalities and histories in place, "Memorandum" suggests that this co-presentness involves a mutual making of history within the temporal frames furnished by settler national(ist) historiography.[59]

What, precisely, does this history look like? Rifkin points to the limits of asserting Native American and settler co-participation in a shared present, noting that such assertions can actually work to normalize settler colonialism. In particular, co-participation in modernity, that construction of European and US historicism, is premised on conquest and so-called modern temporalities of progress, linearity, and simultaneity.

As Rifkin writes, even if modernity is understood as a product of Native American and settler co-participation, this modernity is still the hallmark of "a world whose condition of possibility lies in 'conquest'"; it is still the signature of a world with "its own temporal formation, with its own particular ways of apprehending time . . . (such as plotting events with respect to their place in national history and seeing change in terms of forms of American progress)."[60] The fictionalized slice of southwestern (US) history contained in "Memorandum" displaces the modern nation's temporalities of progress, linearity, and simultaneity and replaces them with temporalities that exceed the timescale and presumed progressive direction of national history. The frame narrator's notion that Karslake's notes are "more a picture of things seen than a transcription of things thought" (153) seems rather unfitting once we read the notes from the final day of the skirmish: at one point, as his fellow soldier Bunt is dying, Karslake writes, "This is the first violent death I have ever seen, and it astonishes me to note how unimportant it seems. . . . Possibly my mental vision is scaled to a larger field since this Friday, and as the greater issues loom up one man more or less seems to be but a unit—more or less—in an eternal series" (160). Dying for one's country is here lifted out of its national(ist) context and placed into "an eternal series" that, by Karslake's reckoning, empties this one death of the importance that it should have carried. The "greater issues" of which Karslake writes appear to be, at least in part, what he later describes as the utter insignificance of human life vis-à-vis deep biblical time: "human life an atom of microscopic dust," and at the "summit" of existence, "God himself."[61] Karslake's expanded "mental vision" perceives time as what Benedict Anderson describes as a form of Christian theological simultaneity "wholly alien" to the historically progressive simultaneity of modern national time; Karslake's perception, following Anderson's reading of Walter Benjamin's "Messianic time," is on the order of "a simultaneity of past and future in an instantaneous present."[62] This "Messianic" temporal perception is brought on by Karslake's sense that the Native American fighters clearly have the upper hand, as they have forced him and his remaining fellow soldiers into a geographical position where Karslake senses his "approaching death."[63] In other words, the Native American characters in "Memorandum" exercise a kind of co-presentness that results, not in a completion or assertion of a US national(ist) modernity (in other words, a US settler colonial modernity) that merely includes Natives, but in a displacement of the modern temporalities that relegate Natives to the past in the first place. The crucial point to note here, though, is that this displacement shifts us to another European(American) temporal frame of reference, Christian theological simultaneity. Norris's Native American characters might exercise a form of control over the narrative, but the narrative is captivated by the temporalities of Euroamerican and Christian civilization.

By nestling this displacement in a set of fictional notes that bespeak Karslake's death after "intense struggle,"[64] "Memorandum" also displaces the temporal structure named above as settler-frontier primitivity, a temporal structure defined by the temporary, ultimately regenerative inhabitation of an indigenizing primitivity. This temporal structure of settler-frontier primitivity can be understood as a key component of the "temporal formation" of US settler colonialism around the turn of the twentieth century, when fears over the supposedly ill effects of urban modernity helped to spawn such phenomena as the "West Cure." As I have mentioned, save his death, Karslake sounds like a fictional amalgam of figures such as Owen Wister and Teddy Roosevelt: he is a genteel Easterner with ambitions to write about the West despite not actually living in the region, and he engages in US military exploits at the turn of the twentieth century. Of course, Wister and Roosevelt emerged rejuvenated from their experiences in western "nature" (i.e., their positive experiences with the West Cure), with the latter also standing alive and victorious in the wake of military conflicts along the US frontier(s). Karslake's radically different fate contrasts not only with Wister's and Roosevelt's stories but also with the typical narrative arc of the Eastern "brain worker" who goes west to engage in vigorous physical activity as a respite from the overly civilized life to which he will return rejuvenated.[65] Although the frame narrator does not explicitly state that Karslake is out West to cure strained nerves, we know that Karslake intends to write about his experiences in the region, which calls to mind the West Cure prescription to "record this experience in writing."[66] Karslake is a case of western rejuvenation and remasculinization gone awry, skewed away from the triumphant trajectory that allegorically forecasts a future populated and dominated by supposedly intellectually advanced, racially superior Anglo-Saxons, and instead directed toward death.

But the frame narrative with which "Memorandum" begins, and which reasserts its presence at the end of the text in a note that "*The* [manuscript] *ends here*," reminds us that the settler polity was never really at stake.[67] We are returned to the reality that the settler polity continued to assert its right to North American land, and we are again made aware that Native American agency in Euroamerican histor(io-graph)y is necessarily limited and easily coopted without a thorough reckoning with the colonization of time itself. It is in the settler continuity that the frame narrative conjures, in the colonization of time that it and Karslake's manuscript herald, that "Memorandum" participates in the settler tensing of white ascendance, racialized death, and Indigenous genocide.

Jack London's "To Build a Fire" (1908) deploys its own unique version of the overly civilized Anglo-Saxon in a narrative that evades the violence of settler colonial conquest by paring it down to its dynamic of mastery over the land. As Patrick Wolfe has written, "The primary object of settler colonization is the land itself" in the form of ownership over it and its resources, and in "Fire" not even the imperative to eliminate and replace Indigenous people stands between the unnamed male protagonist and the land that he feels entitled to plunder.[68] But against the unnamed man's confidence in his mastery over the Klondike's harsh conditions, which is presented as also mastery over pace and timing when the man thinks to himself that "If he kept [his pace] up, he would certainly be with the boys by six," "Fire" counterposes a paradoxical representation of settler connectedness to the land as alienation, death, and narrative stasis.[69]

The portrayal of the unnamed man in "Fire" evokes *fin-de-siècle* fears about the supposed ill effects of what London biographer Earle Labor refers to as "overcivilization."[70] If an aristocratic turn-of-the-twentieth-century culture of "regeneration through violence" viewed the West Cure as a corrective to the enervating effects of urban-industrial modernity, the unnamed man of "Fire" appears to be unable to capitalize on the salubrious effects of frontier adventure. London's short story stages the ability to persevere over unforgiving "nature" as the difference between the capacity for unreflective "judgment" and the possession of inherited "instinct." The unnamed man "was quick and alert in the things of life, but only in the things, and not in the significance. Fifty degrees below zero . . . impressed him as being cold and uncomfortable, and that was all." On the other hand, for the dog working as the unnamed man's "toil slave," "Its instinct told it a truer tale than was told to the man by the man's judgment. . . . Possibly in its brain there was no sharp consciousness of a condition of very cold such as was in the man's brain. But the brute had its instinct."[71] The narrator's foreshadowing of the unnamed man's eventual death appears at first to suggest that the man has been hopelessly corrupted by "civilization," left unable to inhabit the indigenizing and revitalizing primitivity—what is called "instinct" in the dog—that frontier adventure should engender. But the unnamed man's relationship to "instinct," or, more precisely, his (in)ability to hear its "truer tale," is not as clear-cut as this opening opposition between the man and the dog would suggest.

I am interested here in tracing how "judgment" and "instinct," as opposed concepts in the story, are mapped onto the temporal structure of settler-frontier primitivity. If settler-frontier primitivity names the temporal structure whereby white settlers temporarily inhabit qualities associated with indigeneity so as to appropriate and subsequently transcend it, the portrayal of the unnamed man (re)figures such transcendence as alienation and death. Scholars often focus on how "Fire" attributes the unnamed man's death to his own failings of morals or character, a reading that captures the narrator's tendency, especially early in the story, to fault the man for his ultimately poor, unreflective "judgment."[72] Unfortunately, such a reading all too easily occludes those moments when the protagonist's will to survive—what we might call his "instinct" to survive—aligns him with the dog, who, "warm and secure in its natural covering," serves as a figure of indigenous belonging in the Klondike. Despite the story's establishment of a division between the man and the dog, when the man falls through the ice, wetting his legs and prompting a desperate but controlled attempt to build a life-saving fire, images of "instinct" temporarily replace the narrator's wonted emphasis on the man's (unreflective) thought. Having been forced to stand relatively still in order to build the fire, the man feels (in contrast to thinking about) the extreme cold: "The blood of his body recoiled before it. The blood was alive, *like the dog, and like the dog it wanted to hide away and cover itself up from the fearful cold.*" The implicit separation of the man from his blood (i.e., in the notion of the blood as alive and desirous of cover) is consistent with the story's tendency to syntactically strip the man of agency (as seen in sentence constructions such as "Once in a while *the thought reiterated itself* that it was very cold").[73] But this separation also serves as an occasion for aligning the man, as an embodied entity, with the dog, who, like the man's blood, is referred to throughout the story as "it," in marked contrast to the male pronouns used for the man. For the briefest of moments, spanning not even two whole paragraphs, the man bodily inhabits instinctual feeling, the mode of response that helps the dog to remain alive while he eventually perishes. The text temporarily suspends what Bruno Latour and Donna Haraway describe as the "Great Divide" between humans and all the other animals, the conceit that informs dominant settler (and, more broadly, Western) imaginings of humanity as "free" rather than part of "a spatial and temporal web of interspecies dependencies."[74]

This narrative suspension of the "Great Divide" can be read as itself a settler-indigenizing move, aligning London's text with Cherokee scholar Brian K. Hudson's observation that "many Native ideologies do not define humans as categorically different from or superior to nonhuman animals."[75] Moreover, the text's language suggests an identity between the man and the inhuman nature that he is appropriating in an attempt to stay alive: "He was feeding [the fire] with twigs the size of his finger. In another minute he would be able to feed it with branches the size of his wrist."[76] Jeanne Reesman argues that this language integrates the human and the nonhuman and thus leaves the unnamed man unable to exercise the mastery of quantification over "nature."[77] But this language of human and nonhuman mirroring also gestures toward a white settler connection to the land that evokes the settler imperative to appropriate indigeneity.

Consistent with the temporal structure of settler-frontier primitivity, the man's temporary inhabitation of an indigenizing primitivity, here figured as instinctual response, gives way to a transcendence (back) into thought: soon after the man is "safe," with a fire burning "with strength," his thoughts again become the focal point of narration, such as his remembering the advice and thinking about the sometimes "womanish" sentiments of the "old-timers." Yet this transcendence (back) into thought functions, not as an important moment for the completion of a revitalizing drama of salubrious frontier adventure, but as a moment of hubris leading, seemingly inexorably, to the unnamed man's alienation from his own freezing body and eventually to his death. The emphasis on the man's alienation from his own body that proliferates in the narrative after the fire is extinguished (we see this proliferation in, for example, bits of narration like "the absence of sensation in his feet left him unrelated to the earth" and "He seemed . . . to have no connection with the earth") turns "Fire" into a drama of failed settler subjectivity: once mastery over self and land dissolve, the only alternative is death figured as the end of narrative.[78]

Norris's *McTeague* and "Memorandum" and London's "Fire," all published within nine years of each other, chart the development of a "degenerative frontier" chronotope in which settler binaries and categories—settler vs. Native, land as exploitable *terra incognita*—frame the narration of (white) settler death. These texts pare down the heterogeneity of settler society, not to (re)forge a shared settler identity in a post-frontier moment but to imagine the effects of settler-frontier primitivity when, as Norris puts it in *McTeague*, "nature" is "savage, sullen, and magnificently indifferent to man"—in other words, when nonhuman "nature" figures as an uneasy mix of the romantic and the naturalistic, the benevolent and the "magnificently indifferent."[79] Yet these texts undercut their own critical potential in relation to settler tensing. Norris's and London's displacements of Euroamerican (settler) apprehensions of time as linear, progressive, and national are tied to the end of narrative itself, which recenters settler temporalities as the frame of reference and path to futurity. The two texts that I turn to in the next section, London's "In a Far Country" and *The Call of the Wild*, work to consolidate the phenomenological orientations that subtend settler tensing by emphasizing the agency of racialized characters who are positioned vis-à-vis the US settler state quite differently than are the Native American fighters of "Memorandum."

## Race and Frontier Regeneration

Like *McTeague*, "Memorandum," and "Fire," "In a Far Country" (1899) and *The Call of the Wild* (1903) portray white settler death on the frontier, but in these two latter texts the elision of settler heterogeneity is replaced by narratives that highlight intra-settler difference. While in *McTeague*, "Memorandum," and "Fire" white settler death representationally cancels settler appropriation and transcendence of primitivity, in "Far" and *Call* white settler death is channeled into reconfigurations of intra-settler racial hierarchies. Such reconfigurations buttress frontier representation's performative utility for conquest, for Native genocide and settler replacement, by portraying racialized characters as agents of settler futurity within narratives that recapitulate the phenomenological orientations that underwrite US settler colonialism. In other words, the degenerative frontier chronotope as it manifests and governs representation in "Far" and *Call* produces, as did the California fiction of Bret Harte discussed in chapter 1, a vision of settlement without heteronormativity and nationalism without racial purity.

The primary narrative focus of "In a Far Country," of narrating the degeneration and death of the two white men Carter Weatherbee and Percy Cuthfert, appears at first blush to work in much the same way as the death of the unnamed man in "Fire." Thrust into what the narrator describes as "the savage youth, the primordial simplicity of the North," the two men transform so profoundly that they take on "the appearance of wild beasts."[80] The narrative of "Far" gains initial impetus from Weatherbee and Cuthfert's decisions to pursue adventure and wealth in the Klondike Gold Rush. The two join a gold-seeking group whose plan is overly ambitious and decidedly dangerous, and when Weatherbee and Cuthfert find themselves uninterested in continuing on the arduous path ahead of them, they settle into a cabin along the trail to wait out the winter. The cabin's resources allow them to forgo any strict discipline, the lack of fresh vegetables and exercise sickens them, and their lack of common interests and general isolation turn them against one another. No longer resembling the men they were in their former lives, save for their lack of fortitude, they end up killing each other. "Far" is careful to remind us at every turn that Weatherbee and Cuthfert's reversion is not the kind of temporarily self-preserving transformation (into an "American" for McTeague, into a soldier thrilled by violence for Karslake of "Memorandum," and into "instinct" for the unnamed protagonist of "Fire") that ultimately fails the characters who perish in the three texts considered in the previous section. Weatherbee and Cuthfert never actually inhabit any of the stages that comprise the temporal structure of settler-frontier primitivity. Their deaths read as articulations of a need to inhabit the temporal structure of settler-frontier primitivity in a world where survival is premised on the appropriation and disappearance of indigeneity.

"In a Far Country" begins with a long series of proverb-like statements about what a masculine subject must do in order to leave civilization successfully and prosper in the Klondike. Save the narrator's mention of "the North," the two opening paragraphs of the story proceed in a de-historicizing mode and read like advice that one might give to Turner's archetypal, decades-spanning frontier "colonist": he

> may estimate success at an inverse ratio to the quantity and quality of his hopelessly fixed habits. He will soon discover, if he be a fit candidate, that the material habits are the less important. The exchange of such things as a dainty menu for rough fare, of the stiff leather shoe for the soft, shapeless moccasin, of the feather bed for a couch in the snow, is after all a very easy matter. But his pinch will come in learning properly to shape his mind's attitude toward all things, and especially toward his fellow man.[81]

Unlike Turner's "colonist," though, the implied masculine subject to whom the narrator's advice is addressed is not on a providential path through the wilderness, as indicated by the use of the conditional tense ("if he be a fit candidate"). In other words, this masculine subject is not necessarily destined to be mastered by, and then become master of, the space into which he is venturing—indeed, as historian Kathryn Morse relates, settler gold-seekers in the Klondike often "struggled for the words to convey the physical and mental experience of hauling their bodies and their heavy packs and sleds" over the trails to the goldfields, witnessing along the way "pack animals, dogs, and mules, cruelly beaten and starving" alongside "the rotting carcasses of dead horses" and "human beings dead and dying from accidents, meningitis," and events such as the deadly Chilkoot avalanche of April 3, 1898.[82]

Weatherbee and Cuthfert, a couple of "effete scions of civilization," call to mind the supposedly agency-robbing, feminizing conditions of urban life at the turn of the twentieth century: Weatherbee, formerly a clerk, has "no romance in his nature,—the bondage of commerce had crushed all that; he was simply tired of the ceaseless grind"; while Cuthfert, a turn-of-the-twentieth-century version of the contemporary trust fund baby, "suffered from an abnormal development of sentimentality." Gold mining in the Klondike presents these two with an opportunity not only to strike it rich but also to (re)gain the agency and masculinity that elude them in their urban lives. As is the case in many of London's Klondike short stories, Weatherbee and Cuthfert's expedition party is composed of a racially heterogeneous mix of characters; although Weatherbee and Cuthfert's racial identities are not stated explicitly, their English-sounding names and the contrasts drawn between them and "half-breed voyageurs" such as the half-Anishinaabe/Ojibwe, half-French Canadian Jacques Baptiste suggest that they are not just white men but Anglo-Saxons, and therefore members of a valorized group of white people within the US's hierarchy of white "races" in the second half of the nineteenth and first quarter of the twentieth century.[83] While Anglo-Saxon racial heritage or (white) wealth mixed with frontier struggle leads some naturalist characters to (re)find their virility—examples include Humphrey Van Weyden of London's *The Sea Wolf* (1904), the aforementioned Ross Wilbur of Norris's *Moran of the Lady Letty*, and Harvey Cheyne Jr. of Rudyard Kipling's *Captains Courageous* (1897)—Weatherbee and Cuthfert do not undergo any such transformation and eventually elect to settle into a mysterious cabin along the expedition party's trail while the rest of the party continues its journey.

Weatherbee and Cuthfert degenerate and eventually perish in the cabin while the other members of the party, composed of white men, so-called "half-breeds," women, and children, ostensibly survive their travels in the harsh environment. The divergent paths of these Anglo-Saxons and their heterogeneous crew complicate the racially purifying and masculinizing meanings associated with the frontier and "nature" at the turn of the century. For one, "In a Far Country" severs any necessary link between the "natural" conditions of the frontier and Anglo-Saxon racial dominance; if anyone does indeed survive the expedition (we never find out what happens to the other members of the party), the most likely candidate is Jacques Baptiste.[84] Sloper, the only racially "superior" ("Teutonic") character identified as supremely capable on the frontier like Baptiste, stands at an emaciated ninety pounds, is "[y]ellow and weak" after "fleeing from a South American fever-hole," and is past his prime.[85] He seems as likely to be overcome by the environment around him as to exert any form of mastery. The story also sets Weatherbee and Cuthfert's degeneration in a cabin that, despite its frontier setting, initially evokes the civilizational ease and boredom that these men were trying to escape.[86] Like "Fire," "Far" ends with a suggestion of human and nonhuman mirroring, in this case the mutual frozenness of the land and Weatherbee and Cuthfert's bodies, as the two men are left to freeze as the frost permeates the now fire-less cabin. In other words, "Far" ends with a vision of (white settler) connection to the land that perversely evokes the settler imperative to appropriate indigeneity, so that "Far" also figures settler connectedness to the land as alienation and death.

In contrast to "Fire," "Far" is interested in the racial, cultural, and linguistic heterogeneity of the milieu it depicts, as reflected in the sled crew who leave Weatherbee and Cuthfert behind. Kathryn Morse has noted that Klondike gold-seekers "who could afford to hire help in moving their supplies immediately turned to local Native Alaskans and Native Yukoners," and "From the earliest days of Yukon steamboating, captains relied on Native pilots to guide them."[87] In other words, reliance on Native guides and laborers, particularly Tlingit and Tagish guides and laborers, was common during the Klondike Gold Rush. "Far" obliquely registers this history in the supposedly "disreputable contingent of half-breed voyageurs with their women and children" who initially help the journey's progress but reasonably abandon the expedition when gold proves elusive, because, according to the narrator, they are "overcome by the common dread of the Unknown Lands." It is after this parting of ways, and after summer's passing, that Weatherbee and Cuthfert elect to settle into the cabin. To what is left of the crew's still heterogeneous but now much less Indigenous milieu, composed of eight individuals including Baptiste, Sloper, and a "heavy-going Westerner from the Dakotas," the story assigns a future premised on the appropriative absorption of indigeneity. Jacques Baptiste reads not only as the most likely individual to survive the expedition but also as the one character fully capable of stewarding the crew safely and successfully. Baptiste, we are told, was born of a Chippewa [Anishinaabe/Ojibwe] woman and a renegade voyageur (having raised his first whimpers in a deerskin lodge north of the sixty-fifth parallel [a measure of latitude that roughly bisects Alaska] and had the same hushed by blissful sucks of raw tallow).

Baptiste, I would like to suggest, serves as a figure of robust but disappearing indigeneity in this story, given the absence by narrative's end of any other partly or fully Indigenous characters who have "the protean faculty of adaptability" that the story takes as requisite for survival. Within settler logics of Native genocide via extermination or assimilation, Baptiste's paternal parentage casts him as a figure of Native genocide through assimilation in whom the dilution of Anishinaabe/Ojibwe blood by French Canadian blood works to eliminate indigeneity.[88] Moreover, in the 1890s context of the story's setting and publication, the Canadian government had already extended to the Northwest Territories programs that forced people of mixed Indigenous and European ancestry to choose a "Métis" or "Indian" identity and to agree to the "extinguishment of their Aboriginal title either by entering treaty or taking scrip [a voucher for land or money]."[89] When we are told that, in response to Sloper's joke about Weatherbee and Cuthfert as the two "Kilkenny cats" who pettily fight to mutual death, "The Frenchman in Baptiste shrugged his shoulders, but the Indian in him was silent," that silence signifies more than just a stoic Indian stereotype.[90] It suggests as well the "silent" disappearance of indigeneity under the influence of Eurocanadian and Euroamerican penetration (literally) and colonization. Like settler nations, the future of the expedition's heterogeneous crew relies on the appropriation and disappearance of indigeneity, dramatizing Jodi Byrd's provocative insight that "ideas of Indians and Indianness have served as the ontological ground through which U.S. settler colonialism enacts itself as settler imperialism" into the present.[91]

*The Call of the Wild*'s (1903) diverse cast of human, canine, and lupine characters points to a similar interest in heterogeneous settler "types," in this case within a narrative where indigeneity is not so much disappearing or being assimilated as instead merely ancillary to the ascendance of an uncannily human-yet-not-human dog hero. *Call* has been adapted many times over, in film at least seven times, with the latest adaptation the 2020 Hollywood film *The Call of the Wild*, directed by Chris Sanders. The film stars Black French actor Omar Sy, Ojibwe Canadian actor Cara Gee, and Jewish-Irish Catholic American actor Harrison Ford, the latter receiving top billing. Jack London's original 1903 novella tells the story of the dog Buck, who lives "at a big house in the sun-kissed Santa Clara Valley" of California until he is stolen away and sold into servitude as a sled dog in the Klondike, delivering mail for the Canadian government before being turned to pulling gold-seekers along their paths to anticipated fortune.[92] At the end of *Call*, a fictional Indigenous People called the Yeehats are left to continue existing similarly to how they had before their appearance near the end of the narrative, a particularly blood-soaked appearance that involves their killing Buck's human associates before Buck kills some of the Yeehats. Yet the Yeehats' role as those who kill Buck's owner, John Thornton, thus freeing Buck from his final master, and the Yeehats' role as those who give Buck his first taste of human flesh, thereby affirming Buck's physical superiority, reduces the Yeehats' continuing existence to that of enabling subordinates in a "wild" world ruled by Buck. (All of this, of course, is on top of the fact that London devised a fictional, violent, superstitious

THE END(S) OF REGENERATION

tribe to appear while Buck and his human associates are along *Nä`chòo ndek* (the Stewart River, a tributary of the Yukon River) on land likely inhabited by living, breathing, still existing Tr'ondëk Hwëch'in, Na-cho Nyak Dun, or Dënéndeh people.)[93] Moreover, Buck's trajectory over the course of *Call*'s narrative is unmistakably reminiscent of the temporal structure of settler-frontier primitivity: Buck undergoes an indigenizing transformation into wildness that feeds into an appropriation of Native land, as he installs himself at the head of a pack of timber wolves who wrest away from the Yeehats "a certain valley which they [the Yeehats] never enter" anymore.[94]

Although critics have tended to read London's novella through variously autobiographical and anthropomorphizing lenses, recent work informed by posthumanism and animal studies—two overlapping frames that seem particularly germane in the context of Frank Norris's and Jack London's tendencies to decenter human subjectivity and agency—calls for caution in reading Buck as an autobiographical projection and the novella as, in Mark Seltzer's words, a story about "men in furs."[95] London's and his contemporaries' writings on differences within and between humans and other animals also push us, however speciously, toward reading *Call* as, at least in one sense, a story about a "civilized" dog (not London himself or one of Seltzer's furry men) who becomes properly "wild" with the help of a racially heterogeneous cast of human characters. My intent here is to situate *Call* within a turn-of-the-twentieth-century moment when US settler colonialism remained in the process of consolidation, a process that frontier logics and performative frontier representation abetted.[96] If we understand Buck as a dog and attend to the racial heterogeneity of the human characters who accompany him in his journey to "wildness," *Call* reads as a narrative that questions imperial and settler colonial notions of racial and species hierarchies but ultimately (re)affirms the appropriative, genocidal dynamics of US settler colonialism.

Older, influential readings of *Call*, such as those in Mark Seltzer's *Bodies and Machines* (1992) and Jonathan Auerbach's *Male Call* (1996), have viewed the novella, and London's writings more generally, as complicit in the capitalist ideology and economic system of the late

127

nineteenth and early twentieth centuries.[97] This emphasis on London's reproduction of the dominant ideology of his historical moment is unsurprising given the New Historicist orientation that Seltzer's and Auerbach's studies and the present chapter share, an orientation that Walter Benn Michaels pithily encapsulated in his notion that "the only relation literature as such has to culture as such is that it is part of it."[98] Literature, the (in)famous New Historicist position maintains, cannot criticize or endorse the culture from which it springs; instead, it "exemplifies" that culture's dominant logic.[99] Combining a New Historicist approach with Michael Lundblad's work on animality and the "discourse of the jungle" allows us to see how Buck and his narrative reproduce settler colonialism's appropriative logic.[100]

In *The Birth of a Jungle* (2013), Lundblad locates the origins of this "discourse of the jungle" in the years around the turn of the twentieth century, when evolutionary ideas had already taken hold in the minds of most educated Europeans and US Americans. This discourse is centrally concerned with questions related to "the figure of 'the animal.'" As such, it conceives of humans and other animals as "Darwinist-Freudian animal[s]" in order to produce an understanding of a trans-species "animality" that is violent so as to ensure survival and heterosexual so as to ensure reproduction. One of the effects of this kind of continuum between humans and nonhuman animals is that animality was (and continues to be) constructed and situated differently in relation to various human groups. Thus, the purview of the discourse of the jungle includes the kind of eugenic, scientific racism-informed thinking that would maintain that all humans manifest "animal instincts," but that white people, as supposedly more evolved humans, are more in control of these instincts than are (colonized) people of color. Such thinking, Lundblad suggests, accounts for Teddy Roosevelt's critical response, in what came to be known as the Nature Fakers controversy, to London's representations of animals such as Buck as thinking and feeling, rather than instinctual, beings: "Roosevelt's interest in this debate over the nature of animality can be mapped onto his investment in the discourse of the jungle, in which 'higher animals'—such as nonhuman primates —could be equated with 'lower humans,' both within the United States, in terms of African Americans and Native Americans, and abroad, at sites of U.S. imperialism, such as Cuba, the Philippines, and Panama."[101]

In short, Roosevelt took issue with London's animal stories because their modeling of animal subjectivity potentially cast a negative light on US settler colonial and imperial endeavors, as the "humanness" of London's dog heroes cast doubt on the species and racial logics that helped to legitimize violence in North America and abroad. Lundblad's work demonstrates that Buck and the narrative of *The Call of the Wild* enter into contemporaneous debates about the difference between human and animal, debates that were connected to ideas about (racial) differences among humans, in ways that trouble the species and racial hierarchies that figures like Teddy Roosevelt saw in the world. To be clear, though, this troubling of species and racial hierarchies does not represent genuine resistance to US settler colonialism but, rather, a unique "expression" of US settler colonialism's appropriative logic.

*McTeague* focalizes around the ethnically ambiguous McTeague, who is momentarily an "American" before he perishes in Death Valley; "Memorandum," "Fire," and "Far" portray white men who are overcome, rather than revitalized, on the frontier. In all four of these texts, frontier spaces consume these men in ways that reconfigure, if not refute, the narratives of western regeneration associated with figures including Turner and Roosevelt. Against characters such as Norris's Karslake and London's unnamed man, Buck's trajectory represents something much closer to Turner and Roosevelt's triumphalist takes on western experience. But Buck's narrative is irreducible to those of Turner and Roosevelt, and part of what accounts for this difference inheres in the fates of the humans who own Buck over the course of his initiation into life in the Klondike.

In *The Call of the Wild*, the men and one woman who take charge of Buck at various points are a racially heterogeneous group. Similar to "Far," survival is linked to race in ways that privilege those who are marked as racially and culturally other vis-à-vis the Anglo-Saxon and the "American." In this way, notions of white western regeneration are challenged, and any hierarchical ordering of human (racial) groups that might be deduced from the text favors those "'lower humans'" to which Lundblad refers above. In "The Strenuous Life" (1899), Teddy Roosevelt argued that if the US were to "stand idly by" rather than take paternalistic charge of Hawaii, Puerto Rico, and the Philippines, "the bolder and stronger people will pass us by, and will win for themselves the domination of the world."[102] In the immediate context of places including the Philippines, these "bolder and stronger people" are the Spanish, another imperial power vying for influence in the Pacific and Caribbean. More broadly, though, Roosevelt's rhetoric breaks the world's peoples and nations into two groups: the lighter-skinned peoples of US and European imperial powers, and the darker-skinned peoples of nations supposedly in need of imperial stewardship. For Roosevelt, there is no question that "the domination of the world" will fall to a nation in the former group.[103] This view of geopolitics, as Lundblad perceptively suggests, is inseparable from Roosevelt's overarching investment in the racial and species hierarchies whose logic dictated that lighter-skinned peoples and nations would come out on top in the wake of "intense struggle, whether in war, in the capitalist economic system, on the frontier, or anywhere else away from the constraints of female civilization,"[104] to use Alfred Habegger's memorable description of the thematic preoccupation of London and other turn-of-the-twentieth-century male naturalists, a preoccupation that applies equally to Roosevelt.

Confronted by the outcomes of Buck's various "masters," Roosevelt's logic falls apart. Buck's first "masters" in the Klondike are Perrault, a "swarthy" French-Canadian, and François, a "French-Canadian half breed . . . twice as swarthy" as the former.[105] In other words, François is part-Native and Perrault calls to mind the supposedly morally and politically inferior "swarthy" white "races" of late nineteenth and early twentieth-century US racial thought and classification.[106] These men are portrayed through the perspectives of Buck and the narrator as "fair men" who are well-equipped, in temperament and knowledge, for survival in the Northland. Unsurprisingly, these men are able to complete their object of bringing important news from the Canadian government into the recesses of the Klondike. Buck and his fellow sled dogs next fall under the control of a "Scotch half-breed" in charge of "the mail train, carrying word from the world to the men who sought gold under the shadow of the Pole." Like Perrault and François, this half-Native man is able to carry out his task successfully.

Having offered these portrayals of survival and success, the text then puts Buck under the ownership of a group of gold-seekers, two men and a woman from "the States" named Charles, Hal, and Mercedes. Like Weatherbee and Cuthfert of "Far," these three are woefully incapable of adapting to their new environment and end up bickering with one another once "Arctic travel became to them a reality too harsh for their manhood and womanhood." Charles, the patriarchal figure in relation to his "dainty" and "pretty" wife Mercedes and her "callow[]" brother Hal, "was a middle-aged, lightish-colored man, with weak and watery eyes and a mustache that twisted fiercely and vigorously up, giving the lie to the limply drooping lip it concealed." This characterization of this ostensible authority figure alludes to his phenotypical whiteness ("lightish-colored") and thus invites comparison with the "half-breed" and "swarthy" men who have proven themselves eminently capable in the Klondike. The comparison decidedly favors the darker men from the very moment that Charles and his "family" enter the narrative. In drawing attention to Charles's "limply drooping lip," the narrator implies that he is lacking in firmness or vigor or vitality. Perhaps most telling, though, is that Charles, Hal, and Mercedes die when their sled falls through the ice of the trail that was supposed to lead them to riches. Their deaths are unsurprising; what is perhaps less expected is the way in which whiteness, impotence, and death are aligned.

Buck's final "master," John Thornton, saves him from the fate that befalls Charles, Hal, Mercedes, and the rest of their sled dogs, and for a while Thornton seems like a figure who might reverse the connection between whiteness and futility that is established in Charles's and his crew's fate. Thornton, another seeker of Arctic gold, is more seasoned and comports himself in ways considerably more conducive to survival, yet he too perishes before the end of the narrative. Furthermore, as if to drive home the racial meanings of Thornton's death, he is killed by the Yeehats: "Thornton's desperate struggle" against the force of the Yeehats "was fresh-written on the earth, and Buck scented every detail of it down to the edge of a deep pool."[107] As with the stories of white men in the "wilderness" that I have analyzed above, the white men of *Call* are overcome by their experiences of "the strenuous life."

Buck then kills the Yeehats in an act of violence that represents the narrative's final inversion of the interconnected racial and species hierarchies that circulated in contemporaneous debates about animality. The narrator's language signals this inversion of hierarchy, as Buck drags the Yeehats "down like *deer* as they raced through the trees"; the importance of this comparison of the Yeehats to deer will become clear shortly.[108] Were we to read Buck as an autobiographical projection, such as Auerbach does, his coming out on top might be (mis)taken as a metaphor for the white supremacy that London sometimes espoused. Yet London's own words about *The Call of the Wild* and companion text *White Fang* (1906) in his *Collier's* article "The Other Animals" (September 5, 1908) show him pushing readers to view his "dog-heroes," Buck and White Fang, as animals whose mental capacities are closer to those of the "savage" than they are to the intellectual and cognitive abilities of a white man such as London himself.[109] Buck, as one who toils so as to circulate writing, certainly seems like a vector for London's views on being a writer within what Christopher Wilson has described as a culture of "Progressive-era literary professionalism."[110] But Buck is also a vector for London's complicated views on race/species as much as he is a transfiguration of London the writer.

In "The Other Animals," London writes that *Call* and *White Fang* were "in truth a protest against the 'humanizing' of animals." In an attempt to truthfully represent animal subjectivity, one of London's intentions in writing these stories was "to hammer into the average human understanding that these dog-heroes of [his] were not directed by abstract reasoning, but by instinct, sensation, and emotion, and by simple reasoning." London argues that humans share "kinship with the other animals," but that this kinship is hierarchical, moving downward from "higher" to "lower" human "types" and subsequently to "higher" and then "lower" nonhuman animal "types." In London's Darwinian–white supremacist taxonomy, the "savage[s]" of Tahiti are just above monkeys in the "animal scale," individuals such as himself and his (white) readers are at the top, and birds represent the kinds of nonhuman animals that dwell at the bottom.[111]

In short, London might disagree with Roosevelt's charge of "faking" it, but he agrees with Roosevelt that there is something like a "natural" order. Roosevelt's belief in such an order provided a convenient basis for violence against racialized populations, violence that Roosevelt was particularly well positioned to oversee as a statesman and military leader.[112] Despite the racist aspects of London's "The Other Animals," we need to remember that the article is a response to Roosevelt and John Burroughs, the naturalist who lent scientific support to Roosevelt's notions about nonhuman animals. As such, the article attempts to engage in a kind of ambivalent advocacy for racialized populations and nonhuman animals. For although London maintains a hierarchical ordering topped by "civilized" whites, he also argues for greater proximity and similarity between various human groups and nonhuman animals: "From the robin to the monkey, where is the impassable gulf? and where is the impassable gulf between the monkey and the feeding-child? between the feeding-child and the savage who seeks the man behind the partition? ay, and between the savage and the astute financiers Mrs. Chadwick fooled and the thousands who were fooled by the Keeley Motor swindle?"[113] In the case of Roosevelt the statesman and military leader, we can look to his speeches (such as "The Strenuous Life") and military action (namely, violence against racialized populations at home and abroad) for a larger picture of his ideas about race and animality. With London the writer, we should look to the fiction that he wrote.

London's fictional engagement with race and animality in *Call* is not only or even primarily about who survives and who perishes in the Northland in the specific historical moment of the Klondike gold rush. Rather, London offers a vision of who survives and thrives over the longer sweep of evolutionary history. At every turn in Buck's journey to self-ownership, temporal displacements seep into his consciousness and behavior. These curious displacements manifest in such things as Buck's "instinctive" "fear of the wild thing for the trap . . . a token that he was harking back through his own life to the lives of his forebears," for how else, the narrator surmises, could a "civilized dog" act so? An even stranger displacement takes the form of dream-like visions of a "hairy man" who ostensibly represents primitive (hu)man. Such displacements in a sense follow through on the suggestive title of the first chapter, "Into the Primitive," which frames Buck's story as a movement backward through the deep time of evolutionary history. But such displacements, as Auerbach recognizes, are irreducible to the naturalist plot of decline, of descent into atavism. The signs of primordial reversion that Buck exhibits in such things as his "fear . . . for the trap" are accompanied throughout the narrative by episodes that show him learning, through the use of "simple reasoning," how to survive. One such instance is when he learns from his fellow sled dogs that he must dig a hole in the snow to sleep in at night, so as to stay warm. The narrator is quick to point out that this is not instinctual or primordial behavior, but, instead, "[a] nother lesson" that Buck has learned in the Northland. The narrator's early indecision as to whether Buck's changed behavior in the Klondike represents a process of "development" or "retrogression" is apt, for his changes represent not one or the other, but both. Like the "hairy man," whose instincts give him "a quick alertness as of one who lived in perpetual fear of things seen and unseen," Buck's instinctual reflexes suit him to the Klondike. Even more ably than a white man like John Thornton, Buck is able to learn how to comport himself as he navigates his embodied relationship to this harsh environment.

Instinctually and intellectually, Buck is primed to survive. Importantly, the narrator is careful to note that his survival informs the composition and future of the lupine/canine population in the Klondike. A few paragraphs before the end of the text, the narrator says, "here may well end the story of Buck," but the text then proceeds to tell the story of how the wolves' fur began to look like Buck's, with his characteristic "splashes of brown on head and muzzle" and "rift of white . . . down the chest." In these last paragraphs, narrative attention focuses entirely on Buck's new pack and the remaining Yeehats, the two collectivities that remain at the end of Buck's narrative of toil and transformation, when "the claims of man"—i.e., the constraints of "civilized" life—have been transcended.[114] "Higher" nonhuman animals and "lower" humans, to use London's own terms in "The Other Animals," turn out to be the most "fit" once the constraints of "civilization" have been traded for the (racial) testing ground of the frontier.

Yet as I gestured toward earlier, the coexistence of Buck's pack and the Yeehats is also a kind of performative frontier representation, functioning as a narrative conclusion that turns the racial and species inversions of *Call* into a preamble to a canine version of settler colonial appropriation. Having created a fictional Klondike where imperial and settler colonial racial and species hierarchies are reversed, London uses a seemingly new configuration—a new top dog—to tell an all-too-familiar story: the supremacy of a formerly "civilized" figure on the frontier, at the cost of Native life and land. Like *McTeague, Call* moves away from matters of intra-settler difference at its end, to a settler-Native binary. This paring down functions in *Call* as an occasion to narrate the generational futurity of Buck and the pack that begins to phenotypically resemble him, genetically carrying him across time and into the future. Buck not merely becomes pack leader and sovereign force over land from which the Yeehats formerly fed themselves but also exerts formative influence on the making of historical time, for his killing of Yeehats marks for them "the advent of the Evil Spirit" that now threatens their lives and livelihood.[115] In dictating these fictional Native Americans' relationship to historical time, Buck carves out his settler future.

## Conclusion: (Re)generating Settler Futures

Frank Norris's and Jack London's works call for a new category alongside naturalist "plots of decline" and "plots of triumph": naturalist "plots of appropriation." I use the word appropriation here in its verbal sense of "to take exclusive possession of" in order to signal my understanding of the five texts considered in this chapter as settler authors' laying claim to exclusive possession of the right to dictate temporality. I also use the word appropriation in another of its verbal senses, that of "to take or make use of without authority or right," to indicate that I view these narratives of white settler death as instances of settler authors representing racialized and Indigenous subjects in service of the settler colonial project without sanction from those being represented.[116] While "plots of triumph" are premised on a white supremacist vision of racial hierarchy explicitly consonant with settler colonialism's informing dynamic of genocidal appropriation and replacement, the plots of appropriation in the five texts that I have considered in this chapter question this premise without unseating that informing dynamic. As such, these plots of appropriation perform the hegemonic function of representing and defusing "resistance" to the settler colonial state's biopolitics. This biopolitics, dependent on the ideological support furnished by the idea of white frontier regeneration, is confronted with narratives that contradict this vision of racial supremacy, in some cases simply by killing off their white settler characters, and in others by also installing racialized figures as the victors when "nature, left to its own devices, . . . sort[s] out who belongs on top."[117] But the ongoing, endlessly reproduced goal of the logic of white frontier regeneration (i.e., the naturalization of settler colonialism and settler subjectivity) persists in these narratives: perhaps it comes as no surprise that white frontier regeneration need not actually unfold in front of reader's eyes for settler literary narrative to support the settler colonial project.

Naturalist "plots of appropriation" point to the seemingly intractable durability of US settler colonial logics. And while Norris's and London's narratives of white settler death do not necessarily point us out of those logics, they do point us toward the potential utility of recognizing and specifying the profound flexibility of frontier representation as an instrument of settler colonial power. In particular, these narratives suggest that settler literature necessarily works in support of the US settler colonial project so long as Euroamerican, settler temporalities remain the *sine qua non* of settler literary representation. For settler authors—and settler critics such as myself—denaturalizing settler colonial temporalities and their Euroamerican forebears is the bare minimum for remaking our world(s) beyond the narrow limits of time as settler colonialism has made us know it.

# CHAPTER 4

# "Mix with the Whole Thing"

GENRE INHERITANCES AND QUEERLY
SETTLER COLONIAL COMMUNITY
IN OWEN WISTER'S *THE VIRGINIAN*
AND ZANE GREY'S *RIDERS OF THE
PURPLE SAGE*

E ven when they are not the focus, marriage plots always seem to surface. Polly Mullins and Ramon Martinez are married in Bret Harte's short story "An Ingénue of the Sierras" (1893), analyzed in chapter 1. Dick and Jane get married in Edward Wheeler's *Deadwood Dick's Doom* (1881), one of the texts considered in chapter 2. Frank Norris's *McTeague* (1899), discussed in chapter 3, portrays the marriage of Trina and titular character McTeague, replete with a sumptuous banquet. But there is always something a bit off, temporally, about these marriage plots.

Marriage plots are supposed to provide a snapshot of generational futurity. Polly Mullins and Ramon Martinez's coupling, conversely, seems merely expedient for their outlawry, even if it is, as chapter 1 argued, a portrayal of settler futurity. Dick and Jane's marriage would have left devoted readers of the Deadwood Dick series expecting Dick to eventually find himself single again after losing his mate in some way in a subsequent novel—as Henry Nash Smith and Richard Etulain have noted, Dick courts and marries (and sometimes fails to marry) female characters many times over as the series runs its length.[1] Trina's murder by her own husband, and McTeague's bleak situation in the desert without any conceivable way out, articulate a much different relationship to time than the middle-class nuclear family that Trina and McTeague seemingly intended to create.

In contrast to those marriages from Harte's, Wheeler's, and Norris's writings, this chapter focuses on two novels that seem to promise the kind of heteronormative futurity associated with the marriage plot: Owen Wister's *The Virginian* (1902) and Zane Grey's *Riders of the Purple Sage* (1912). These Westerns participate in the settler tensing of Native genocide, racialized expendability, and white ascendance by narratively folding queerness into the settler nation as a central rather than peripheral component. Rather than articulate queerness and its timelines as complements to heteronormative forms of settler colonial power, these novels collapse queerness into settler heteronormativity.

In *The Virginian*, heteronormative futurity is explicitly portrayed in the marriage of the Virginian and Molly Stark Wood and the highly compacted closing paragraphs of the novel, which tell of their many children, their general happiness in matrimony, and the Virginian's business successes. Grey's ending is rather less neat, but it nonetheless marks the future as the site of heterosexual couplehood and nuclear family: after defeating Mormons who are vilified in ways similar to the Mormon characters of the Deadwood Dick dime novels analyzed in chapter 2, gunslinger hero Lassiter, Mormon heroine Jane Withersteen, and former orphan girl Fay find themselves locked into bounteous Surprise Valley, where, despite the absence of marriage and biological connections between parents and child, the three of them live as a nuclear family. Moreover, the other heroic figures in the novel, Bern Venters and Elizabeth Erne, exit the narrative of *Riders* on their way back to Venters's hometown in Illinois with the intention of getting married.

As these descriptions of the endings of *The Virginian* and *Riders* suggest, these novels seem intent on valorizing a sexual and social normativity that is either absent, muted, or derailed in most of the texts analyzed in previous chapters. Wister and Grey forward visions that are easily read as blunt valorizations of those who are middle-class, white, and more or less normatively heterosexual. But the most compelling scholarship of the last thirty or so years on *The Virginian* and *Riders*, including books by Forrest Robinson, Lee Clark Mitchell, and William Handley and Melody Graulich and Stephen Tatum's edited collection, *Reading* The Virginian *in the New West*, has found a range of complexities, ambiguities, and contradictions within these texts—texts that, at first blush, might seem to be straightforwardly nationalist, racist, and heterosexist in outlook.[2] In *Marriage, Violence, and the Nation in the American Literary West* (2002), William Handley highlights literary form in his consideration of the intersections of race and sexuality in *The Virginian* and *Riders*. For Handley, Wister's novel portrays a range of affective relationships that flourish in the relatively unencumbered West, and it locates the strongest emotions in homosocial and homoerotic bonds. The Virginian and Molly's marriage at the end of the novel thus represents a sacrifice of the personal for the political, as tender feelings between close male friends are subordinated to the imperative that the Virginian and Molly, two Anglo-Saxons, marry "for the sake of a nation's racial future out West."[3] In *Riders*, Handley finds a narrative of Mormon assimilation or, in other words, a narrative of the group's incorporation into the nation through a process of literary familiarization along with Mormon Church President Wilford Woodruff's 1890 manifesto "proclaiming an end to the practice of plural marriage within the borders of the United States."[4] For compelling reasons, Handley reads the novels as narratives of (white) national incorporation and consolidation.

Handley's analysis of *The Virginian* ties queer desire in the novel to the formal and affective disjunctures that result in part from Wister's incorporation of separate, shorter fictional pieces into the novel. Rather than attribute the novel's formal and affective inconsistencies (for example, the shifts in narrative perspective and the emotionally flat honeymoon of the Virginian and Molly) to mere authorial clumsiness in the incorporation of previously published, separate stories, Handley reads these inconsistencies as signs of the personal costs, for Wister, of raising *The Virginian* to a level of (white) national(ist) significance. This chapter also focuses on the formal and narratological peculiarities of *The Virginian* and of *Riders*, but shifts the emphasis away from the kind of biographical-symptomatic reading in which Handley and Jane Tompkins engage, the latter of whom reads *The Virginian*'s "double story, the surface one of glamour and success and an understory of unhappiness hidden deep within," as symptomatic of Wister's personal unhappiness.[5]

This chapter (re)theorizes how queer desire functions in Wister's novel by focusing less on the author and more on his readers and the generic coordinates of his text. For the most part, in Handley's and Tompkins's accounts, *The Virginian*'s homoeroticism and homosociality appear as what must be sacrificed or, alternatively, as expressions of male solidarity that index Wister's animosity toward his mother. This chapter accords with Handley's recognition that "the novel itself barely conceals . . . a type of love not legitimated by law": namely, deep emotional attachments between men.[6] It also reads these attachments in a way that builds from Valerie Rohy's reading in *Anachronism and Its Others* (2009) of nineteenth and twentieth-century American literature as an archive that refracts the co-constitution of "straight time" and the abject, racialized, sexually "perverse" temporalities that straight time defines itself against and contains within itself.[7] As Rohy writes, "the anachronism assigned to blackness and queerness is in fact not external, but internal to and constitutive of the white, heterosexual norm."[8]

In *The Virginian* and *Riders* the white, heterosexual settler norm coheres around "appropriate" pairings and familial formations, as manifested in the Virginian and Molly's marriage and fecundity and the nuclear family formations that begin to take shape at the end of *Riders*, after an intense struggle against the machinations of Mormon villains. But in order to arrive at these "appropriate" endings, the novels must pass through the queerness of same-sex intimacy and eroticism in *The Virginian* and Mormon polygamy in *Riders*. In each novel, the queerness that must be transcended is marked prominently, if not chiefly, as some sort of anachronism against which settler futurity takes shape. Wister's text begins with a preface that explicitly locates this story of cowboys and cowboy heroism in a bygone moment, a move that serves to place the novel's homosociality and homoeroticism in the past. As the preface laments, the figure of the horse-riding cowboy with whom the narrator is so taken "will never come again. He rides in his historic yes-terday."[9] In Grey's novel, Mormonism is portrayed as a politically anach-ronistic phenomenon that bears a racialized accent, as the Mormons embody a "mysterious despotism" and a racially redolent "blackness" that are at odds with white, Christian US civilization.[10] As early as the 1856 Republican Party platform, "polygamy was [portrayed], with slav-ery, [as] one of the last 'twin relics of barbarism.'"[11] As the language of "relics" and "barbarism" attests, anti-Mormon discourse conjoined two elements that often are rhetorically fused together: anachronism and (racial) alterity. Ultimately, the novels are consonant with Rohy's argument that "straight time" and the white, heterosexual norm contain within themselves their abject others in order to construct themselves as primary, hegemonic, and altogether natural formations. For the per-mutations of normalcy that emerge at the ends of *The Virginian* and *Riders* are structurally dependent on the queer, racialized threats that assail the normalcy that each text takes as primary, as given, as natural.

It is worth slowing down here so as to emphasize the kind of rela-tionship that obtains between the queer and the normative, or, in more concrete terms, between same-sex intimacies and heterosexual fecundity in *The Virginian* and between Mormon polygamy and gentile monog-amy in *Riders*. It is not that these figures of queerness simply provide a constitutive other against which these forms of normalcy gain coher-ence. In these novels the "normal" also partakes of—is itself partly made out of—the queerness and anachronism that supposedly oppose and threaten it. This seemingly paradoxical constitution of the queer and the normal is a function of two intertwined aspects of Wister and Grey's texts: their curious uses of generic conventions with which readers would have been familiar, and the ways in which commonplace links between queerness and anachronism on the one hand, and between normativity and futurity on the other, are in certain ways upheld and in other ways violated.

Forrest Robinson has argued that rather than containing or manag-ing potentially subversive issues, popular texts including *The Virginian* and *Riders* "present themselves as sites for the negotiation of competing perspectives on the issues of race and gender" and, more broadly, as sites for the negotiation of "central, painfully vexing questions on power and authority."[12] As announced in the title to the 1993 book from which that last quote is drawn, *Having It Both Ways: Self-Subversion in Western Popular Classics*, texts including Wister's and Grey's have it both ways, as they assert salient political and social ideals at the same time that they contain elements that depart from these ideals—all without fully acknowledging that they are violating what they purport to champion. Working from Robinson's insights, this chapter suggests that these novels participate in settler tensing by negotiating the relationship between normalcy and queerness. This negotiation is rife with contradictions, inconsistencies, evasions, and the implicit espousal of what these texts would otherwise seem to disavow and oppose. For if the normal partakes of the queer—and in these novels, as we will see, the normal partakes of the queer not simply in a theoretical sense but in salient thematic and formal elements as well—then what these novels espouse, despite any explicit disavowals, are the very qualities and timelines, the very queerness, that they seem to be bent on banishing in the name of (white) settler consolidation.

This (white) settler consolidation thus is more properly conceived as a movement toward incorporation that strategically coopts the qualities and timelines that each novel attaches to sexual and racial alterity. *The Virginian* and *Riders* turn the narration of (white) settlement out West into a scene of readerly identification with a curious mix of (hetero)normative and queer temporalities and sexual-social arrangements. Wister's and Grey's narratives represent queer (re)configurations of the regional writing and romance genres, genres whose work is in part to define the nature and boundaries of the social order.[13] Intentionally or not, Wister and Grey manipulate familiar conventions of existing genres to redefine and revalue binary pairings including self/other and (hetero)normative/queer. Like the Bret Harte short stories and Deadwood Dick dime novels discussed in chapters 1 and 2, these Westerns assign value and a future within the nation to practices, arrangements, and desires that are perverse vis-à-vis contemporaneous white, middle-class, Christian settler norms. Since the "perversity" of these alternative formations is informed in part by their discursively constructed relation to time and history, the assignation of value to these alternative formations endows queer temporalities with an integral place in the past, present, and future of the idealized visions of the settler nation that Wister and Grey offer. What is peculiar about this aggregation of heteronormative and queer temporalities is its incorporation into the novels' marriage plots, which unite white settlers into bourgeois nuclear families. *The Virginian* and *Riders* (re)produce settler colonialism by making queerness look straight, and vice versa. There is always a future for US settlers in these Westerns.

## Consolidating the Western: Genre and Queerly Settler Colonial Incorporation

For many a critic, the Western was a boys' club up until quite recently. The publication of Christine Bold's *The Frontier Club* (2013) and Victoria Lamont's *Westerns: A Women's History* (2016) provided essential correctives to the "one-man-genre narrative" that, spanning critical statements from Leslie Fiedler in 1968 to Lee Clark Mitchell in 1996, took *The Virginian* as *the* narrative pattern for the Western.[14] For good measure, Mitchell also identified *Riders* as a generically significant text, one that played a key role in "consolidating formal aspects of the Western."[15] Bold's and Lamont's work demonstrates that *The Virginian* and *Riders* do indeed occupy prominent, central places in the history of the Western, so long as that history is acknowledged for what it is: an androcentric one, a discourse long controlled by white male settler authors and white male settler critics and scholars. From this perspective, *The Virginian* and *Riders* are significant pieces of a genre history that stretches back through James Fenimore Cooper's Leatherstocking Tales and the dime novel Westerns of the nineteenth century such as those analyzed in chapter 2.

But Wister's and Grey's novels also partake of the conventions of other prominent literary forms in US literary history. Such generic borrowing is not on its own a particularly significant phenomenon. After all, Mikhail Bakhtin's "Forms of Time and of the Chronotope in the Novel" suggests that discrete genres are actually just modifications of other, previous genres.[16] At the same time, Fredric Jameson contends that discrete literary texts are sites of genre mixing that often work in the service of ideological containment.[17] Jameson's emphasis on genre mixing as a mechanism of ideological containment is in certain ways applicable to Wister's and Grey's novels. Both novels attempt to contain or defuse the sexual and racial threats that they countenance, and in each case this attempted containment is carried out through recourse to the armature of the marriage plot, a staple of late nineteenth-century genteel realism. But attempting is not the same as achieving, and the genre mixing that takes place in *The Virginian* and *Riders* often devalues and even denaturalizes what at first look like conclusions modeled on white, middle-class, Christian norms and heteronormative generational futurity. These novels do the work of settler tensing by situating protagonists and readers in spaces where all available temporalities and timelines produce white settler ascendance.

Although Wister's own comments about the genre status of *The Virginian* are perhaps more promotional than accurate, the novel's prefatory remarks "To the Reader" immediately draw the attention of readers and critics to the problem of defining just what this "novel" is. Wister writes that some early newspaper reviewers, upon seeing the novel's original subtitle, *A Tale of Sundry Adventures*, made the "mistake" of thinking that they were in the presence of a "historical novel," a label that Wister takes to mean "colonial romance" (3). Yet he ultimately concludes just two sentences later that "when you look at the root of the matter, [*The Virginian*] is a colonial romance" (3). This paradox of mistaken yet accurate generic identification becomes even more baffling once we actually start to read through the chapters of the text, as we find that many of these "chapters" are self-contained short stories that all happen to feature the Virginian and were therefore (somewhat) amenable to being thrown together and passed off as a novel. Ultimately, this canonical Western reads as a strained attempt to incorporate a set of connected short stories into one longer fictional text, an attempt that relies heavily on the marriage plot involving the Virginian and Molly Stark Wood to create a sense of novelistic coherence.

Perhaps the most accurate description of *The Virginian* is that it is a particularly unified collection of local color stories with a marriage plot like that of a realist novel appended to it. If we go back to the antebellum

Southwestern humor of writers such as Thomas Bangs Thorpe and Augustus Baldwin Longstreet, we find that Wister's tenderfoot Eastern narrator can be read as a variation on the cosmopolitan Eastern narrator of this early form of local color.[18] Moving forward to the postbellum texts more often associated with the labels "local color" and "regional writing," we find, as John Cobbs has argued, that the Virginian looks like a more fully fleshed out version of the regional characters that circulate through the fiction of writers including Bret Harte, George Washington Cable, and Joel Chandler Harris—and we can probably add characters from minority and female authors including Charles Chesnutt and Sarah Orne Jewett to this list.[19] Perhaps even more so than a Bret Harte character such as the card sharp John Oakhurst, the Virginian acts as a stand-in for the traits of the imagined region, in this case an imagined West defined by physical vastness and a strict code of behavior, qualities embodied in the physically imposing Virginian, who kills his beloved friend Steve out of adherence to a code. But whereas the narrator of a story like Longstreet's "The Horse-Swap" distances himself from the conduct of the regional characters with whom he comes into contact (and for good reason, perhaps: "The Horse-Swap" is about two men who try to swindle each other in a trade), Wister's narrator tries to learn how to be more like the Virginian and the western type that he embodies.[20]

This relationship between the narrator and the Virginian is characterized by a mode of narrator–regional character affinity that resembles the narrator–regional character affinity familiar to readers of texts in the female-centered tradition of regionalism that Judith Fetterley and Marjorie Pryse delineate in *Writing Out of Place*.[21] Wister's novel maintains the relative urbanity of the narrator and the regional representativeness of the regional character, the Virginian, but shifts the narrator's relationship to the regional character from one of quasi-ethnographic distancing or condescension to one of adoration and emulation. The narrator's adoration of the Virginian is from the start tinged with eroticism; in the narrator's first impression of him, the Virginian is "a slim young giant, more beautiful than pictures."[22] It is in these uses of the conventions of regional writing, coupled with the emotional flatness of the genteel marriage plot involving the Virginian and Molly, that

Handley locates queer desire in the novel, although he does not offer his reading in quite these terms.[23] Wister almost certainly was aware that the kind of writing contained in many of the novel's chapters looked like intact pieces of what was often referred to as local color in the nineteenth century. A significant portion of the novel was originally published as short stories in magazines such as *Harper's*, and Wister "himself said that a reader looking carefully could see the scissor marks of the author's cut-and-paste job" of incorporating previously published short stories into the novel.[24]

The Eastern tenderfoot narrator, who is often read as a stand-in for Wister himself, is, logically enough, a main point of readerly identification. The reader not only gets the story through the tenderfoot's perspective but also ostensibly shares his touristic relationship to an imagined American West. In Thorpe's and Longstreet's writing, as Lloyd Pratt has argued, readers' identification with the narrator is supposed to work as a prophylactic. This identification is supposed to function as a reassurance that reader and cosmopolitan narrator are part of a translocal, Andersonian "imagined community" knit together by a shared present and sealed off from the premodern obsolescence of supposedly "backward" regional characters.[25] But by the end of *The Virginian*, the titular character is not some moribund regional "other." On the contrary, the novel marks him as the sign and source of a desirable present and future in which Anglo-Saxon racial identity, heterosexuality, and middle-class capitalist achievement align. The morally and racially "inferior" characters who bring into relief the nobility of the Virginian, such as Trampas and Shorty, step in to fulfill the role of the regional other who, in Richard Brodhead's influential reading of regional writing, is fated to die out—tellingly, both of these "inferiors" perish in the novel.[26] The narrator stands somewhere in between these regional others and the Virginian. The narrator, as Handley has argued, undergoes a "gradual coming to equality with this man of quality [the Virginian]."[27] But whereas the Virginian ends up married and a father, the narrator is almost as absent as Trampas and Shorty at the end of the novel: the last two chapters are narrated in the third person, and the narrator is ostensibly still the bachelor that he was at the beginning of the narrative. As with Trampas and Shorty, no clear connections are drawn between the narrator and future generations, in contradistinction to the novel's closing description of the Virginian and Molly's prosperity and multiple children (rather than actually note how many children they have, the omniscient narrator who takes over toward the end of the text refers to an "eldest boy" to signal the existence of multiple children).[28] The narrator's only significant attachment, ultimately, is to the Virginian, an attachment that calls to mind Fetterley and Pryse's observation of "regionalism's insistence on foregrounding characters who do not participate in heterosexual plots and who thus do not participate actively in the reproduction of heterosexuality."[29]

In *The Virginian*, the identification with a relatively urbane Eastern narrator that regional writing fosters asks readers to identify with the homosocial, homoerotic, and implicitly racialized position from which the novel's marriage plot attempts to remove the Virginian. Like the narrator, readers are drawn into a position of observing but not necessarily being a part of the idealized (Anglo-Saxon, heterosexual, bourgeois) settler national community for which the Virginian, Molly, and their children are a metonym. Crucially, we readers are never quite made to think that the Virginian's fate is an ideal one; on the contrary, ambivalence surrounds his marriage, his children, his domestication. The novel marks the Virginian's transition from bachelor cowboy to married, middle-class man of consequence as a social and economic boon, and yet the transition is also marked by loss. For the narrator essentially loses the man whom he admired, loved, and would have given himself to "had [he] been a woman" (206), and the Virginian essentially gives up his playful cowboy existence and idealized cowboy code for the comforts of the settled life that he had avoided up to that point.[30] The Virginian and Molly's marriage plot seems designed to contain the queer orientations that the novel articulates in its portrayal of homosocial and homoerotic bonds. But because this marriage plot culminates, as Handley eloquently puts it, in a mood of "hypertrophied sentimentalism"[31] bereft of the poignant emotions that characterize male-male bonds in the novel, *The Virginian* casts doubt on what was ostensibly intended to be a happy, desirable ending. As readers, we are left in a rather queer position, oriented at once toward a homosocial and homoerotic past and the futurity articulated in the Virginian and Molly's marriage and family. The queer contours of that futurity are the subject of the concluding section of this chapter.

As this chapter has noted, Wister was forthright about labeling *The Virginian* a romance—specifically, a "colonial romance"—and he came rather close to calling his "novel" a patchwork of local color stories when he remarked that an attentive reader would notice the seams around the stories that he had incorporated. Zane Grey's *Riders of the Purple Sage* does not share this patchwork quality, but it does follow Wister's text in reading like a romance. First off, *Riders* partakes of the symbolic and allegorical qualities that Richard Chase, building on the work of fellow mid-twentieth century critics including F. O. Matthiessen and Lionel Trilling, famously argued were cornerstones of the American romance form.[32] Perhaps more to the point, *Riders* shares with the American romance "a tendency towards melodrama."[33] As Keith Newlin writes, melodramatists tend to portray the world in terms of "a Manichaean struggle between opposing forces," and in certain respects Grey's text strives to present its central characters and its overall narrative in terms of the clashing of opposed forces, namely, the Gentile heroes who represent US settler civilization and the Mormon villains who stand in for Mormon "empire."[34] Such Manichaeanism, Jameson suggests, also characterizes the romance in its earlier, medieval forms, such as the romances of Chrétien de Troyes and Wolfram von Eschenbach.[35] This is not to say that *The Virginian* does not share in these romantic and melodramatic qualities. But Grey's novel is where these qualities more clearly engage in settler tensing, by appropriating queer temporalities to underwrite settler futurity. Like the queer temporality of Wister's reader, situated in the space where desire for a prior moment of homosociality and homoeroticism meets the generational futurity of marriage and family, *Riders* ends in a note of ahistorical seclusion that appropriates the anachronism of Mormons and the Anasazi (Ancestral Puebloans) in the name of US hegemony in Utah.

For Chase, the American romance, as a descendant of the medieval romance, shies away from the novel's "requirements of verisimilitude, development, and continuity" in favor of a more sensational, idealized mode of representation. In contrast to the realist novel's privileging of character over plot, the American romance's symbolic and allegorical mode subordinates characters to plot in such a way that these characters are often flatter, "two-dimensional *types*."[36] Handley implicitly addresses *Riders'* participation in the romance's mode of characterization when he writes that the text "typologiz[es] its characters."[37] Drawing a more explicit genre link, Forrest Robinson argues that Grey's novel simply "is a romance" because it "makes no pretense to realism or verisimilitude."[38] More precisely, for Robinson *Riders* is an example of what Wayne Ude refers to as the "'romance-adventure-novel,'" a genre whose plot twists and obfuscations lead to morally acceptable, if somewhat superficial, conclusions.[39]

*Riders* certainly is full of plot twists and obfuscations, but Grey's romance does more than just offer superficially ethical conclusions to its narrative of struggle between "evil" Mormons and "good" Gentiles. The kinds of oppositions that Jameson identifies as distinguishing features of the romance "as a mode," by which Jameson means a theoretical formulation of the romance that can reduce each individual instance (text) of the genre to a common meaning, do not play out neatly in *Riders*. Jameson argues that a defining attribute of the romance is "the conceptual opposition between good and evil, under which all the other types of attributes and images (light and darkness, high and low, etc.) are clearly subsumed."[40] Throughout, *Riders* dispenses with any neat oppositions in favor of a mysterious blackness and darkness that pervade gunslinger hero Lassiter and Mormon and rustler antagonists alike. (This is not to say that, among texts that might be classed as members of the romance genre, *Riders* is singular in its tangling of oppositions, but Grey's tangling is noteworthy.) Lassiter's entrance into the narrative is marked by an abstract, symbolic mode of characterization that focuses on his black garb and black guns: the word "black" is used six times to describe him in the first few pages after he makes his entrance. The accompanying dialogue of one of the Mormon elder Tull's henchmen emphasizes Lassiter's blackness, as the color black is mentioned three of those six times in the space of one sentence: "He packs two black-butted guns—low down—they're hard to see—black agin [*sic*] them black chaps." Just a few pages earlier, Tull is introduced as a "leader" among Mormons, "a tall, dark man, [and] an elder of Jane's church." When the rustler Oldring, another symbol of evil, is introduced, his distinguishing features are his "huge bulk" and his "black-bearded visage," and we are told at the end of the scene in which he first appears that "the darkness swallowed" him and his band of rustlers.[41] Handley shows that this imagery of blackness and darkness is but one of the ways in which the text curiously aligns its heroes and villains, and he concludes that Mormon "Other" and US "imperial Self" unsettlingly come to resemble one another as *Riders* works to assimilate Mormon difference into dominant US culture.[42] Handley does not explicitly view this collapsing of self and other as a function of how Grey handles the romance form, but his recognition of Grey's typological characterization and allegorical narrative machinery points to how the conventions of the American romance are foundational to Grey's attempt to pruriently entertain, and then defuse, the Mormon "threat."

What are the effects of *Riders*' attempt to defuse this Mormon threat? Is Mormon difference, a difference based in sexuality and politics, folded fairly seamlessly into the dominant (white, Christian) settler culture for which Lassiter, Jane, and Fay, as well as Venters and Bess, stand as representatives at the end of the text? We can begin to formulate an answer here by referring to Jameson's account of the ideological function of the romance. When properly historicized, Jameson argues, the Manichaeanism of the romance form is not some transcendent "fact" of human ethics that one might find in any of a number of literary forms spread across human history. Instead, this Manichaeanism is intimately linked to the nature of class society, as well as to the animosities and divisions created by nationalism and the concept of race. Once we penetrate the surface of the romance, which is marked, as just noted, by an emphasis on the organizing principle of good versus evil, we can see the latent meaning of these opposed categories: what is evil is whatever or whomever is other, and what is good is whatever or whomever is self.[43] The function of the romance, then, is to "draw[] the boundaries of a given social order and provid[e] a powerful internal deterrent against deviancy or subversion."[44]

The romance, like any other literary genre, performs its ideological work in part through its configuration of time and space. Bakhtin, in his accounts of "The Greek Romance" and "The Chivalric Romance" in "Forms of Time and of the Chronotope in the Novel," tends to stress how these older forms of the romance present character in fundamentally static terms.[45] For example, whereas the bildungsroman tends to be about character development in historical time, the romance in its Greek and chivalric forms tends to resist the novelistic commonplaces of individual development and historical specificity. Northrop Frye articulates this fundamentally static presentation of character in transhistorical terms in *Anatomy of Criticism*: "At its most naïve [the romance] is an endless form in which a central character who never develops or ages goes through one adventure after another until the author himself collapses." If we think back to this book's discussion in chapter 2, we should hear resonances between Bakhtin's and Frye's accounts and the temporality of the dime novels. While Bakhtin's interest in historically-specific variations on the romance keeps him away from making transhistorical claims about the form, Frye's more synthetic approach leads to the conclusion that "the hero of romance is analogous to the mythical Messiah or deliverer who comes from an upper world, and his enemy is analogous to the demonic powers of a lower world."[46] As we have seen, in *Riders* this binary conception of the romance's "hero" and "enemy" is violated from within the very symbolic aesthetic vocabulary that, in Chase's estimation, is one of the defining qualities of the form. Moreover, Grey's "hero," Lassiter, is not the kind of static, unchanging character that Bakhtin and Frye accord a prominent place in the romance. Yet Lassiter is like Frye's archetypal "hero" in that he is a Messianic figure: more precisely, he is a secular savior who swoops in to save white womanhood from the supposed evils of Mormonism. In so doing, Lassiter plays a central role in impelling *Riders* along a narrative trajectory informed by the redemptive temporality of the romance. This temporality, to be clear, is not the same as Benedict Anderson's well-known understanding of Benjamin's "Messianic time" as "a simultaneity of past and future in an instantaneous present."[47] Rather, the redemptive temporality of the romance resembles the socially reproductive narrative temporality that

Frye and Jameson locate in the genre of comedy. Crucially, however, this redemptive temporality aims not at the status quo that comedy often reproduces—one famous example of this fundamentally conservative vision being Shakespeare's *As You Like It* and its quadruple marriage conclusion, which puts all the characters back into their "proper" social places—but at the creation of something higher and better, in other words, something redeemed. Translated to Jameson's social and ideological register, this "something" that has been redeemed is the social order that the romance works to demarcate. What I wish to highlight here is the profound extent to which the function of social order definition that Jameson finds in the romance, and which this chapter finds in *Riders*, depends on a genre-defining, redemptive narrative temporality that Frye gestures toward in his emphasis on Messianic figures and deliverance and redemption.

The redeemed social order around which boundaries are being drawn in *Riders* bears elements that strikingly resemble the supposed evils and excesses of Mormonism. One such evil was the perception among prominent anti-polygamists that Mormon plural marriage amounted to the enslavement of women. Harriet Beecher Stowe, for instance, expressed hope in her preface to Mormon wife Fanny Stenhouse's 1875 autobiography *Tell It All* that "the hour is come to loose the bonds of a cruel slavery [i.e., polygamy] whose chains have cut into the very hearts of thousands of our sisters."[48] *Riders'* rather dramatic ending, where Lassiter, Jane, and Fay lock themselves into Surprise Valley by tipping into place the "Balancing Rock" perched near "Deception Pass," amounts to Jane trading her potential "enslavement" under Mormonism for captivity in a valley with a man to whom she is not wedded and a young girl whom she has de facto adopted.[49] As Handley points out, Lassiter's "rescue" of Jane from the supposed (sexual) slavery of Mormon womanhood looks less like a rescue and more like the initial moment of actual captivity for a woman who formerly owned her own land and cattle.[50] Even more evocative of supposed Mormon unsavoriness is *Riders'* mimicking of two major thematic coordinates of what Lori Merish calls the "anti-Mormon narratives" of the second half of the nineteenth century. Jane's situation in Surprise Valley features a unique twist on those narratives' "twin ideas of captivity and sexual danger."[51] For Lassiter does not just lead Jane into captivity. His desire for vengeance against the men who harmed his sister also leads Jane to conclude relatively early in the narrative that she is willing to leverage her sexuality to prevent violence, as she "came finally to believe that if she must throw herself into Lassiter's arms to make him abide by 'Thou shalt not kill!' she would yet do well."[52] Such risking of feminine sexual virtue almost certainly scandalized a large swath, if not all, of Grey's readership in 1912. The only way in which *Riders* is somewhat able to get around its own contradictions is by aligning this captivity and "sexual danger" with the nuclear family form of the man, woman, and child trio of Lassiter, Jane, and Fay.

There are at least two ways of reading what this sexually dangerous captivity-as-rescue conclusion does to the relationship between marginalized Mormons and majority US settler culture. These two readings are premised on Handley's conclusion that *Riders* acts as an agent, in literary form, of Mormon incorporation through the collapsing of difference between Mormon and "American." Such incorporation might be read as the effacement, after the actual historical dismantling of Mormon "empire" out West, of the perceived threats that the Mormons posed: their "perverse" sexuality, their imperilment of white womanhood, and their theocratic ways, all of which threatened civilization itself in the eyes of some politicians as well as journalists including Alfred Henry Lewis.[53] The fact that the last image of Tull is of him "shrouded" in dust "as he fell on his knees with uplifted arms"—in other words, the fact that this symbol of Mormonism exits the narrative in a pose of defeat and supplication while he is visually erased from the landscape—lends credence to the notion that *Riders* does the work of incorporating Mormons through erasure of their threatening differences.[54] In this reading, Jane's new place alongside Lassiter and Fay represents a transcendence or escape from the alternative sexual and religious practices of Mormons like Tull and the quasi-ethnic status that came with such deviancy. In the sense that Jane is locked into a valley where her only option is to play a role like that of wife and mother within a nuclear family, it does appear, at least superficially, that she has been rescued.

Yet the situation in which Jane finds herself at the end of Grey's romance contains deviations from a Christian settler norm of monogamous marriage (including its promise of generational futurity, which will be addressed shortly) that point to the redrawing of the boundaries of the settler social order so as to coopt the supposedly subversive energies of Mormonism. Fittingly, Grey's romantic mode of characterization—that is, his dependence on abstract, symbolic presentation of character—clues us in to *Riders'* redrawing of the boundaries of the social order. As noted just a few pages prior, Lassiter, in his "blackness," resembles the Mormon men against whom he struggles in the narrative, and the meanings with which this "blackness" is invested reinforce the resemblance. For example, Lassiter's black guns, phallic symbols whose status as such is driven home by Jane's seductive caresses of them, call to mind the racialized sexual excess associated with polygamous Mormon men.[55] One telling example of the eroticism invested in Lassiter's guns comes in the chapter "Faith and Unfaith": "Jane slipped her hands down to the swinging gun-sheaths, and, when she had locked her fingers around the huge, cold handles of the guns, she trembled as with a chilling ripple over all her body."[56] It would be a mistake, in my view, to conclude that Lassiter and Mormon men like Tull and Bishop Dyer are mirror images of one another, but the symbolic implication of Lassiter's sexual excess is, significantly, transformed into actual deviance at the end of the text. Before Lassiter, Jane, and Fay seal themselves into Surprise Valley, Lassiter gives up his guns in a move that suggestively allows for the exclusion of these symbols of sexual excess from the scene of nuclear familiality that Surprise Valley will become. There is thus a sense that everything has been set aright, so to speak. Lassiter and Jane are moving into a monogamous relationship in Surprise Valley that resembles a normative domestic arrangement, seeing as they already have a child in Fay and Surprise Valley has already had at least two sets of inhabitants (Venters and Bess and, well before them, the Anasazi, referred to dismissively in the novel as simply ancient "cliff-dwellers") who have shown just how amenable the space is to settled life. Moreover, Lassiter has divested himself of the symbols of excessive sexuality that were responsible in part for his unsettling proximity to racialized Mormon men. Whiteness, or, more precisely, the sexual propriety associated with whiteness, is symbolically wedded to the monogamous, normatively domestic form that we assume will take hold among Lassiter, Jane, and Fay in Surprise Valley. Yet the marriage contract is conspicuously absent from this (future) scene of domestic life. This absence, when located in the form of the romance, suggests a redrawing of the social order that allows for, indeed celebrates, social and sexual lives that mimic but are not identical to settler Christian norms of marriage and domesticity.

Jane Tompkins's (in)famous reading of the Western as a rejection of Christianity and domesticity in favor of the secular and the masculine[57] is thus partly right but in need of a bit of modification in the case of *Riders*. *Riders* certainly does perform a certain rejection of Christianity in celebrating the form of monogamous couplehood without the formality of Christian marriage. Yet even in this rejection of Christianity, the text still endorses the religion's nucleus of social life, and *Riders* even goes so far as to grant the (impending) sanctification of marriage to Venters and Bess, who exit the narrative with the intention of getting married and heading east to Venters's old home in Illinois. "'Do you know—,'" Venters asks Bess near the end of *Riders*, "'have you thought that very soon—by this time to-morrow—you will be Elizabeth Venters?'" The sheer excitement and happiness conveyed in Venters's breathless question offers further evidence of the text's endorsement, rather than rejection, of domesticity; in contrast, Venters was not particularly happy in his former life of masculine solitude in the Utah uplands, sleeping alone and "bitterly comparing [the night stars'] loneliness to his own."[58] But because Grey's romance ends with the image of Lassiter, Jane, and Fay locking themselves into Surprise Valley—in other words, because this romance's concluding image of the triumph of good over evil locates good in a trio who cannot be called comfortably Christian in their ways—Tompkins's counterposing of Christianity and domesticity versus secularity and masculinity seems less analytically useful here than a consideration of how these categories' meanings and relationships to one another are shifted within the pages of the text. In particular, the metonymic connection between US settlement, Christianity, and heteronormative domesticity is sundered.

This connection is sundered in such a way that the foundational settler domestic "norm" out in the wild Western space of 1871 Utah, as opposed to the Christian domesticity that Venters and Bess presumably will practice in Illinois, looks both reassuringly Christian and "perversely" Mormon at the same time. To put this another way, *Riders'* ending mixes the monogamous form of Christian domesticity with conventions of early twentieth-century literary representations of Utah and Mormonism. This strange mixture, significantly, also is overlain with evocations of Frederick Jackson Turner's well-known image of the European colonist who begins to become "American" and enacts his own settler indigenization—and Native American erasure—by planting corn in the wilderness.[59] Surprise Valley, as this chapter noted above, is occupied not only by Lassiter, Jane, and Fay, but also by Venters and Bess earlier in *Riders*. While Venters and Bess inhabit the valley, Venters leaves to pay Jane a visit at her estate and acquire the supplies necessary to make Surprise Valley a properly domestic(ated) home for himself and Bess. He tells Jane that Surprise Valley is "a wonderful place. I intend to stay there. It's so hidden I believe no one can find it. There's good water, and browse, and game. I want to raise corn and stock."[60] Venters's agricultural plans are commonplace enough, but the strongly allegorical and mythological character of *Riders* that scholars including Handley and Richard Slotkin[61] have remarked upon makes it hard to read Venters's choice of crop as merely incidental. Instead, Venters's choice calls to mind the equally mythological scene in which Turner's frontier colonist makes his first appearance and, along with living and dressing like the imagined Natives he is displacing, plants Indian corn as part of a set of acts that begins Turner's grand, settler-indigenizing drama of "Americanization." Of course, in that opening scene of Turner's drama, women are conspicuously absent. In Surprise Valley, on the other hand, women and monogamous domestic life are foregrounded: within the Utah of *Riders*, the valley is the only place where such a life seems at all safe from Mormonism.

As a retrospective allegory of the US's clash with Mormon "empire," Venters and Bess's stay in Surprise Valley, and the symbolic defeat of Mormonism that transpires when Lassiter, Jane, and Fay lock themselves into it, seem at first to dramatize the very historical progression of Utah in the years between 1871 and 1912: from Mormon territory to "Americanized" domestic space. And yet the space in which victory over Mormonism is achieved, a space that has been marked as a bright, paradisiacal place of monogamy and settler colonial consolidation, is shut off from the world and from history. Richard Slotkin observes that rather than conclude with "general social renewal," a common trope of what he calls the Myth of the Frontier, *Riders* leaves our protagonists in a space of ahistorical seclusion.[62] The parallels between this ahistorical seclusion and the representational conventions of nineteenth and early twentieth-century literary portrayals of Mormonism are unmistakable. Terryl Givens notes that popular adventure fiction including Burt Standish's *Frank Merriwell Among the Mormons; or, The Lost Tribe of Israel* (1896) and James Oliver Curwood's *The Courage of Captain Plum* (1908) portray Mormonism as culturally, socially, and geographically isolated—and, we can add, temporally isolated. In that 1896 Frank Merriwell dime novel, the common theme of Mormon isolation finds expression in the fictional Valley of Bethsada, a sentry-guarded space in the Utah wilderness that Gentiles cannot enter and Mormon women cannot leave.[63] Consciously or unconsciously, Grey reconfigured the trope of ahistorical seclusion and created a perverse amalgam of Mormon and "American." In *Riders*, Grey weds symbols and temporalities that connote Mormon and "American" social forms and identities and folds this curious mix into a literary form, the romance, that historically has done the work of defining which people and practices rightfully belong in a collectivity and its future.

## The Heterogeneity of Settler Time

Benedict Anderson's *Imagined Communities* (1983) gave the realist novel a central place in considerations of the temporality of nationalism. This section argues that the regional writing and romance forms as practiced in *The Virginian* and *Riders* articulate the peculiar temporality of hegemonic US settler nationalism. If the function of the romance form is to draw boundaries around the people and practices that properly belong in a collectivity, then the regional writing on which much of *The Virginian* is modeled is best understood as a parallel form that cloaks its own work of settler social order definition in the guise of picturesque tourism. In the Southwestern humor of Longstreet and Baldwin discussed earlier in this chapter, the opposition between cosmopolitan narrator (and reader) and grotesque local other is not far off from the romance's traditional structuring binary of good versus evil. Brodhead's and Jameson's work on, respectively, regional writing and romance glosses each of these genre formations as a means through which a group's identity and coherence are forged. Of course, a number of other genres can be described in similar terms. The genteel realist novel in the mold of William Dean Howells, for example, can be said to do the work of defining the urban middle-class self in the late nineteenth century. But the crucial difference between, on the one hand, the genteel realist novel and, on the other, the romance and regional writing is that we would be hard-pressed to read a text like Howells's *A Hazard of New Fortunes* (1889) as an attempt to expel or write out of existence the working-class people of New York. As Amy Kaplan has argued, realism instead should be conceived as a "strategy" for negotiating social conflicts so as to construct through narrative a "common ground among classes both to efface and reinscribe social hierarchies."[64] In other words, the realism of authors including Howells and Henry James attempts to fabricate social harmony and unity, in contrast to the romance's Manichaeanism and regional writing's tendency to polarize cosmopolitan narrator/reader and regional other.

Despite meaningful differences, Kaplan's reading of realism echoes Benedict Anderson's account of the realist novel as a form for representing the social totality of the nation. The premise behind this theory of textually mediated national affiliation that Anderson hints at but never quite articulates is the assumption of the heteroreproductive temporality of the nation. Anderson is careful to specify that the textual construction of the nation does not cultivate in readers just a sense of simultaneity but also a sense of the nation as a "sociological organism," "a solid community moving steadily down (or up) history."[65] Any given realist novel will necessarily present only a few characters and events that stand in for the larger national collectivity, the aggregate of people that actually exists historically. But Anderson's language of "a solid community" moving "steadily" and in linear fashion through history suggests that these few characters and few slices of national life also cultivate a readerly con-sciousness of the nation as an entity marked by permanence over the sweep of history, over generations.

It is not simultaneity but, rather, the reproductive temporality tra-ditionally associated with heterosexuality that secures this imagining of permanence. As Annamarie Jagose has argued, in Anderson's account of nationalism "heterosexuality, via its overdetermined claims to repro-duction, is taken for a universal figure for meaningful continuity."[66] In other words, simultaneity unites individuals synchronically, but it is the rhythms traditionally reserved for heterosexuality that unite individuals diachronically. As Jagose and other queer theorists including Elizabeth Freeman have argued, belonging, whether to the nation, the "race," or some other collectivity, is produced through the inhabitation of forms of sexual(ized) simultaneity that are "less geotemporally precise" and more directly implicated in diachronic national permanence than the simulta-neity of which Anderson writes.[67] These are forms of simultaneity such as the simultaneous orgasm of husband and wife that Jagose discusses in *Orgasmology* and the heteronormative habitus that Freeman identifies via the work of Pierre Bourdieu, both of which engender belonging in the moment and over the broader sweep of history.[68]

Jagose's and Freeman's work helps to train our attention on the ways in which myriad acts connected to (hetero)sexuality—from simulta-neous orgasm to the rituals associated with marriage and death to the performances of motherhood and fatherhood—have been imbued with national significance, tasked with cultivating, on the synchronic plane, the scripts for "anonymous, simultaneous activity" that enable the imag-ining of the nation as a diachronic entity.[69] Diachronic permanence involves the passing on, through everyday activity and cultural represen-tations, of the heteronormative scripts, the temporalities such as those that Jagose and Freeman discuss, that underwrite the nation's historical permanence. In other words, it is safe to say that hegemonic—but by no means all—forms of nationalism, as idea and as lived experience, are strongly inflected by heteronormative rhythms.

The early 1990s saw an emerging critical consensus that "there is no privileged narrative of the nation, no 'nationalism in general' such that any single model could prove adequate to its myriad and contradictory historical forms."[70] Perhaps, then, the realist novel is not the best or only place to look for a US settler national narrative. And perhaps the heteroreproductive temporality of the nation implicit in Andersonian nationalism is but one of the temporalities through which the nation narratively (re)presents and (re)produces itself in a hegemonic tune. Instead, as I have been suggesting throughout this chapter, we should think of Westerns like *The Virginian* and *Riders*, texts marked by the conventions of regional writing and romance, as exemplary articulations of a US settler national narrative.

A crucial part of that 1990s critical energy around nationalism was Homi Bhabha's important theoretical contribution of identifying the "double-time" of national representation, the "split between the continuist, accumulative temporality of the pedagogical, and the repetitious, recursive strategy of the performative."[71] While the "pedagogical" totalizes and homogenizes, the "performative" is the modality through which subjects lay claim to national belonging and engage in the constant remaking of a national narrative, and a national community, characterized by contentious and unequal practices and identities. I rehearse Bhabha's distinction between the "pedagogical" and the "performative" because I wish to borrow his notion that heterogeneities of time and identity are more proper to the narration of nation, particularly in settler colonial contexts, than are the homogeneities of time and identity associated with Anderson and the work of other theorists of nationalism such as Ernest Gellner.[72] Lee Bebout's theorization of "the *mythohistorical*, [composed of] an integrated network of myths and histories," as the materials out of which shared narrative, identity, and community are forged, illuminates the specificity of settler, as opposed to postcolonial, national narration. For Bebout, hegemonic as well as subordinated groups use manipulations of the mythohistorical to "imagine new communities and new boundaries as well as fashion new citizenships."[73]

Contrary to Bhabha's emphasis on the spaces of resistance that heterogeneities of time and identity make available in *postcolonial* nations, *settler colonial* nations such as the US consolidate hegemonic national identity and nationhood through a heterogeneous mix of the primitive and the modern and the Native and the European, all of which coalesces into the figure of the settler. For the US settler nation, then, "pedagogical" narration simultaneously includes and excludes indigeneity and primitivity, integrating an imagined Native identity and intimate connections to the land into settler identity while also erasing actual, living and breathing Native Americans.[74] Louis Owens, Jennifer Tuttle, and Neil Campbell have made versions of this point in their essays in Graulich and Tatum's edited collection, *Reading The Virginian in the New West*. For Owens and Campbell, Wister's novel relegates Native Americans to fixed points in time and space, "frozen . . . in American mythic time [and . . .] expected to remain where they are put in Wister's West," as Owens writes, and "consign[ed] . . . to the past," in Campbell's words. For Tuttle, *The Virginian* is precisely about a white settler appropriation and integration of an imagined nativeness: as she succinctly puts it, "Wister's novel attempts to construct an 'indigenous' white identity—an authentic American whiteness entitled to dominance on all fronts—through an appropriation of the 'native.'"[75]

Building from Owens's, Campbell's, and, in particular, Tuttle's insights, my point throughout this chapter and in the following section is to articulate *The Virginian*'s and *Riders*' appropriation of imagined Indigenous and racialized others as part and parcel of the temporal-biopolitical formation that this book has called settler tensing. Whereas most of the texts analyzed in the first three chapters of this book variously resist (if always incompletely) the heteroreproductive temporality of the nation to which an appropriation of indigeneity and primitivity is wedded in the US settler colonial context, *The Virginian* and *Riders* integrate settler heterogeneities of time and identity into this heteroreproductive temporality. It is in this integration that the novels express the queerness of hegemonic US settler identity. The following section focuses on the marriage plot resolution of *The Virginian*, which exemplifies a US settler "pedagogy" in which indigeneity and primitivity are simultaneously rendered queer and coopted as bases of hegemonic settler identity and futurity.

## The Queerness of Settler National Narration in *The Virginian*

*The Virginian* caps off its contribution to the settler tensing of white ascendance, racialized death, and Native genocide by beginning and ending with episodes that turn queer relations to time and evolution into the foundation for settler indigenization and futurity. In *The Virginian*, "pedagogical" narration begins to take form before we even get to the narrative proper. Addressed "To the Reader" is a preface that claims for the novel the "epochal" temporality of national narratives grounded in an originary past, the kind of national narrative temporality that excludes the "everyday" time of the heterogeneous actors and acts that actually comprise the nation and its history.[76] Like many, if not all, pedagogical nationalisms, Wister announces that his narrative offers an account of individuals and events that are representative of "a vanished world" rich with significance for US national identity—as significant, Wister implies, as the Revolutionary War moment that his cousin S. Weir Mitchell dramatized in the "historical novel" *Hugh Wynne*. *The Virginian* thus addresses its readers in a manner that Bhabha identifies with a "nationalist pedagogy": "the [nation's] people are the historical 'objects' of a nationalist pedagogy, giving the discourse an authority that is based on the pre-given or constituted historical origin *in the past*."[77]

Yet the exploits of the Virginian in Wyoming between the years of 1874 and 1890, the years covered in *The Virginian*, are less obviously the materials of a national origin story than are the events and historical figures that feature in the Revolutionary War narrative of *Hugh Wynne*. For one, the years 1874 through 1890 do not, chronologically speaking, correspond to a moment of national beginnings. But Bhabha's point is not that pedagogical narratives locate national identity only in founding, or historically first, figures and events. Rather, the point is that pedagogical narratives locate national identity in a series of originary moments and figures that comprise the major scenes and characters of the national plot and furnish the individual national subject with points of identification. This seems to be the very issue that Wister is addressing in his pedagogical address to the reader: perhaps for Wister, if not for US Americans more generally, the story of a "superior" cowboy in late nineteenth-century Wyoming had not yet, in 1902, acquired the significance accorded to the Revolutionary War and the founding fathers.[78] What Wister is doing, then, is promoting a new point of identification for the settler nation, one that introduces its own unique exclusions and surprising inclusions into the national narrative. In *The Virginian*, the queerness of settler national narration inheres in the Virginian's simultaneous claims to primitivity and heterosexuality, which integrate an indigenizing relationship to primitivity into the (white) settler heterosexuality that provides much of the contours and continuity of the US settler nation.

*The Virginian*'s exclusions begin to clarify in the first chapter, which focuses on the Virginian and a character named Uncle Hughey's divergent orientations vis-à-vis social mores around marriage. In his essay "What Is a Nation?" Ernest Renan claimed that "Forgetting, I would even go so far as to say historical error, is a crucial factor in the creation of a nation."[79] Renan's point is that the aggregation of hitherto unaffiliated people into a nation requires that elements of national history that suggest conflict, disunity, and violence must be forgotten in order for the nation to create and perpetuate itself. *The Virginian* is full of moments redolent with national forgetting, among them chapter sixteen's ("The Game and the Nation—Last Act") portrayal of the Apsáalooke (Crow) as beneficiaries of the commodification of "painted bows and arrows and shiny horns" and "beef... and game, and fish." This pattern of occluding historical conflict actually begins with the verbal shots that the Virginian aims at Uncle Hughey's history with marriage, a series of playful remarks that transmute the historical persecution of polygamous Mormons into ultimately harmless teasing. The Virginian asks Uncle Hughey, "Off to get married *again?* Oh, don't!" Thus begins an exchange between the two men in which the "Mormon"-like Uncle Hughey and, implicitly, any man who cannot find a (as in one) wife and settle down is made to look ridiculous:

> He [the Virginian] had by no means done with the old man [Uncle Hughey].
>
> "Why, yu've hung weddin' gyarments on every limb!' he now drawled, with admiration. "Who is the lucky lady this trip?"
>
> The old man seemed to vibrate. "Tell you there ain't been no other! Call me a Mormon, would you?"
>
> "Why, that—"
>
> "Call me a Mormon? Then name some of my wives. Name two.

Name one. Dare you!"

"—that Laramie wido' promised you—"

"Shucks!"

"—only her doctor suddenly ordered Southern climate and—"

"Shucks! You're a false alarm."[80]

The conversation continues in this general direction, with the Virginian continuing to playfully mock Uncle Hughey's misfortunes in marriage. If we take Uncle Hughey at his word, we find out that he indeed has been somewhat unlucky and is not, as he seems to think the Virginian is suggesting, a "Mormon." Nonetheless, this dialogue on marriage performs a certain kind of rhetorical work regarding national unity, since national unity in the face of the supposed Mormon threat often was cast as a function of the US's vigilance in protecting the institution of monogamous marriage.[81]

"Forgetting" and "historical error" are not just about omission. They are also carried out through the resignification of a denigrated category such as "Mormon." *The Virginian* was published twelve years after the Church of Jesus Christ of Latter-day Saints officially renounced polygamy and thus took an all-important step in quelling the US's targeting of Mormons and Mormonism. The general levity around the "Mormon" label in the opening chapter of Wister's text suggests an ease about Mormon polygamy, a supposedly dead institution by 1902, that would seem out of place in earlier texts such as the Deadwood Dick dime novels of the late 1870s and 1880s discussed in chapter 2. But this ease does not hide the sense that "Mormon" denotes something undesirable within Wister's settler national narrative. For Wister's initial audience, knowledge of the historical weight of the "Mormon" label would have been necessary to understand how the term functions in this opening chapter, but the text simultaneously glosses over any potentially unsavory aspects of Mormon persecution to (re)install "Mormon" as a figure for any man who acts in a supposedly inappropriate manner regarding marriage.

A curious and contradictory movement of inclusion and exclusion thus is performed. "Mormon" sexual deviance is given a place in the national narrative by virtue of the Virginian's implicit claim of kinship with the man he calls *Uncle* Hughey, as well as through the simple fact that Uncle Hughey even appears in *The Virginian*. Yet this avuncular figure is marked as kin only to be cast as one of the Virginian's foils, in this case on the terrain of conduct in marriage and family life. When readers next encounter Uncle Hughey, he has just gotten married to a woman who, in the narrator's estimation, "could easily have been his granddaughter." It almost certainly is not a coincidence that this difference in age looks forward to the proposed marriage between the actually Mormon Elder Tull and Jane Withersteen in *Riders*. In his last appearance, Uncle Hughey is accused by the Virginian of "'gambol-lin' around'"[82] without proper regard for his wife and twin babies, so oblivious to his familial responsibilities that the Virginian and another cowboy, Lin McLean, are able to switch Hughey's babies with other babies at a party without the gag being noticed until after the sets of parents have parted ways. Granted, other married men commit similar indiscretions in *The Virginian*: like Uncle Hughey, the other men at the party in chapter 10 ("Where Fancy Was Bred") dance with Molly and provoke the Virginian's jealousy, and fail to notice that their babies have been switched. But Uncle Hughey is the only character whose behavior around courtship, marriage, and family life is roundly, if lighthearted-edly, criticized by the Virginian and the narrator. This sustained note of lighthearted disapproval is crucial to the nationalist pedagogy that *The Virginian* strives to articulate, and not simply because it papers over actual historical conflict and Mormon suppression. It also lumps together a whole set of nonnormative or "inappropriate" behaviors in the character of Uncle Hughey to promote the fiction that deviations from "proper" conduct are met with laughter, not violence. Rather than the outright omission of marginalized practices and identities, the treat-ment of sexual-social deviants is given a place but sanitized in the name of the nation.

In one sense, then, this pedagogical sanitization of violence against sexual and social deviants promotes a national unity that is founded on the withering tolerance of "inappropriate" individuals. At the same time, however, the figuration of national identity in Wister's text, the Virginian, is occasionally no less transgressive than Uncle Hughey.

Having nearly finished with his jests at Uncle Hughey's expense, the Virginian drops a curious line given his overarching movement within the narrative toward marriage with Molly: "'What's the use o' being married?'" The strangeness of this comment in a narrative that can be read as being precisely about the use of being married (namely, for the sake of symbolically uniting North and South as well as bringing together the "aristocratic" bloodlines of the Virginian and Molly) is subdued to an extent by the Virginian's declaration that his aversion to marriage is "proper" to his age of twenty-four. Indeed, his comments seem relatively insignificant until the last chapter, "At Dunbarton." While on his and Molly's honeymoon, the Virginian asks, "What's the gain in being a man?" The question obliquely recalls his question to Uncle Hughey in the first chapter and invites doubt about whether the Virginian has revised his earlier views on marriage now that he has aged a bit and gotten married. But it is not just the evolution of the Virginian's views on marriage that is placed in doubt. As Handley observes, the value of the social Darwinian evolutionary model that would prioritize the Anglo-Saxon Virginian also is questioned when he tells Molly of his desire "to become the ground, become the water, become the trees, mix with the whole thing. Not know myself from it. Never unmix again."[83] In place of his perch atop the "natural order," the Virginian desires self-dissolution into "an undifferentiated natural world."[84]

While this desire sounds somewhat fitting in the context of the trials that the Virginian endures over the course of the narrative, it sounds rather unsuitable coming from a writer who ardently admired Theodore Roosevelt (Wister was so fond of Roosevelt that he dedicated *The Virginian* to him). As discussed in chapter 3, Roosevelt's spat with Jack London over the latter's supposed inaccuracies in portraying animals had quite a bit to do with the matter of violence against racialized populations at the turn of the twentieth century, as the US engaged in imperial exploits in the Pacific and Caribbean. Portray nonhuman animals like the domesticated-turned-wild dog Buck of Jack London's novella, *The Call of the Wild*, as creatures of reason, and the species and racial logics that authorize violence against "lower" humans lose their power to excuse brutality against racialized populations. The Nature

Fakers controversy involving Roosevelt and London did not see its signal contributions from the two men until 1907's "Nature Fakers," by
Roosevelt, and 1908's "The Other Animals" from London. Nonetheless,
later versions of *The Virginian*, notably the 1911 edition to which Wister
added a "Re-dedication and Preface," maintained the Virginian's wish
to dissolve into "nature" while on his honeymoon. In so doing, Wister
fictionally violates the social Darwinian principle of Roosevelt's geopolitics and his own nationalism alike.[85]

*The Virginian*'s settler nationalist pedagogy is in important, indeed
central, ways dependent on the social Darwinism that Wister articulates
in, for example, chapters 12 through 16. In these chapters, authorial
addresses to the reader and the Virginian's dialogue mount an argument
for the superiority of "quality" individuals, those who are racially and
economically privileged in relation to the "equality" of the nation. The
logic of the argument is rather obviously premised on a social Darwinian
logic that would have been familiar to Wister, his initial readers, and those
of us looking back from the present day—the argument is, in essence,
that racially and economically "superior" individuals like the Virginian
are most fit to succeed in the environment that US democracy furnishes.
The narrator/author makes the point most bluntly when he says, "It was
through the Declaration of Independence that we Americans acknowledged the *eternal inequality* of man. . . . Let the best man win! That is
America's word. That is true democracy. And true democracy and true
aristocracy are one and the same thing."[86] As an originary figure, a nodal
point in the procession of figures and events that comprise a hegemonic
settler national narrative, the Virginian's primacy relies on our accep-
tance of the principles of differentiation and hierarchy that he seeks to
escape in one of the last scenes of the text.

The Virginian's complaints against marriage and humanity appear to
take on a subversive aspect when read in the context of *The Virginian*'s
social Darwinism and, in particular, when read in the context of the deep
evolutionary time that subtends social Darwinism's logic. Although the
many and various articulations of social Darwinism that have cropped
up over the last roughly century and a half often have not followed
very closely the biological formulations of Charles Darwin, all social

Darwinisms are at some level dependent on the generations-spanning time scale of his evolutionary theory. *The Virginian* is no exception, and Wister's 1895 essay "The Evolution of the Cow-Puncher," which stakes the Anglo-Saxon's claim to supremacy across multiple historical periods and environments, actually invites us to think about *The Virginian* in terms of generations and centuries, rather than individuals and decades. Moreover, Wister's fictional narrative tends to follow evolutionary theory's principle of natural selection, or the process whereby individuals who possess traits conducive to survival and success within the given environment are more likely to reproduce and pass on those favorable characteristics. Variously "inferior" in moral, economic, or racial endowments, characters such as Steve, Shorty, and Trampas perish while the Virginian passes on his supposedly superior stock in the form of the multiple children that he and Molly have together. Uncle Hughey, who may or may not share ancestry with the Virginian, has more success in propagating than these three other men, but even he, as a different kind of inferior, seems liable to lose out over the course of deep evolutionary time if he is not more careful in ensuring that his twin babies actually make it to puberty. Most crucial for this chapter's purposes, the Virginian's desire to "mix with the whole thing" and relinquish all the differentiating characteristics that prime him for victory in the evolutionary fight appears to run contrary to the logics of time and evolution that the narrative fulfills, in part, via his and Molly's fruitful marriage.

This seeming contradiction between the Virginian's words and *The Virginian*'s narrative trajectory offers a key glimpse into the queerness of settler national narration: the Virginian and his story function as anchoring points for settler national identity precisely because they turn queer relations to time and evolution into the foundation for settler indigenization and futurity. Although Freud's *Three Essays on the Theory of Sexuality* would not be published until three years after the publication of *The Virginian*, the links between homosexuality, racial alterity, and evolutionary regression had already been established by 1879 thanks in large part to Ernst Haeckel's now-defunct recapitulation theory, captured in the formulation "ontogeny recapitulates phylogeny."[87] In this context, the Virginian's desire for deep, ultimate regression into the undifferentiated depths of evolutionary history violates the linked racial and sexual timelines of the evolutionarily (hence racially and sexually) advanced Anglo-Saxon. His desire for a self-dissolving plunge into the past does not, however, equate to an unqualified adoption of racial and sexual alterity, even if his desired place in an undifferentiated natural world is an extreme logical extension of the position that racialized and queer subjects began to inhabit in scientific discourses of the late nineteenth century. These "scientific" accounts of the relation between race, sexuality, and temporality were imposed upon racial and sexual others. The Virginian, on the other hand, imaginatively adopts an evolutionarily backward self that reads as a negation of the principles of Anglo-Saxon supremacy and futurity that are suggested in the text's closing pages. In envisioning this backward, undifferentiated self, the Virginian only appears to vitiate the (white) nationalist thrust of the relation between race, sexuality, and temporality that his narrative otherwise upholds. As a point of identification in a hegemonic national narrative, the Virginian's desires link the Anglo-Saxon national subject to an abjected backwardness in order to appropriate indigeneity and primitivity for settler identity.

Leslie Fiedler long ago claimed in *Love and Death in the American Novel* (1960) that canonical US literature fails to deal with "adult heterosexual love" and instead holds a "consequent obsession with death, incest and innocent homosexuality."[88] Fiedler (in)famously located this "obsession" in some of the best-known interracial male relationships in US literary history: James Fenimore Cooper's Natty Bumppo and Chingachgook, Herman Melville's Ishmael and Queequeg, Mark Twain's Huck Finn and Jim. As Valerie Rohy has argued, Fiedler's fusion of homosexuality, racial alterity, and infantilism demonstrates the long lineage in US literary history of the racial, sexual, and temporal assemblage for which Haeckel provided a scientific formulation in his 1879 recapitulation theory. But while Fiedler's reading of US literary history emphasizes the connection between infantile, "innocent homosexuality" and racial others, *The Virginian* explicitly links its titular white male character to a fantasy of regression while he is on his honeymoon with his white wife. In *The Virginian* there is no racial other in whom the white protagonist invests his (homo)erotic energy. Earlier in the text, we might point to the Virginian's relationship with Steve as a variation on the "innocent homosexuality" that Fiedler finds in US literary history, but it is difficult to see Steve as an analogue of Chingachgook or Queequeg or Jim, as these latter three characters are explicitly racialized figures. Moreover, as Rohy has observed, in Fiedler's model of US literary perversity, male-male attachments are something that comes before mature, adult heterosexuality and, paradoxically, after the failure of this very same adult heterosexuality.[89] The Virginian's regressive desire, on the other hand, comes after the success of adult heterosexuality, namely, his union with Molly.

The narrative plotting of Wister's text thus introduces a wrinkle into the dynamic for which Fiedler argued in *Love and Death*, wherein "innocent homosexuality" and the racial and temporal meanings attached to it can only exist before or after the *failure* of adult heterosexuality. More precisely, the Virginian's deep attachment to Steve and subsequent marriage to Molly loosely follow Fiedler's plotting of sexual succession (from infantile/homo to adult/hetero) without the marriage plot being done away with altogether as in, for example, Twain's *The Adventures of Huckleberry Finn*. Rather than supplanting the marriage plot, the Virginian's relationship with Steve literalizes the timeline that Fiedler constructs through readings of texts in which male intimacy is not, in terms of narrative progression, the antecedent to heterosexuality. Huck does not take leave of Jim to enter into a marriage plot. Ishmael and Queequeg's relationship is suffused with the language and imagery of marriage, but Ishmael does not survive the wreck of the *Pequod* to then move on to a "proper" (heterosexual) marriage plot. At the level of literal narrative conclusion, then, the Virginian's perverse desire for ultimate regression is folded into his and Molly's marriage plot in a way that normalizes it. In normalizing this perverse desire, the politically significant relationship between "perverse" and normative temporal orientations undergoes a fundamental shift. Rather than simply represent the underdeveloped or future-negating temporality of abjected racialized and queer subjects, in this instance the perverse temporality of regression and the normative, future-oriented temporality of the marriage plot are sutured together without the former derailing the latter. Like Bret Harte, Edward L. Wheeler, Frank Norris, and Jack London before him and Zane Grey after him, Wister makes queerness and its temporalities into materials for settler hegemony. More strikingly than any of his fellow authors, Wister makes queerness look straight.

# Conclusion

## AGAINST SETTLER TENSES

A closing that opens onto new beginnings: that is the hope for this conclusion. Elizabeth Povinelli has argued that in the British settler colonies of North America, Australia, and New Zealand, "all people may belong to nationalism, [but] not all people occupy the same tense of nationalism": "the relationship between settler and Native/Indigenous was transformed from a mutual implication in the problem of prior occupation to a hierarchical relationship between two modes of prior occupation, one oriented to the future, the other to the past."[1] Literature, as this book has sought to demonstrate, participates in this temporal-political dynamic in rather queer ways, at least in white male US settler writing of the late nineteenth and early twentieth centuries. But one of the theoretical implications of this book's chronotopic method, as I mentioned in the introduction, is that there indeed are (have been, will be) literatures and politics that genuinely resist, and offer decolonial alternatives to, the queer (re)production of settler tensing.

Recuperating and aligning queerness for and with sustainable futurity is a project that Sarah Ensor has undertaken in a queer ecocritical mode, reading the spinster as the locus of an ecologically sustainable temporality and futurity, a figure who "practices an avuncular form of stewardship, tending the future without contributing directly to it."[2] Although Ensor does not explicitly say so, her work carves out a space for thinking about settler queerness as a relationship to time that stewards all of us, whether Indigenous, settler of color, or white settler, through potentially more just and sustainable pasts, presents, and futures. Yet Ensor's queer spinsters ultimately seem only obliquely related to the task of reconceiving time against the grain of settler colonialism's investments in white ascendance, racialized expendability, and Native genocide; they seem, in other words, to be invested in a settler temporal queerness that has yet to fully reckon with the imperative to unsettle the presumed naturalness of settlement.

Indigenous futurisms have been up to the task of denaturalizing settlement and its temporalities, queer or otherwise. The subgenre of speculative fiction called "Native slipstream," writes Grace Dillon, "views time as pasts, presents, and futures that flow together like currents in a navigable stream." Slipstream "allows authors to recover the Native space of the past, to bring it to the attention of contemporary readers, and to build better futures."[3] Native artists, scholars, and writers including Lisa Brooks, Diane Glancy, Joy Harjo, Stephen Graham Jones, Jarrett Martineau, Eric Ritskes, Gerald Vizenor, and Kyle P. Whyte have participated in this work of recovery and the building of better futures, often through engagements with an ontology of time as a spiral rather than a line.[4] The work of denaturalizing straight and queer settler temporalities is underway in the work of Native artists, scholars, and writers. But it seems as yet that the transgressive potential of settler queerness, its potential to ally itself with decolonial projects, remains largely untapped. Queerness has been rightly critiqued as part of settler imperial power since at least Jasbir Puar's 2007 book *Terrorist Assemblages*. The art, writing, and scholarship that engages in this critique of the connections between queerness and settler imperial power is of vital importance; I would not have written this book if I did not believe this to be the case, which perhaps goes without saying given that the aim of this book has been to elucidate how settler literary forms and settler queernesses intersect to (re)invigorate the settler colonial project.

Now, as always, is the time for settler artists, scholars, and writers of all stripes and social locations to commit to the work of thinking and practicing queerness and temporality in truly transgressive rhythms, in dialogue with Indigenous artists, scholars, and writers, and against the dictates of settler colonial time. Projects such as Mark Rifkin's *Settler Common Sense* (2014) and my own in this book have done some of the work of showing how literature re-presents and (re)produces the naturalness of settlement in a queer key.[5] The capacity to apprehend and describe the queerness of settler hegemony is no mean feat. But too often it seems as though settler critics of varying social locations leave to a closing gesture, a near-footnote, the crucial next step: the work of thinking and creating temporalities and spaces outside or beyond the settler colonial. *Settler Tenses* is no better in this regard. There are crucial exceptions to this tendency in, for example, the work of Iyko Day, Beenash Jafri, Juliana Hu Pegues, Malissa Phung, Rita Wong, and other scholars who engage Asian-Indigenous relationalities. Their work might serve as inspiration and one potential model for settler critics working across multiple fields and disciplines.[6] We need (even more) criticism and scholarship devoted to the possibilities that emerge from thorough reckonings with the recognition of being part of a simultaneously marginalized *and* colonizing population under settler imperialism. Our Indigenous colleagues have been doing the work of imagining and building better pasts, presents, and futures—in short, better temporalities—for a long time. The least we can do is to earnestly and respectfully offer our support and our efforts in that work, not in the form of closing gestures or footnotes as I am doing here, but as a central creative, intellectual, and political concern that we are obligated to address while we inhabit a world structured by settler privilege.

# Notes

## Introduction

1.  Edward L. Wheeler may have been a pen name under which multiple writers produced texts for the Deadwood Dick dime novel series discussed in chapter 2. For the purposes of this book, what is important is that these novels were published under a masculine name of ostensibly English (settler) origin.

2.  "Collections: Currier & Ives Prints," *Internet Archive*, last modified December 18, 2002, https://web.archive.org/web/20130512005153/http://www.hfmgv.org/exhibits/collections/Collections/library/special/prints/currier.asp.

3.  Patrick Wolfe, *Settler Colonialism and the Transformation of Anthropology: The Politics and Poetics of an Ethnographic Event* (New York: Cassell, 1999), 2.

4.  Mikhail Bakhtin, "The *Bildungsroman* and Its Significance in the History of Realism," in *Speech Genres and Other Late Essays*, trans. Vern W. McGee, ed. Caryl Emerson and Michael Holquist (Austin: University of Texas Press, 1986), 25.

5.  Frank B. Wilderson III, *Red, White & Black: Cinema and the Structure of US Antagonisms* (Durham, NC: Duke University Press, 2010).

6.  Victoria Lamont, *Westerns: A Women's History* (Lincoln: University of Nebraska Press, 2016).

7.  Michel Foucault, *The History of Sexuality, Volume 1: An Introduction*, trans. Robert Hurley (New York: Pantheon, 1978), 43. Foucault famously declared that up to the late nineteenth century, "The sodomite had been a temporary aberration; the homosexual was now a species" (43).

8.     One of the most compelling and theoretically rich accounts of the post–Civil Rights era alliance of queerness and nationalism is Jasbir Puar, *Terrorist Assemblages: Homonationalism in Queer Times* (Durham, NC: Duke University Press, 2007). For an account that, like mine, extends that alliance further back in time and into the nineteenth century, see Hiram Pérez, *A Taste for Brown Bodies: Gay Modernity and Cosmopolitan Desire* (New York: New York University Press, 2015).

9.     Hsuan Hsu, "Chronotopes of the Asian American West," in *A Companion to the Literature and Culture of the American West*, ed. Nicolas Witschi (Malden, MA: Wiley-Blackwell, 2011), 146.

10.    Ibid.

11.    On the lineage and antecedents of the cattle range cowboy figure, see, for example, John G. Cawelti, *The Six-Gun Mystique Sequel* (Bowling Green: Bowling Green State University Popular Press, 1999), 11–98. On the formation of modern sexuality, see, in particular, Foucault, *History of Sexuality*; David M. Halperin, *One Hundred Years of Homosexuality: And Other Essays on Greek Love* (New York: Routledge, 1990); and Eve Kosofsky Sedgwick, *Epistemology of the Closet* (Berkeley: University of California Press, 1990). Despite meaningful debates and disagreements about the nature of "modern sexuality," scholars tend to agree that it began to take definite shape in the late nineteenth century.

12.    Scott Lauria Morgensen, *Spaces between Us: Queer Settler Colonialism and Indigenous Decolonization* (Minneapolis: University of Minnesota Press, 2011), 23.

13.    Foucault, *History of Sexuality*, 95–96.

14.    Dana Luciano, *Arranging Grief: Sacred Time and the Body in Nineteenth-Century America* (New York: New York University Press, 2007), 9–12.

15.    See Morgensen, *Spaces between Us*, 1–53, and Luciano, *Arranging Grief*, particularly 69–117.

16.    Ibid., 42; Luciano, *Arranging Grief*.

17.    Luciano, *Arranging Grief*, 69–117; Morgensen, *Spaces between Us*, 42.

18. Foucault, *History of Sexuality*, 157, 155.

19. Michel Foucault, *Discipline and Punish: The Birth of the Prison*, trans. Alan Sheridan (New York: Vintage, 1995 [1977]); Foucault, *History of Sexuality*; Michel Foucault, *Society Must Be Defended: Lectures at the Collège de France, 1975–76*, trans. David Macey, ed. Arnold I. Davidson (New York: Picador, 1997).

20. Mikhail Bakhtin, "Forms of Time and of the Chronotope in the Novel," in *The Dialogic Imagination: Four Essays*, trans. Caryl Emerson and Michael Holquist, ed. Michael Holquist (Austin: University of Texas Press, 1981), 85.

21. Ibid., 84, emphasis added. Cf. Katerina Clark and Michael Holquist, *Mikhail Bakhtin* (Cambridge, MA: Harvard University Press, 1984), 280: "Time assuming flesh is something more than a trope here, for those who enflesh the categories are people."

22. Bakhtin, "Forms of Time," 84.

23. In this notion of the sexual production of (US) settler colonialism, I follow scholars including Morgensen and Mark Rifkin in regarding the colonial imposition of discourses and institutions of modern sexuality as a key method for establishing and maintaining settler colonialism and the settler state. See Morgensen, *Spaces between Us*, particularly 42–49; and Mark Rifkin, *When Did Indians Become Straight?: Kinship, the History of Sexuality, and Native Sovereignty* (New York: Oxford University Press, 2011).

24. Amy Kaplan, *The Anarchy of Empire in the Making of U.S. Culture* (Cambridge, MA: Harvard University Press, 2002); Laura Wexler, *Tender Violence: Domestic Visions in an Age of U.S. Imperialism* (Chapel Hill: University of North Carolina Press, 2000).

25. Lisa Duggan, "The New Homonormativity: The Sexual Politics of Neoliberalism," in *Materializing Democracy: Toward a Revitalized Cultural Politics*, ed. Russ Castronovo and Dana Nelson (Durham, NC: Duke University Press, 2002), 175–94; Puar, *Terrorist Assemblages*.

26. Rifkin, *When Did Indians Become Straight?*; Morgensen, *Spaces*

*between Us.*

27. On racialization and gender (un)differentiation and the temporal arrest imputed to the ungendered, racialized body, see, for example, Hortense Spillers, "Mama's Baby, Papa's Maybe: An American Grammar Book," *Diacritics* 17, no. 2 (Summer 1987): 64–81, and Kyla Schuller, *The Biopolitics of Feeling: Race, Sex, and Science in the Nineteenth Century* (Durham, NC: Duke University Press, 2018).

28. Bret Harte, "Notes by Flood and Field," in *The Luck of Roaring Camp and Other Sketches,* Portland ed. (Boston: Houghton, Mifflin and Company, 1894), 200, 217.

29. Axel Nissen, *Manly Love: Romantic Friendship in American Fiction* (Chicago: University of Chicago Press, 2009), 52; Harte, "Notes by Flood and Field," 200.

30. Harte, "Notes by Flood and Field," 209, 226.

31. Peter Coviello, *Tomorrow's Parties: Sex and the Untimely in Nineteenth-Century America* (New York: New York University Press, 2013), 10.

32. Jonathan Ned Katz, *The Invention of Heterosexuality* (Chicago: University of Chicago Press, 2007), 15–16.

33. Morgensen, *Spaces between Us*; Puar, *Terrorist Assemblages.*

34. Morgensen, *Spaces between Us,* 42.

35. Harte, "Notes by Flood and Field," 199, emphasis added, 233–34.

36. Wolfe, *Settler Colonialism,* 163.

37. Harte, "Notes by Flood and Field," 206.

38. Patricia Limerick, *The Legacy of Conquest: The Unbroken Past of the American West* (New York: Norton, 1987), 259–61; Harte, "Notes by Flood and Field," 228.

39. Elizabeth Anker and Rita Felski, "Introduction," in *Critique and Postcritique*, eds. Elizabeth Anker and Rita Felski (Durham, NC: Duke University Press, 2017), 1.

40. Louis Althusser, "Ideology and Ideological State Apparatuses (Notes towards an Investigation)," in *Lenin and Philosophy and Other Essays* (New York: Monthly Review Press, 1971), 127–86; Jacques Lacan, Écrits, trans. Bruce Fink (New York: W. W.

Norton, 2007).

41. Gary Saul Morson and Caryl Emerson, *Mikhail Bakhtin: Creation of a Prosaics* (Stanford: Stanford University Press, 1990), 71.

42. Mikhail Bakhtin, "Art and Answerability," in *Art and Answerability: Early Philosophical Essays*, trans. Vadim Liapunov, ed. Michael Holquist and Vadim Liapunov (Austin: University of Texas Press, 1990), 1–2.

43. Bakhtin, "Forms of Time," 254.

44. Anker and Felski, "Introduction," 5.

45. Raymond Williams, "Base and Superstructure in Marxist Cultural Theory," *New Left Review* 1, no. 82 (November/December 1973), 6. We should note that Williams was careful to specify that such social change is often eventually integrated into "the dominant culture" without changing the main lineaments of the society in question (ibid.).

46. Gary Saul Morson, "Bakhtin, Genres, and Temporality," *New Literary History* 22, no. 4 (1991), 1087.

47. Morgensen, *Spaces between Us*, 3.

48. Bakhtin, "Forms of Time," 84.

49. Cf. Morson and Emerson, *Mikhail Bakhtin*, who write that "Chronotopes provide the ground for particular kinds of activity and carry with them a particular sense of experience" (426).

50. See Bakhtin, "Forms of Time," 254 for the discussion upon which I base my notion of literature's "speaking back" to settler colonial reality.

51. Wolfe, *Settler Colonialism*, 2; Morgensen, *Spaces between Us*, 42.

52. Morgensen, *Spaces between Us*, 24.

53. Puar, *Terrorist Assemblages*, 211.

54. Mikhail Bakhtin, "Epic and Novel," in *The Dialogic Imagination: Four Essays*, trans. Caryl Emerson and Michael Holquist, ed. Michael Holquist (Austin: University of Texas Press, 1981), 5–7.

55. Benedict Anderson, *Imagined Communities: Reflections on the Origin and Spread of Nationalism* (London: Verso, 2006).

56. Homi Bhabha, "DissemiNation: Time, Narrative, and the

Margins of the Modern Nation," in *The Location of Culture* (New York: Routledge, 1994), 199–244.

57.    On national forgetting, see Ernest Renan, "What Is a Nation?," trans. Martin Thom, in *Nation and Narration*, ed. Homi Bhabha (New York: Routledge, 2003), 8–22.

58.    Mark Rifkin, *Manifesting America: The Imperial Construction of U.S. National Space* (New York: Oxford University Press, 2009), 7.

59.    Anderson, *Imagined Communities*, 26.

60.    See Morgensen, *Spaces between Us*, 1–53.

61.    "Following the Frontier Line, 1790 to 1890," United States Census Bureau, September 6, 2012, https://www.census.gov/dataviz/visualizations/001/#:~:text=In%201890%2C%20the%20Superintendent%20of,previous%20100%20years%20was%20complete.

62.    On longer periodizations of the California genocide that stretch the event into the twentieth century, see, for example, Benjamin Madley, "Patterns of Frontier Genocide 1803–1910: The Aboriginal Tasmanians, the Yuki of California, and the Herero of Namibia," *Journal of Genocide Research* 6, no. 2 (2004), 167–92, 176–81. On the continuation of small-scale conflicts between Apaches and US Americans after 1890, see, for example, Paul Andrew Hutton, *The Apache Wars: The Hunt for Geronimo, the Apache Kid, and the Captive Boy Who Started the Longest War in American History* (New York: Crown, 2016), 415–24.

63.    Frederick Jackson Turner, *The Frontier in American History* (Tucson: University of Arizona Press, 1986), 3–4.

64.    See Bakhtin, "Forms of Time."

65.    On Harte's constructed centrality and originary role in local color writing, see, for example, Wallace Stegner, "Western Record and Romance," in *Literary History of the United States*, ed. Robert E. Spiller, et. al. (New York: Macmillan, 1948), 867, and Cleanth Brooks, R. W. B. Lewis, and Robert Penn Warren, *American Literature: The Makers and the Making, Volume II, 1861 to the Present* (New York: St. Martin's Press, 1973), 1252. On the

centrality of Edward L. Wheeler's *Deadwood Dick, the Prince of the Road* to the dime novel tradition, see, for example, Bill Brown, "About This Volume," in *Reading the West: An Anthology of Dime Westerns*, ed. Bill Brown (Boston: Bedford/St. Martins, 1997), who writes that Wheeler's novel has "more than arbitrary representative value" because it is "often named the paradigmatic Western thriller [and] shows the radical transformation of the Western" (vii). Numerous studies of US literary naturalism from the 1960s through the first two decades of the twenty-first century have focused on Norris's *McTeague* and London's *The Call of the Wild*. On *McTeague*, see, for example, Donald Pizer, *Realism and Naturalism in Nineteenth-Century American Literature* (Carbondale: Southern Illinois University Press, 1966), 11–32; June Howard, *Form and History in American Literary Naturalism* (Chapel Hill: University of North Carolina Press, 1985); Walter Benn Michaels, *The Gold Standard and the Logic of Naturalism: American Literature at the Turn of the Century* (Berkeley: University of California Press, 1987); Donna Campbell, *Resisting Regionalism: Gender and Naturalism in American Fiction, 1885–1915* (Athens: Ohio University Press, 1997); and Jennifer Fleissner, *Women, Compulsion, Modernity: The Moment of American Naturalism* (Chicago: University of Chicago Press, 2004). On *The Call of the Wild*, see, for example, Donald Pizer, *Realism and Naturalism in Nineteenth-Century American Literature*, rev. ed. (Carbondale: Southern Illinois University Press, 1984), 166–79; Christopher P. Wilson, *The Labor of Words: Literary Professionalism in the Progressive Era* (Athens: University of Georgia Press, 1985); Mark Seltzer, *Bodies and Machines* (New York: Routledge, 1992); Earle Labor and Jeanne Campbell Reesman, *Jack London*, rev. ed. (New York: Twayne, 1994); Jonathan Auerbach, *Male Call: Becoming Jack London* (Durham, NC: Duke University Press, 1996); and Michael Lundblad, *The Birth of a Jungle: Animality in Progressive-Era U.S. Literature and Culture* (Oxford: Oxford University Press, 2013). On the constructed generic significance and popularity of Owen Wister's *The Virginian* and Zane Grey's *Riders of the Purple Sage*, see, for example, Lee Clark Mitchell, *Westerns: Making the Man in Fiction and Film* (Chicago: University of Chicago Press, 1996); William Handley, *Marriage, Violence, and the Nation in the American Literary West* (Cambridge: Cambridge University Press, 2002); and William Handley, "Introduction," in Zane Grey, *Riders of the Purple Sage* (New York: Modern Library, 2002).

66. Gary Saul Morson, "Bakhtin, Genres, and Temporality," *New Literary History* 22, vol. 4 (1991): 1087.

67. For accounts of regional writing's ethnographic production of anachronism, see Richard Brodhead, *Cultures of Letters: Scenes of Reading and Writing in Nineteenth-Century America* (Chicago: University of Chicago Press, 1993), 107–41, and Amy Kaplan, "Nation, Region, and Empire," in *The Columbia History of the American Novel*, ed. Emory Elliott (New York: Columbia University Press, 1991), 240–66.

68. On dime novel seriality, see Daniel Worden, *Masculine Style: The American West and Literary Modernism* (New York: Palgrave Macmillan, 2011).

69. Rifkin, *When Did Indians Become Straight?*, 37.

70. Morgensen, *Spaces between Us*, 16.

71. Wolfe, *Settler Colonialism*, 165.

72. Ibid.

73. On these theorizations of regional writing and romance, see Brodhead, *Cultures of Letters*, 107–41, and Fredric Jameson, "Magical Narratives: Romance as Genre," *New Literary History* 7, no. 1 (1975): 135–63.

74. For instance, Geoffrey Bateman, "Queer Wests: An Introduction," *Western American Literature* 51, no. 2: 129–41, recently reminded scholars of western American literary and cultural studies of the "many nationalist and heteronormative myths associated with and promoted through the literatures and cultures of the American West" (138).

75. See, for example, Blake Allmendinger, *The Cowboy:*

*Representations of Labor in an American Work Culture* (New York: Oxford University Press, 1992); Susan Lee Johnson, *Roaring Camp: The Social World of the California Gold Rush* (New York: W. W. Norton and Co., 2000); Axel Nissen, *Bret Harte: Prince and Pauper* (Jackson: University Press of Mississippi, 2000) and *Manly Love*; Nayan Shah, *Contagious Divides: Epidemics and Race in San Francisco's Chinatown* (Berkeley: University of California Press, 2001) and *Stranger Intimacy: Contesting Race, Sexuality and the Law in the North American West* (Berkeley: University of California Press, 2011); Handley, *Marriage, Violence, and the Nation*; Peter Boag, *Same-Sex Affairs: Constructing and Controlling Homosexuality in the Pacific Northwest* (Berkeley: University of California Press, 2003); and Chris Packard, *Queer Cowboys: And Other Erotic Male Friendships in Nineteenth-Century American Literature* (New York: Palgrave Macmillan, 2005).

76.  Bateman, "Queer Wests," 133.

## Chapter 1

1.  For an authoritative biography of Bret Harte, see Gary Scharnhorst, *Bret Harte: Opening the American Literary West* (Norman: University of Oklahoma Press, 2000). Scharnhorst writes that "Plain Language from Truthful James" "was transformed into a culture-text that was appropriated for a variety of purposes, few of them intended by the poet" (55).

2.  See, for example, Margaret Duckett, "Bret Harte's Portrayal of Half-Breeds," *American Literature* 25, no. 2 (1953): 193–212, and Hsuan Hsu, "Vagrancy and Comparative Racialization in *Huckleberry Finn* and 'Three Vagabonds of Trinidad.'" *American Literature* 81, no. 4 (2009): 687–717.

3.  Matthew Watson, "The Argonauts of '49: Class, Gender, and Partnership in Bret Harte's West," *Western American Literature* 40, no. 1 (2005): 33–53, provides an illuminating discussion of the economic and social dimensions of the "mining partnership" and Bret Harte's writing (37).

4.     Bret Harte, "The Luck of Roaring Camp," in *The Luck of Roaring Camp and Other Writings*, ed. Gary Scharnhorst (New York: Penguin, 2001), 16, emphasis mine.

5.     Richard Brodhead, *Cultures of Letters: Scenes of Reading and Writing in Nineteenth-Century America* (Chicago: University of Chicago Press, 1993), identifies the term "development" as "a prime historical referent [of the] regionalist genre" (121).

6.     I am referring here to Benedict Anderson, *Imagined Communities: Reflections on the Origin and Spread of Nationalism* (London: Verso, 2006), which theorizes the novel and the newspaper as media that produce the citizen's sense of a shared time inhabited by herself and her fellow citizens. For Anderson, the novel and the newspaper "provided the technical means for 're-presenting' the *kind* of imagined community that is the nation" (25), and one of the principal means by which these literary forms performed this unifying function was by furnishing readers with a vision of a national social totality "moving steadily down (or up) history" (26). For a fuller description, see "Chapter 2: Cultural Roots," particularly the chapter's last section, "Apprehensions of Time."

7.     John Demos, *Circles and Lines: The Shape of Life in Early America* (Cambridge: Harvard University Press, 2004), 22, 45.

8.     Lloyd Pratt, *Archives of American Time: Literature and Modernity in the Nineteenth Century* (Philadelphia: University of Pennsylvania Press, 2010), 5, 36.

9.     For a list of some of the critics who have claimed that Harte founded local color/regionalism/regional writing, see, for example, Harold Kolb Jr., "The Outcast of Literary Flat: Bret Harte as Humorist," *American Literary Realism, 1870–1910* 23, no. 2 (1991): 52–63. Kolb writes, "eventually [Harte] came to be seen as the originator of what was called the local color movement" (54).

10.    June Howard, *The Center of the World: Regional Writing and the Puzzles of Place-Time* (Oxford: Oxford University Press, 2018), 17, 18.

11.    Cleanth Brooks and Robert Penn Warren, *Understanding Fiction*

(New York: F. S. Crofts, 1943), 219–20.

12. Howard, *The Center of the World*, 22.

13. The critical history of Harte's writing is characterized by a curious contradiction: on the one hand, critics tend to *generically* affiliate Harte's work with the condescending and acquisitive disposition of the postbellum elite; on the other hand, critics also often read Harte as *thematically* sympathizing with and advocating for historically marginalized groups. For example, Judith Fetterley and Marjorie Pryse (*Writing Out of Place: Regionalism, Women, and American Literary Culture* [Urbana: University of Illinois Press, 2003]) place Harte among a group of "local color" writers (as opposed to a female-centered tradition of "regionalism") who are more or less unsympathetic toward the "quaint" regional characters whom they portray (1–33). Conversely, George Stewart, *Bret Harte, Argonaut and Exile* (Boston: Houghton Mifflin, 1931), considers Harte's treatment of (regional) mixed-race characters "unusually sympathetic" (16); Margaret Duckett, "Bret Harte's Portrayal of Half-Breeds," adds that "Harte's sympathy for the underdog—including Chinese, Indians, Mexicans, Negroes, and Spanish Californians, who as members of minority groups were victims of prejudice and wanton cruelty—is apparent throughout his writings" (193).

14. Pratt, *Archives of American Time*, 151. The "new consensus view" that Pratt describes is exemplified in Brodhead, *Cultures of Letters*; Amy Kaplan, "Nation, Region, and Empire," in *The Columbia Literary History of the United States*, ed. Emory Elliott (New York: Columbia University Press, 1991), 240–66; and Sandra Zagarell, "Troubling Regionalism: Rural Life and the Cosmopolitan Eye in Jewett's *Deephaven*," *American Literary History* 10, no. 4 (1998): 639–63. The "traditional consensus" is exemplified in Warner Berthoff, *The Ferment of Realism: American Literature, 1884–1919* (Cambridge: Cambridge University Press, 1981), and Jay Martin, *Harvests of Change: American Literature, 1865–1914* (Englewood Cliffs: Prentice-Hall, 1967). As Mark Storey writes, this "traditional consensus" "viewed 'local color' writing

as a 'cultural elegy' that performed 'the work of memorializing a cultural order passing from life at that moment and of fabricating, in the literary realm, a mentally possessable version of a loved thing lost in reality'" ("Country Matters: Rural Fiction, Urban Modernity, and the Problem of American Regionalism," *Nineteenth-Century Literature* 65, no. 2 (2010): 192–213, 196).

15.  Pratt, *Archives of American Time*, 145.

16.  Michael Warner, *Fear of a Queer Planet: Queer Politics and Social Theory* (Minneapolis: University of Minnesota Press, 1993), viii.

17.  Valerie Rohy, *Anachronism and Its Others: Sexuality, Race, Temporality* (Albany: Suny Press, 2009); Sarah Ensor, "Spinster Ecology: Rachel Carson, Sarah Orne Jewett, and Nonreproductive Futurity," *American Literature* 84, no. 2 (2012): 409–35; Peter Coviello, *Tomorrow's Parties: Sex and the Untimely in Nineteenth-Century America* (New York: New York University Press, 2013); and J. Samaine Lockwood, *Archives of Desire: The Queer Historical Work of New England Regionalism* (Chapel Hill: University of North Carolina Press, 2015).

18.  Fetterley and Pryse, *Writing Out of Place*, 316. See Axel Nissen, "The Feminization of Roaring Camp: Bret Harte and *The American Woman's Home*," *Studies in Short Fiction* 34, no. 3 (1997): 379–88. Also see J. David Stevens, "'She War a Woman': Family Roles, Gender, and Sexuality in Bret Harte's Western Fiction," *American Literature* 69, no. 3 (1997): 571–93.

19.  Coviello, *Tomorrow's Parties*, 94.

20.  Elizabeth Freeman, *Time Binds: Queer Temporalities, Queer Histories* (Durham, NC: Duke University Press, 2010), 3.

21.  This view is associated most closely with Richard Brodhead's *Cultures of Letters*.

22.  Harte, "The Luck of Roaring Camp," 25.

23.  On Harte's portrayals of intimacy between men, see in particular the work of Axel Nissen.

24.  Elizabeth Freeman, "Time Binds, or, Erotohistoriography," *Social Text* 23, nos. 3–4 (2005): 57–68, 57.

25.  Harte, "The Luck of Roaring Camp," 16.

26. Benjamin Madley, *An American Genocide: The United States and the California Indian Catastrophe, 1846–1873* (New Haven, CT: Yale University Press, 2016), 6–7; Theodora Kroeber and Robert F. Heizer, *Almost Ancestors: The First Californians*, ed. F. David Hales (San Francisco: Sierra Club, 1968), 19. On longer periodizations of the California genocide, see, for example, Benjamin Madley, "Patterns of Frontier Genocide 1803–1910: The Aboriginal Tasmanians, the Yuki of California, and the Herero of Namibia," *Journal of Genocide Research* 6, no. 2 (2004), 167–92, who writes that "Long after the war was over, reservation policies continued to destroy the Yuki [an Indigenous people of Northern California]. According to Sherburne Cook, starvation and sickness combined with settler encroachment and attacks to destroy 80% of the Yuki on the reservation between 1873 and 1910. . . . Thus, the reservation system continued the genocide into the twentieth century" (181).

27. Harte, "The Luck of Roaring Camp," 18, 22, 25.

28. Ibid., 17.

29. Nissen, "The Feminization of Roaring Camp," 379–88, 381.

30. Warner, *Fear of a Queer Planet*, xxvi. For example, Catharine Beecher and Harriet Beecher Stowe's *The American Woman's Home* (Bedford: Applewood Books, 2008 [1869]) underscores (even in its title) the centrality of *women* in the composition of normative domesticity.

31. See the introduction to Mark Rifkin, *When Did Indians Become Straight?: Kinship, the History of Sexuality, and Native Sovereignty* (New York: Oxford University Press, 2011).

32. Harte, "The Luck of Roaring Camp," 19, 22.

33. Rifkin, *When Did Indians Become Straight?*, 37.

34. Harte, "The Luck of Roaring Camp," 25.

35. Neil Campbell, *The Rhizomatic West: Representing the American West in a Transnational, Global, Media Age* (Lincoln: University of Nebraska Press, 2008), 6–9.

36. Harte, "The Luck of Roaring Camp," 25.

37. Brodhead, *Cultures of Letters*, 125. For a discussion of the

*Overland Monthly*'s aspirations to be a West Coast version of publications such as the *Atlantic Monthly*, see, for example, Scharnhorst, *Bret Harte: Opening the American Literary West.*

38. Brodhead, *Cultures of Letters*, 125–26.

39. Ibid., 123. On processes of postbellum (re)unification and incorporation, see note 8, specifically the works identified as examples of the "new consensus view" of regional writing. Also see Lloyd Pratt's *Archives of American Time*, 125–26, which provide a succinct account of the influential historical reading of the postbellum US as the scene of "market culture's dissolution of the hardscrabble premarket peoples and the frozen-in-time geographic domains that had made America what it was" (125).

40. Rohy, *Anachronism and Its Others*, 59.

41. See, for example, Sigmund Freud, *Three Essays on the Theory of Sexuality* (New York: Basic, 2000).

42. Harte, "The Luck of Roaring Camp," 25.

43. See, for example, the introduction to Stephanie LeMenager, *Manifest and Other Destinies: Territorial Fictions of the Nineteenth-Century United States* (Lincoln: University of Nebraska Press, 2004), for a discussion of how "the rhetoric of US expansion turned the varied cultures and climates of the American West into 'destiny,' a simple temporal marker of the nation's future settlement" (3).

44. See Homi Bhabha, "DissemiNation: Time, Narrative, and the Margins of the Modern Nation," in *The Location of Culture* (New York: Routledge, 1994), 199–244.

45. Harte, "The Luck of Roaring Camp," 22.

46. John L. O'Sullivan, "Annexation," *The United States Magazine and Democratic Review* 17, no. 1 (1845): 5–10, 9, emphasis added.

47. Pratt, *Archives of American Time*, 128. See, in particular, Anthony Giddens, *The Consequences of Modernity* (Stanford: Stanford University Press, 1990), and Anderson, *Imagined Communities.*

48. See, for example, Pratt, *Archives of American Time*, 127–29.

49. Harte, "The Luck of Roaring Camp," 25.

50. Ibid.

51. Ibid., 24, 25.

52. Dana Luciano, *Arranging Grief: Sacred Time and the Body in Nineteenth-Century America* (New York: New York University Press, 2007).

53. Harte, "The Luck of Roaring Camp," 20, 24.

54. Brodhead, *Cultures of Letters*, 121.

55. Giddens, *The Consequences of Modernity*, 143.

56. Bret Harte, "The Iliad of Sandy Bar," in *The Luck of Roaring Camp and Other Writings*, ed. Gary Scharnhorst (New York: Penguin, 2001), 94.

57. Stephanie Palmer, "Travel Delays in the Commercial Countryside with Bret Harte and Sarah Orne Jewett," *Arizona Quarterly* 59, no. 4 (2003): 71–102, 74.

58. Ibid.

59. Anderson, *Imagined Communities*, 36.

60. Ibid., 24.

61. Peter Stoneley, "Rewriting the Gold Rush: Twain, Harte and Homosociality," *Journal of American Studies* 30, no. 2 (1996): 189–209, 199.

62. Watson, "The Argonauts of '49," 33–53, 36, 37.

63. Bret Harte, "Tennessee's Partner," in *The Luck of Roaring Camp and Other Writings*, ed. Gary Scharnhorst (New York: Penguin, 2001), 50.

64. Harte, "The Iliad of Sandy Bar," 87.

65. Watson, "The Argonauts of '49," 45.

66. Luciano, *Arranging Grief*, 1.

67. Ibid., 36.

68. Watson, "The Argonauts of '49," 45.

69. Harte, "Tennessee's Partner," 49, 50.

70. Lee Edelman, *No Future: Queer Theory and the Death Drive* (Durham, NC: Duke University Press, 2004), 4.

71. Harte, "Tennessee's Partner," 57.

72. Luciano, *Arranging Grief*, 8, 44.

73. Harte, "The Iliad of Sandy Bar," 90, 97.

74. Watson, "The Argonauts of '49," 47.

75. Harte, "The Iliad of Sandy Bar," 91. See Manu Karuka, *Empire's Tracks: Indigenous Nations, Chinese Workers, and the Transcontinental Railroad* (Berkeley: University of California Press, 2019), for an illuminating account of Chinese labor under conditions where "State and corporation supplied the organizational basis for colonialism in nineteenth-century California" (85).

76. Luciano, *Arranging Grief*, 8.

77. Harte, "The Iliad of Sandy Bar," 97.

78. Ibid., 97, 96, emphasis added.

79. Stephen Tatum, "Postfrontier Horizons," *Modern Fiction Studies* 50, no. 2 (2004): 462.

80. Rohy, *Anachronism and Its Others*, 94.

81. Scharnhorst, *Bret Harte: Opening the American Literary West*, 45.

82. Amy Kaplan, *The Anarchy of Empire in the Making of US Culture* (Cambridge, MA: Harvard University Press, 2002), 27.

83. O'Sullivan, "Annexation," 9.

84. Pratt, *Archives of American Time*, 39.

85. O'Sullivan, "Annexation," 5.

86. Reginald Horsman, *Race and Manifest Destiny: Origins of American Racial Anglo-Saxonism* (Cambridge, MA: Harvard University Press, 2009), 4.

87. Bret Harte, "The Idyl of Red Gulch," in *The Luck of Roaring Camp and Other Writings*, ed. Gary Scharnhorst (New York: Penguin, 2001), 61, 63, emphases added.

88. Harte, "The Idyl of Red Gulch," 64.

89. Gary Scharnhorst, *Bret Harte* (New York: Twayne, 1992), 32.

90. Administration for Children and Families, "Healing from the Trauma of Federal Residential Indian Boarding Schools," accessed January 3, 2023, https://www.acf.hhs.gov/blog/2021/11/healing-trauma-federal-residential-indian-boarding-schools#:~:-text=The%20Indian%20Civilization%20Act%20of%201819%20was%20enacted%20for%20the,emotional%20suffering%2C%20physical%20illness%2C%20immediate.

91. Northern Plains Reservation Aid, "History and Culture:

Boarding Schools," accessed January 3, 2023, http://www.native-partnership.org/site/PageServer?pagename=airc_hist_boarding-schools #:~:text=The%20boarding%20school%20experience%20for,in%20the%20state%20of%20Washington.

92. Scharnhorst, *Bret Harte: Opening the American Literary West*, 46.

93. "An Ingénue of the Sierras" was first published in the New York *Sun* on May 7, 1893.

94. Bret Harte, "An Ingénue of the Sierras," in *The Luck of Roaring Camp and Other Writings*, ed. Gary Scharnhorst (New York: Penguin, 2001), 138, 145, 153, 149, 154.

95. For a useful overview of the dissemination of Murrieta stories, see Shelley Streeby, *American Sensations: Class, Empire, and the Production of Popular Culture* (Berkeley: University of California Press, 2002), chapter 9: "Joaquín Murrieta and Popular Culture."

96. Streeby, *American Sensations*, 252.

97. Susan Lee Johnson, *Roaring Camp: The Social World of the California Gold Rush* (New York: W. W. Norton and Co., 2000), ebook, 39.

98. Harte, "An Ingénue of the Sierras," 146, 143.

## Chapter 2

1. Harte's "The Luck of Roaring Camp" (1868), for instance, was published in the first issue of the *Overland Monthly*, a leather-bound monthly magazine, while dime novels were named for their relatively cheap sales price. Many of the texts referred to broadly as dime novels actually sold for less and were named and marketed accordingly.

2. Frank Norris, "The Literature of the West," in *Frank Norris: Novels and Essays*, ed. Donald Pizer (New York: The Library of America, 1986), 1179.

3. Frank Norris, "A Neglected Epic," in *Frank Norris: Novels and Essays*, ed. Donald Pizer (New York: The Library of America, 1986), 1202.

4. Ibid., 1201.

5. Critics tend to cite 1860 as the year of the dime novel's inception

and the opening years of the twentieth century as the end of the form's dominance; see Daryl Jones, *The Dime Novel Western* (Bowling Green, OH: The Popular Press, 1978), 4, and Bill Brown, "Reading the West: Cultural and Historical Background," in *Reading the West: An Anthology of Dime Westerns*, ed. Bill Brown (Boston: Bedford, 1997), 1. For a brief discussion of the large readership of dime novel Westerns, which included members of the working and middle classes, see Jones, *The Dime Novel Western*, 14–15. Regarding the relatively short length of dime novel Westerns, Henry Nash Smith, *Virgin Land: The American West as Symbol and Myth* (Cambridge, MA: Harvard University Press, 1978), opines that "they were hardly novels, for they seldom ran to more than thirty thousand words" (90).

6. Smith, *Virgin Land*, 91–92.

7. Michael Denning, *Mechanic Accents: Dime Novels and Working-Class Culture in America* (New York: Verso, 1998), 45–46, 157–66. Contemporary and scholarly accounts offer a fairly hazy picture of dime novel readership. Taken together, these accounts suggest that lots of different kinds of people read dime novels, from shopgirls and factory workers to bankers and businessmen. These accounts also suggest that the majority of this readership were working-class boys and young men. See Denning, chapter 3; Jones, *The Dime Novel Western*, chapter 1; and J. Randolph Cox, *The Dime Novel Companion: A Source Book* (Westport: Greenwood Press, 2000), "Dime Novel Days: An Introduction and History."

8. Daniel Worden, *Masculine Style: The American West and Literary Modernism* (New York: Palgrave Macmillan, 2011), 33.

9. Peter Boag, *Same-Sex Affairs: Constructing and Controlling Homosexuality in the Pacific Northwest* (Berkeley: University of California Press, 2003); Nayan Shah, *Contagious Divides: Epidemics and Race in San Francisco's Chinatown* (Berkeley: University of California Press, 2001); and George Chauncey, *Gay New York: Gender, Urban Culture, and the Making of the Gay Male World* (New York: Basic Books, 1994).

10. Worden, *Masculine Style*; Denise Cruz, "Reconsidering *McTeague*'s 'Mark' and 'Mac': Intersections of U.S. Naturalism, Imperial Masculinities, and Desire between Men," *American Literature* 78, no. 3 (2006): 487–517.

11. Matthew Frye Jacobson, *Whiteness of a Different Color: European Immigrants and the Alchemy of Race* (Cambridge, MA: Harvard University Press, 1998), 93.

12. Roderick Ferguson, *Aberrations in Black: Toward a Queer of Color Critique* (Minneapolis: University of Minnesota Press, 2003).

13. William Handley, *Marriage, Violence, and the Nation in the American Literary West* (New York: Cambridge University Press, 2002), 98.

14. In addition to work on the imbrication of sexuality and settler colonialism and imperialism in the US context (Amy Kaplan, *The Anarchy of Empire in the Making of US Culture* [Cambridge, MA: Harvard University Press, 2002]; Jasbir Puar, *Terrorist Assemblages: Homonationalism in Queer Times* [Durham, NC: Duke University Press, 2007]; Scott Lauria Morgensen, *Spaces between Us: Queer Settler Colonialism and Indigenous Decolonization* [Minneapolis: University of Minnesota Press, 2011]; and Mark Rifkin, *When Did Indians Become Straight?: Kinship, the History of Sexuality, and Native Sovereignty* [New York: Oxford University Press, 2011]), see also Anne McClintock, *Imperial Leather: Race, Gender and Sexuality in the Colonial Contest* (New York: Routledge, 1995), and Ann Laura Stoler, *Race and the Education of Desire: Foucault's History of Sexuality and the Colonial Order of Things* (Durham, NC: Duke University Press, 1995).

15. Zane Grey, *Riders of the Purple Sage* (New York: Modern Library, 2002), 131, 142.

16. Amy Kaplan, "Violent Belongings and the Question of Empire Today," *American Quarterly* 56, no. 1 (2004): 1–18, 3; Puar, *Terrorist Assemblages*, 1.

17. Puar, *Terrorist Assemblages*, 1–36.

18. Kaplan, *The Anarchy of Empire*, 23–50.

19.　Rifkin, *When Did Indians Become Straight?*, 37.

20.　D. W. Meinig, "The Mormon Nation and the American Empire," *Journal of Mormon History* 22, no. 1 (1996): 33–51, 41.

21.　For historical accounts of alternative desires and relationships in the late nineteenth-century and early twentieth-century US, see the historical scholarship cited in note 9 of this chapter.

22.　Mikhail Bakhtin, "Forms of Time and of the Chronotope in the Novel," in *The Dialogic Imagination: Four Essays*, trans. Caryl Emerson and Michael Holquist, ed. Michael Holquist (Austin: University of Texas Press, 1981), 89.

23.　On working-class investments in whiteness, see David Roediger, *The Wages of Whiteness: Race and the Making of the American Working Class*, new ed. (New York: Verso, 2007).

24.　Morgensen, *Spaces between Us*, 16.

25.　Christine Bold, "Malaeska's Revenge; or, The Dime Novel Tradition in Popular Fiction," in *Wanted Dead or Alive: The American West in Popular Culture*, ed. Richard Aquila (Urbana: University of Illinois Press, 1996), 21–42, 23.

26.　Ann S. Stephens, *Malaeska, the Indian Wife of the White Hunter* (New York: Beadle & Adams, 1860), 128.

27.　Harry J. Brown, *Injun Joe's Ghost: The Indian Mixed-Blood in American Writing* (Columbia: University of Missouri Press, 2004), 17.

28.　Edward L. Wheeler, *Deadwood Dick, the Prince of the Road; Or, the Black Rider of the Black Hills* (New York: Beadle & Adams, 1899), 4.

29.　Brian Klopotek, "'I Guess Your Warrior Look Doesn't Work Every Time': Challenging Indian Masculinity in the Cinema," in *Across the Great Divide: Cultures of Manhood in the American West*, ed. Matthew Basso, Laura McCall, and Dee Garceau (New York: Routledge, 2001), 251–73, 251; Lisa Tatonetti, *Written by the Body: Gender Expansiveness and Indigenous Non-Cis Masculinities* (Minneapolis: University of Minnesota Press, 2021), 11; and Ty P. Kāwika Tengan, *Native Men Remade: Gender and Nation in Contemporary Hawaii* (Durham, NC:

Duke University Press, 2008), 10.

30. Wheeler, *Deadwood Dick, the Prince of the Road*, 4, 11.

31. Morgensen, *Spaces between Us*; Rifkin, *When Did Indians Become Straight?*

32. Wheeler, *Deadwood Dick, the Prince of the Road*, 7.

33. See Valerie Rohy, *Anachronism and Its Others: Sexuality, Race, Temporality* (Albany: SUNY Press, 2009), 73–98, for a discussion of the marriage plot and generational futurity.

34. Wheeler, *Deadwood Dick, the Prince of the Road*, 9, 19, 31, emphasis in original.

35. Ibid., 15.

36. Worden, *Masculine Style*, 26.

37. Wheeler, *Deadwood Dick, the Prince of the Road*, 7, 5.

38. Worden, *Masculine Style*, 17–34, makes a similar point about dime novels' detachment of masculinity from male bodies. Worden focuses principally on how dime novels offer a performative masculinity that can function as an "affront to dominant power," e.g., "patriarchy, religion, and the state" (19). I shift the focus here to how masculinity disrupts intra-settler power structures while also uniquely consolidating the overall settler formation.

39. Wheeler, *Deadwood Dick, the Prince of the Road*, 31.

40. Cox, *Dime Novel Companion*, observes, "Dick's continuing attempts to reform and forsake outlaw life form a tenuous theme throughout the saga, as does his failure to establish a home and family. Women tend to turn down his marriage proposals; those who do accept either betray him or die in the next episode" (74).

41. Edward L. Wheeler, *Blonde Bill; Or, Deadwood Dick's Home Base. A Romance of the "Silent Tongues"* (New York: Beadle & Adams, 1899), 31.

42. See Handley, *Marriage, Violence, and the Nation*, 97–124, and Nancy Bentley, "Marriage as Treason: Polygamy, Nation, and the Novel," in *The Futures of American Studies*, eds. Donald Pease and Robyn Wiegman (Durham, NC: Duke University Press, 2002), 341–70.

43. Wheeler, *Blonde Bill*, 4, 5, 8, 9.

44. Ibid., 31.

45. Handley, *Marriage, Violence, and the Nation*, 102.

46. Wheeler, *Blonde Bill*, 31, 29.

47. Ibid., 31.

48. Chapter 2 of *Blonde Bill* offers a moving account of Dick's "terrible grief" (5) upon Edith's death.

49. Ibid., 29, emphasis added.

50. Cathy J. Cohen, "Punks, Bulldaggers, and Welfare Queens: The Radical Potential of Queer Politics?" *GLQ* 3, no. 4 (1997): 437–65, 453.

51. Lee Bebout, *Mythohistorical Interventions: The Chicano Movement and Its Legacies* (Minneapolis: University of Minnesota Press, 2011), 8.

52. Richard Slotkin, *The Fatal Environment: The Myth of the Frontier in the Age of Industrialization, 1800–1890* (New York: Atheneum, 1985), argues that the working class "did not adopt the myth-ideological framework of the Myth of the Frontier as an interpretative scheme" (473). According to Slotkin, when the working-class press did adopt an interpretive scheme associated with the "Myth of the Frontier" and manifest destiny, it tended to identify with those dispossessed and exploited by the racism and capitalism that drove US expansion.

53. Wheeler, *Blonde Bill*, 2.

54. See, for example, Wheeler, *Deadwood Dick, the Prince of the Road*, 4–5.

55. See Jacobson, *Whiteness of a Different Color*.

56. For an illuminating discussion of the links between race, class, and sexuality in the second half of the nineteenth century, see Shah, *Contagious Divides*. For a discussion that considers these links primarily in terms of European immigrants, see, for example, Cruz, "Reconsidering *McTeague*'s 'Mark' and 'Mac.'"

57. Wheeler, *Blonde Bill*, 2.

58. Ibid., 24. See Jacobson, *Whiteness of a Different Color*, 39–90.

59. Richard Etulain, *The Life and Legends of Calamity Jane*

(Norman: University of Oklahoma Press, 2014), 98.

60. Eve Tuck and K. Wayne Yang, "Decolonization Is Not a Metaphor," *Decolonization: Indigeneity, Education & Society* 1, no. 1 (2012): 1–40.

61. Edward L. Wheeler, *Deadwood Dick's Doom; Or, Calamity Jane's Last Adventure. A Tale of Death Notch* (New York: Beadle & Adams, 1881), 3.

62. Ibid., 6, 12.

63. Denning, *Mechanic Accents*, 78.

## Chapter 3

1. Thomas H. Pauly, *Zane Grey: His Life, His Adventures, His Women* (Urbana: University of Illinois Press, 2005), 48.

2. Walter Benn Michaels, *The Gold Standard and the Logic of Naturalism: American Literature at the Turn of the Century* (Berkeley: University of California Press, 1987); Colleen Lye, *America's Asia: Racial Form and American Literature, 1893–1945* (Princeton: Princeton University Press, 2005).

3. Christine Bold, *The Frontier Club: Popular Westerns and Cultural Power, 1880–1924* (Oxford: Oxford University Press, 2013), 2.

4. For example, Lye, *America's Asia*, notes:
"Originating in the debates of evolutionary science and the emergent field of criminal anthropology, a wider fin de siècle discourse of degeneration marked the reversal of earlier progressive expectations of history. While the applications of degeneration should have been reassuring, since atavism was thought to be localized in distinct and immutable individuals, the conceptual possibility of regression that it allowed for led to full-blown anxieties about the decay of the entire social body. In its characteristic fascination with atavism as a way of representing the primitive within civilization, literary naturalism has been viewed as another expressive site for a discourse that predicated the 'survival of the best' on the exclusion of 'bad blood' from the 'national stock.'" (47)

5. Theodore Roosevelt, "The Strenuous Life," in *The Strenuous Life: Essays and Addresses*, ed. Janet Kopito (New York: Dover,

2009), 1–10.

6. Philip Fisher, *Hard Facts: Setting and Form in the American Novel* (New York: Oxford University Press, 1985), 171.

7. Jennifer Fleissner, *Women, Compulsion, Modernity: The Moment of American Naturalism* (Chicago: University of Chicago Press, 2004), 6.

8. Ibid., 6–7.

9. My use of "primitive" here is meant to evoke Turner's capacious use of the word when he writes, in Frederick Jackson Turner, *The Frontier in American History* (Tucson: University of Arizona Press, 1986), of the "continuous touch with the simplicity of primitive society [which] furnish[es] the forces dominating American character" (3).

10. Jodi Byrd, *The Transit of Empire: Indigenous Critiques of Colonialism* (Minneapolis: University of Minnesota Press, 2011), 5, xx.

11. Patrick Wolfe, *Settler Colonialism and the Transformation of Anthropology: The Politics and Poetics of an Ethnographic Event* (London: Cassell, 1999), 165.

12. Turner, *Frontier in American History*, 4.

13. Scott Lauria Morgensen, *Spaces between Us: Queer Settler Colonialism and Indigenous Decolonization* (Minneapolis: University of Minnesota Press, 2011), 17.

14. Fleissner, *Women, Compulsion, Modernity*; Georg Lukacs, "Narrate or Describe? A Preliminary Discussion of Naturalism and Formalism," in *Writer and Critic and Other Essays*, ed. and trans. Arthur Kahn (Lincoln, NE: iUniverse, 2005); on the widespread possibility of degeneration and decline, see Fleissner, *Women, Compulsion, Modernity*, and Lye, *America's Asia*, 47, 95.

15. On the "expressive" conception of the literary, see Michaels, *The Gold Standard*, 1–28.

16. See Fleissner, *Women, Compulsion, Modernity*, 39–52. Also see Brook Thomas, *The New Historicism and Other Old-Fashioned Topics* (Princeton: Princeton University Press, 1991).

17. John Higham, "The Reorientation of American Culture in the

1890s," in *The Origins of Modern Consciousness*, ed. John Weiss (Detroit: Wayne State University Press, 1965), 27–28. See pages 27–30 for Higham's discussion of the sources and meaning of this widespread interest in nature.

18. Turner, *Frontier in American History*, 7.

19. See Nicolas Witschi, *Traces of Gold: California's Natural Resources and the Claim to Realism in Western American Literature* (Tuscaloosa: University of Alabama Press, 2002).

20. For a telling example of the connections that Roosevelt drew between the West and national vitality, see Theodore Roosevelt, "Manhood and Statehood," in *The Strenuous Life: Essays and Addresses*, ed. Janet Kopito (New York: Dover, 2009), 113–19.

21. Fleissner, *Women, Compulsion, Modernity*, 5.

22. For an illustrative example of Roosevelt's evolutionary view of geopolitics, see Theodore Roosevelt, "The Strenuous Life," in *The Strenuous Life: Essays and Addresses*, ed. Janet Kopito (New York: Dover, 2009), 1–10.

23. Theodore Roosevelt, "Prefatory Letter from Theodore Roosevelt," in *The Woman Who Toils: Being the Experiences of Two Gentlewomen as Factory Girls*, ed. Marie Van Vorst (New York: Doubleday, Page & Co., 1903), vii–ix.

24. On Foucauldian and New Historicist conceptions of the immanence of resistance in power, see Michel Foucault, *The History of Sexuality, Volume 1: An Introduction* (New York: Vintage, 1990); and Michaels, *The Gold Standard*.

25. Frank Norris, *Moran of the Lady Letty: A Story of Adventure off the California Coast* (New York: Doubleday, 1898), 222, 212.

26. On naturalist degeneration as metamorphic, see Lye, *America's Asia*, 95.

27. Alfred Habegger, *Gender, Fantasy, and Realism in American Literature* (New York: Columbia University Press, 1982), 65.

28. See Michel Foucault, *Society Must Be Defended: Lectures at the Collège de France, 1975–76*, trans. David Macey, ed. Arnold I. Davidson (New York: Picador, 1997).

29. Lye, *America's Asia*, 95.

30.  Sara Quay, "American Imperialism and the Excess of Objects in *McTeague*," *American Literary Realism* 33, no. 3 (2001): 209–34, 211–2.

31.  Joseph R. McElrath Jr., "The Erratic Design of Frank Norris' 'Moran of the Lady Letty,'" *American Literary Realism* 10, no. 2 (1977): 114.

32.  Frank Norris, *McTeague: A Story of San Francisco* (Blacksburg, VA: Wilder 2010), 584.

33.  Ibid., 593, 628, 719. Critics have long recognized and remarked upon Norris's use of repetition—of words, actions, scenes—as an aesthetic and thematic device. See, for example, pages 186–92 of Ernest Marchand, *Frank Norris: A Study* (Stanford: Stanford University Press, 1942), which claims that Norris's repetitions are sometimes aesthetically pleasing and at other times excessive, and that they are used to drive home the major ideas of his works.

34.  Norris, *McTeague*, 672, 765.

35.  On the salubrious reflection and objectification of the human in the products of her labor, see G. W. F. Hegel, *Phenomenology of Spirit*, trans. A. V. Miller (Oxford: Oxford University Press, 1977), 111–19.

36.  Norris, *McTeague*, 764, 763.

37.  Quay, "American Imperialism," 209–34, 210.

38.  Hugh Dawson, "McTeague as Ethnic Stereotype," *American Literary Realism, 1870–1910* 20, no. 1 (1987): 34–44, argues that McTeague's "highly distinctive name" is among the traits that "mark McTeague as stereotypically Irish-American" (34).

39.  Norris, *McTeague*, 647.

40.  Fleissner, *Women, Compulsion, Modernity*, 19.

41.  See Quay, "American Imperialism," for a discussion of the notion, circulating at the time of *McTeague*'s publication, that multiple generations (three generations in the estimation of one reviewer of the novel) of an ethnic group must live in the US before that group's members can possess the "real refinement" (211) that bespeaks a "fully" American identity.

42.  Norris, *McTeague*, 666, 785.

43. Turner, *Frontier in American History*, 12–16; Denise Cruz, "Reconsidering *McTeague*'s 'Mark' and 'Mac': Intersections of U.S. Naturalism, Imperial Masculinities, and Desire between Men," *American Literature* 78, no. 3 (2006): 487–517, 510.

44. See the closing pages of Quay, "American Imperialism," for a discussion of the novel's eradication of ethnicity via the deaths of its ethnic characters. See Christopher Dowd, *The Construction of Irish Identity in American Literature* (New York: Routledge, 2011), for a discussion of how *McTeague* "denies the Irish a place in the modern city, and by extension, the increasingly urban American community" (96).

45. Frank Norris, "The Literature of the West," in *Frank Norris: Novels and Essays*, ed. Donald Pizer (New York: The Library of America, 1986), 1176–77.

46. Frank Norris, "The Frontier Gone at Last," in *Frank Norris: Novels and Essays*, ed. Donald Pizer (New York: The Library of America, 1986), 1190.

47. Donald Pizer, ed., *The Literary Criticism of Frank Norris* (Austin: University of Texas Press, 2014 [1964]).

48. See, for example, work by Native and settler scholars on conceptions of time as a spiral, including Kyle P. Whyte, "Indigenous Science (Fiction) for the Anthropocene: Ancestral Dystopias and Fantasies of Climate Change Crises," *Environment and Planning E: Nature and Space* 1, nos. 1–2 (2018): 224–42; Lisa Brooks, "The Primacy of the Present, the Primacy of Place: Navigating the Spiral of History in the Digital World," *PMLA* 127, no. 2 (2012); and Wai Chee Dimock, *Through Other Continents: American Literature across Deep Time* (Princeton: Princeton University Press, 2006).

49. Frank Norris, "A Memorandum of Sudden Death," in *The Best Short Stories of Frank Norris* (New York: Ironweed Press, 1998), 154. For a brief account of the history of the Sixth Regiment, see "A Brief History," 6th Cavalry Museum, accessed July 31, 2023, https://www.6thcavalrymuseum. org/regimental-history.

50. On turn-of-the-twentieth-century "aristocratic" forms of

"regeneration through violence," see Richard Slotkin, *Gunfighter Nation: The Myth of the Frontier in Twentieth-Century America* (Norman: University of Oklahoma Press, 1998), 156–93.

51. I use the generic term "fighters" here because "A Memorandum of Sudden Death" is pointedly vague about just who these characters are—hence my hesitance to use politically inflected terms such as warrior, soldier, or rebel.

52. Paul Andrew Hutton, *The Apache Wars: The Hunt for Geronimo, the Apache Kid, and the Captive Boy Who Started the Longest War in American History* (New York: Crown, 2016), writes that Haskay-bay-nay-ntayl disappeared "into the mists of legend" in 1899 (414), while Victoria Smith, *Captive Arizona, 1851–1900* (Lincoln: University of Nebraska Press, 2009), notes that "As late as 1906 to 1907, the hunt continued for Apache Kid" (186). More broadly, although Geronimo surrendered in 1886, skirmishes between Native American rebels and US and Mexican troops in the Southwest continued into the twentieth century. See Smith, *Captive Arizona*, for an account of the many small-scale fights that took place in the region during the second half of the nineteenth century.

53. Norris, "Memorandum," 156; Hutton, *The Apache Wars*, 17–18, 34–36.

54. Wolfe, *Settler Colonialism*, 163–214.

55. Norris, "Memorandum," 152, 153.

56. Johannes Fabian, *Time and the Other: How Anthropology Makes Its Object* (New York: Columbia University Press, 2014), 31.

57. "What 2,000 Years of Traditional Hopi Farming in the Arid Southwest Can Teach About Resilience," Environmental Defense Fund, December 20, 2019, https://blogs.edf.org/ growingreturns/2019/12/20/hopi-farming-resilience-southwest/.

58. Norris, "Memorandum," 163.

59. Mark Rifkin, *Beyond Settler Time: Temporal Sovereignty and Indigenous Self-Determination* (Durham, NC: Duke University Press, 2017), 5–16.

60. Ibid., 9, 2.

61. Norris, "Memorandum," 162.

62. Benedict Anderson, *Imagined Communities: Reflections on the Origin and Spread of Nationalism* (London: Verso, 2006), 24.

63. Norris, "Memorandum," 162.

64. Habegger, *Gender, Fantasy, and Realism*, 65.

65. See, for example, Barbara Will, "The Nervous Origins of the American Western," *American Literature* 70, no. 2 (1998): 293–316, for a discussion of S. Weir Mitchell's "West Cure."

66. Ibid., 293.

67. Norris, "Memorandum," 166, emphasis in original.

68. Wolfe, *Settler Colonialism*, 163.

69. Jack London, "To Build a Fire," in *The Call of the Wild, White Fang & To Build a Fire* (New York: Modern Library, 1998), 261.

70. Earle Labor, *Jack London* (New York: Twayne, 1974), 36.

71. London, "To Build a Fire," 258, 259, 262.

72. See, for example, Labor, *Jack London*, for an example of a reading that stresses the unnamed man's culpability for his fate.

73. London, "To Build a Fire," 266, 264, 260, emphasis added.

74. Donna J. Haraway, *When Species Meet* (Minneapolis: University of Minnesota Press, 2008), 11. See Bruno Latour, *We Have Never Been Modern*, trans. Catherine Porter (Cambridge, MA: Harvard University Press, 1993), particularly pages 97–100, where Latour describes "The Great Divide between Us—Occidentals—and Them—everyone else" as the "*exportation*" of the "other Great Divide between humans and nonhumans" (97, emphasis in original).

75. Brian K. Hudson, "Introduction: First Beings in American Indian Literatures," *Studies in American Indian Literatures* 25, no. 4 (2013), 3–10, 3.

76. London, "To Build a Fire," 264.

77. Jeanne Campbell Reesman, *Jack London: A Study of the Short Fiction* (New York: Twayne, 1999), 44.

78. London, "To Build a Fire," 264, 268, 269.

79. Norris, *McTeague*, 761.

80.  Jack London, "In a Far Country," in *American Local Color Writing, 1880–1920*, eds. Elizabeth Ammons and Valerie Rohy (New York: Penguin, 1998), 374, 385.

81.  Ibid., 374.

82.  Kathryn Morse, *The Nature of Gold: An Environmental History of the Klondike Gold Rush* (Seattle: University of Washington Press, 2003), 4, 6.

83.  London, "In a Far Country," 376, 375. See Matthew Frye Jacobson, *Whiteness of a Different Color: European Immigrants and the Alchemy of Race* (Cambridge, MA: Harvard University Press, 1998), 39–90.

84.  James Giles, "Beneficial Atavism in Frank Norris and Jack London," *Western American Literature* 4, no. 1 (Spring 1969): 15–27, also recognizes that "In a Far Country" represents an exception to the narrative of "beneficial" male Anglo-Saxon atavism on the frontier.

85.  London, "In a Far Country," 378.

86.  Jonathan Auerbach, *Male Call: Becoming Jack London* (Durham, NC: Duke University Press, 1996), similarly reads the cabin as "a surrogate domestic space" (62) in the context of his argument that the Klondike stories respond to a turn-of-the-twentieth-century "crisis in American masculinity" by "reinscrib[ing] communal (white) manhood in relation to the Northland's tribal fathers, who come to represent a solidarity or sense of belonging set against the capitalist marketplace" (57–58). Needless to say, for Auerbach, "In a Far Country" represents a failure to achieve "communal (white) manhood."

87.  Morse, *The Nature of Gold*, 69, 80.

88.  London, "In a Far Country," 375, 376, 379, 374.

89.  Gerhard J. Ens and Joe Sawchuk, *From New Peoples to New Nations: Aspects of Métis History and Identity from the Eighteenth to the Twenty-First Centuries* (Toronto: University of Toronto Press, 2015), 132.

90.  London, "In a Far Country," 379.

91.  Byrd, *The Transit of Empire*, xix.

92. Jack London, *The Call of the Wild*, in *The Call of the Wild, White Fang & To Build a Fire* (New York: Modern Library, 1998), 3.

93. The mythic imprecision of *Call*'s storytelling makes it difficult to determine where, geographically, the Yeehats are supposed to live.

94. London, *Call of the Wild*, 74.

95. Mark Seltzer, *Bodies and Machines* (New York: Routledge, 1992), 167.

96. As elsewhere in this book, here I follow Morgensen, *Spaces between Us*, in regarding the turn of the twentieth century as a time of "tense negotiations of active and contested settlement" (42).

97. Seltzer, *Bodies and Machines*; Auerbach, *Male Call*.

98. Michaels, *The Gold Standard*, 27.

99. Ibid.

100. Michael Lundblad, *The Birth of a Jungle: Animality in Progressive-Era U.S. Literature and Culture* (New York: Oxford University Press, 2013), 1, emphasis removed.

101. Lundblad, *Birth of a Jungle*, 1, emphasis removed, 2, 10, 22.

102. Roosevelt, "The Strenuous Life," 1–10, 10.

103. Roosevelt's thinking on this point had a prominent forerunner: Charles Darwin, in *The Descent of Man, and Selection in Relation to Sex*, Vol. 1 (New York: D. Appleton & Co., 1871), claimed that "At some future period, not very distant as measured by centuries, the civilized races of man will almost certainly exterminate and replace throughout the world the savage races" (193).

104. Habegger, *Gender, Fantasy, and Realism*, 65.

105. London, *Call of the Wild*, 10.

106. See Jacobson, *Whiteness of a Different Color*, 39–90.

107. London, *Call of the Wild*, 10, 34, 40, 45, 72.

108. Ibid., 72, emphasis added.

109. Jack London, "The Other Animals," in *Revolution, and Other Essays 1910* (Ithaca: Cornell University Library Digital Collections, 2010), 67, 75.

110. Christopher P. Wilson, *The Labor of Words: Literary Professionalism in the Progressive Era* (Athens: University of Georgia Press, 1985), 15.

111. London, "Other Animals," 67, 73–74, 75.

112. For example, Roosevelt infamously cabled a congratulatory message to Major General Leonard Wood and those under his command for their indiscriminate killing of hundreds of Moros during the Moro Crater Massacre (First Battle of Bud Dajo) in March 1906. The *New York Times* signaled disapproval of the events and Roosevelt's response by printing a generally admonitory article about the massacre titled, "Women and Children Killed in Moro Battle: Mingled with Warriors and Fell in Hail of Shot. Four Days of Fighting: Nine Hundred Persons Killed or Wounded—President Wires Congratulations to the Troops," *New York Times*, March 11, 1906, https://timesmachine. nytimes.com/timesmachine/1906/03/11/101768986.html? pageNumber=1. Mark Twain offered a more scathing take on the massacre in writings including Mark Twain, "Comments on the Moro Massacre," in *Mark Twain's Weapons of Satire: Anti-Imperialist Writings on the Philippine-American War*, ed. Jim Zwick (Syracuse: Syracuse University Press, 1992), 170–78. Hsuan Hsu, *Sitting in Darkness: Mark Twain's Asia and Comparative Racialization* (New York: New York University Press, 2015), incisively argues that Roosevelt's message, some news reports, and "official reports legitimate the massacre—and lay the groundwork for future massacres—by quietly rendering the dead Moro men, women, and children ungrievable" (153).

113. London, "Other Animals," 75.

114. London, *Call of the Wild*, 15, 35, 74, 73.

115. Ibid., 72.

116. Merriam-Webster.com Dictionary, s.v. "appropriate," accessed June 29, 2020, https://www.merriam-webster.com/dictionary/ appropriate.

117. Fleissner, *Women, Compulsion, Modernity*, 7.

## Chapter 4

1. Henry Nash Smith, *Virgin Land: The American West as Symbol*

*and Myth* (Cambridge, MA: Harvard University Press, 1970), 101; Richard W. Etulain, *Calamity Jane: A Reader's Guide* (Norman: University of Oklahoma Press, 2015), 155–75.

2. Forrest Robinson, *Having It Both Ways: Self-Subversion in Western Popular Classics* (Albuquerque: University of New Mexico Press, 1993); Lee Clark Mitchell, *Westerns: Making the Man in Fiction and Film* (Chicago: University of Chicago Press, 1996), 94–149; William Handley, *Marriage, Violence, and the Nation in the American Literary West* (New York: Cambridge University Press, 2002); Melody Graulich and Stephen Tatum, eds., *Reading the Virginian in the New West* (Lincoln: University of Nebraska Press, 2003).

3. Handley, *Marriage, Violence, and the Nation*, 96.

4. Terryl Givens, *The Viper on the Hearth: Mormons, Myths, and the Construction of Heresy* (New York: Oxford University Press, 1997), 39.

5. See Handley, *Marriage, Violence, and the Nation*, 67–96; Jane Tompkins, *West of Everything: The Inner Life of Westerns* (New York: Oxford University Press, 1992), 138.

6. Handley, *Marriage, Violence, and the Nation*, 83.

7. Valerie Rohy, *Anachronism and its Others: Sexuality, Race, Temporality* (Albany: SUNY Press, 2009), ix–20.

8. Ibid., xv.

9. Owen Wister, *The Virginian* (New York: Simon & Schuster, 2009), 4.

10. Zane Grey, *Riders of the Purple Sage* (New York: Modern Library, 2002), 7, 76.

11. Handley, *Marriage, Violence, and the Nation*, 101.

12. Robinson, *Having It Both Ways*, 2.

13. I borrow this notion that regional writing and the romance work to define and enforce the nature and boundaries of the social order from Fredric Jameson, "Magical Narratives: Romance as Genre," *New Literary History* 7, no. 1 (1975): 135–63, and Richard Brodhead, *Cultures of Letters: Scenes of Reading and Writing in Nineteenth-Century America* (Chicago: University

of Chicago Press, 1993), 107–41.

14. Christine Bold, *The Frontier Club: Popular Westerns and Cultural Power, 1880–1924* (Oxford: Oxford University Press, 2013), xx; Leslie Fiedler, *The Return of the Vanishing American* (London: Cape, 1968), 138; Mitchell, *Westerns*, 95.

15. Mitchell, *Westerns*, 123.

16. See Mikhail Bakhtin, "Forms of Time and of the Chronotope in the Novel," in *The Dialogic Imagination: Four Essays*, trans. Caryl Emerson and Michael Holquist, ed. Michael Holquist (Austin: University of Texas Press, 1981), 84–258.

17. See Jameson, "Magical Narratives."

18. See Lloyd Pratt, *Archives of American Time: Literature and Modernity in the Nineteenth Century* (Philadelphia: University of Pennsylvania Press, 2010), 125–56.

19. John Cobbs, *Owen Wister* (Boston: Twayne, 1984), 81.

20. Augustus Baldwin Longstreet, "The Horse-Swap," in *Georgia Scenes* (Nashville: J. S. Sanders & Company, 1992), 23–31.

21. Judith Fetterley and Marjorie Pryse, *Writing Out of Place: Regionalism, Women, and American Literary Culture* (Urbana: University of Illinois Press, 2003).

22. Wister, *Virginian*, 9.

23. See Handley, *Marriage, Violence, and the Nation*, 67–96.

24. Cobbs, *Owen Wister*, 73.

25. See Pratt, *Archives of American Time*, 125–56.

26. See Brodhead, *Cultures of Letters*, 107–41.

27. Handley, *Marriage, Violence, and the Nation*, 48.

28. Wister, *Virginian*, 409.

29. Fetterley and Pryse, *Writing Out of Place*, 316.

30. Wister, *Virginian*, 206. See Handley, *Marriage, Violence, and the Nation*, 67–96, and Robinson, *Having It Both Ways*, 41–54, for discussions on the ambivalence of the novel's ostensibly happy ending.

31. Handley, *Marriage, Violence, and the Nation*, 71.

32. See Emily Budick, "Sacvan Bercovitch, Stanley Cavell, and the Romance Theory of American Fiction," *PMLA* 107, no. 1

(1992): 78–91, for a brief discussion of Chase's critical forerunners and milieu.

33. Richard Chase, *The American Novel and Its Tradition* (London: G. Bell and Sons Ltd, 1957), ix.

34. Keith Newlin, "Introduction: The Naturalistic Imagination and the Aesthetics of Excess," in *The Oxford Handbook of American Literary Naturalism*, ed. Keith Newlin (London: Oxford University Press, 2011), 15.

35. See Jameson, "Magical Narratives," 138–42.

36. Chase, *American Novel*, ix, 13, emphasis added.

37. Handley, *Marriage, Violence, and the Nation*, 99.

38. Robinson, *Having It Both Ways*, 4.

39. Ibid., 4.

40. Jameson, "Magical Narratives," 139, 140.

41. Grey, *Riders*, 8–12, 8, 4, 22.

42. Handley, *Marriage, Violence, and the Nation*, 121.

43. In the rather different kind of analysis offered in Richard Slotkin, *Gunfighter Nation: The Myth of the Frontier in Twentieth-Century America* (Norman: University of Oklahoma Press, 1998), Slotkin perhaps unintentionally recognizes how neatly the Mormons of *Riders* fit into the category of evil other: "The villainy of the Mormons is also an abstraction and combination of several standard types of literary 'evil'" (214).

44. Jameson, "Magical Narratives," 140.

45. Bakhtin, "Forms of Time," 86–110, 151–58.

46. Northrop Frye, *Anatomy of Criticism: Four Essays* (Princeton: Princeton University Press, 2000 [1957]), 186, 187.

47. Benedict Anderson, *Imagined Communities: Reflections on the Origin and Spread of Nationalism* (London: Verso, 2006), 24.

48. Fanny Stenhouse, *Tell It All: The Story of a Life's Experience in Mormonism* (Hartford, CT: A. D. Worthington & Co., 1875), vi.

49. Grey, *Riders*, 272.

50. Handley, *Marriage, Violence, and the Nation*, 106.

51. Lori Merish, *Sentimental Materialism: Gender, Commodity Culture, and Nineteenth-Century American Literature* (Durham,

NC: Duke University Press, 2000), 168.

52.   Grey, *Riders*, 122.

53.   Handley, *Marriage, Violence, and the Nation*, 106.

54.   Grey, *Riders*, 272.

55.   See Handley, *Marriage, Violence, and the Nation*, 97–124; and Givens, *The Viper on the Hearth*, 121–52.

56.   Grey, *Riders*, 121.

57.   Tompkins, *West of Everything*, 39–45.

58.   Grey, *Riders*, 261, 25.

59.   Frederick Jackson Turner, *The Frontier in American History* (Tucson: University of Arizona Press, 1986), writes that the European colonist's act of "planting Indian corn" is one of the early steps in the making of "a new product that is American" (4). Environment and colonist, in Turner's formulation, mutually transform one another. On settler indigenization, see Lorenzo Veracini, *Settler Colonialism: A Theoretical Overview* (New York: Palgrave Macmillan, 2010), 95–104.

60.   Grey, *Riders*, 170.

61.   See Slotkin, *Gunfighter Nation*, 211–17.

62.   Slotkin, *Gunfighter Nation*, 216.

63.   Givens, *The Viper on the Hearth*, 133. The fictional Valley of Bethsada shows up in at least two other Frank Merriwell adventures, *Frank Merriwell on the Desert; or, The Mystery of the Skeleton* (1897) and *Frank Merriwell's Alarm; or, Doing His Best* (1903).

64.   Amy Kaplan, *The Social Construction of American Realism* (Chicago: University of Chicago Press, 1988), 10, 11.

65.   Anderson, *Imagined Communities*, 26.

66.   Annamarie Jagose, *Orgasmology* (Durham, NC: Duke University Press, 2013), 65.

67.   Ibid., 66.

68.   See Elizabeth Freeman, *Time Binds: Queer Temporalities, Queer Histories* (Durham, NC: Duke University Press, 2010), 1–19.

69.   Anderson, *Imagined Communities*, 26.

70.   Andrew Parker et al., "Introduction," in *Nationalisms*

*and Sexualities*, eds. Andrew Parker et al. (New York: Routledge, 1992), 3.

71. Homi Bhabha, "DissemiNation: Time, Narrative and the Margins of the Modern Nation," in *The Location of Culture*, ed. Homi Bhabha (New York: Routledge, 1994), 209.

72. See Ernest Gellner, *Nations and Nationalism*, 2nd ed. (Ithaca, NY: Cornell University Press, 2006).

73. Lee Bebout, *Mythohistorical Interventions: The Chicano Movement and Its Legacies* (Minneapolis: University of Minnesota Press, 2011), 8.

74. On the settler incorporation of indigeneity and primitivity, see Scott Lauria Morgensen, *Spaces between Us: Queer Settler Colonialism and Indigenous Decolonization* (Minneapolis: University of Minnesota Press, 2011), 1–53.

75. Louis Owens, "White for a Hundred Years," in *Reading* The Virginian *in the New West*, eds. Melody Graulich and Stephen Tatum (Lincoln: University of Nebraska Press, 2003), 72–88, 75; Jennifer S. Tuttle, "Indigenous Whiteness and Wister's Invisible Indians," in *Reading* The Virginian *in the New West*, eds. Melody Graulich and Stephen Tatum (Lincoln: University of Nebraska Press, 2003), 89–112, 90–91; Neil Campbell, "Wister's Retreat from Hybridity," in *Reading* The Virginian *in the New West*, eds. Melody Graulich and Stephen Tatum (Lincoln: University of Nebraska Press, 2003), 213–32, 215.

76. Bhabha, "DissemiNation," 203.

77. Wister, *Virginian*, 4, 3, 208, emphasis in original.

78. See Tristram Coffin, "The Cowboy and Mythology," *Western Folklore* 12, no. 4 (1953): 290–93. Addressing the nationalistic contours of the "cowboy hero myth," Coffin writes that "it is after World War I that Whitman, Lincoln, and the cowboy come to their greatest prominence over here [in the US]" (290, 291).

79. Ernest Renan, "What Is a Nation?," trans. Martin Thom, in *Nation and Narration*, ed. Homi Bhabha (New York: Routledge, 2003), 11.

80. Wister, *Virginian*, 152, 153, 8, 9–10.

81. See Handley, *Marriage, Violence, and the Nation*, 97–124.
82. Wister, *Virginian*, 43–44, 101.
83. Ibid., 11, 401.
84. Handley, *Marriage, Violence, and the Nation*, 76.
85. For a well-known example of Roosevelt's social Darwinian inclinations, see "The Strenuous Life," in *The Strenuous Life: Essays and Addresses*, ed. Janet Kopito (New York: Dover, 2009), 1–10. Although social Darwinism often is associated with laissez-faire policies rather than the interventionism of Roosevelt, his vision of struggle for global dominance bears a strongly social Darwinian accent.
86. Wister, *Virginian*, 123, emphasis in original.
87. See Rohy, *Anachronism and Its Others*, x, for a brief discussion of the establishment of these links in the nineteenth century and their persistence into the twentieth.
88. Leslie Fiedler, *Love and Death in the American Novel* (New York: Criterion, 1960), xi.
89. See Rohy, *Anachronism and Its Others*, 14–20.

## Conclusion

1. Elizabeth Povinelli, *Economies of Abandonment: Social Belonging and Endurance in Late Liberalism* (Durham, NC: Duke University Press, 2011), 37, 36.
2. Sarah Ensor, "Spinster Ecology: Rachel Carson, Sarah Orne Jewett, and Nonreproductive Futurity," *American Literature* 84, no. 2 (2012): 409–35, 409.
3. Grace Dillon, introduction to *Walking the Clouds: An Anthology of Indigenous Science Fiction*, edited by Grace Dillon, 1–12 (Tucson: University of Arizona Press, 2012), 3, 4.
4. See, for example: Lisa Brooks, "The Primacy of the Present, the Primacy of Place: Navigating the Spiral of History in the Digital World," *PMLA* 127, no. 2 (2012): 308–16; the stories and excerpts from "The Native Slipstream" section of Grace Dillon, ed., *Walking the Clouds*; Joy Harjo, *In Mad Love and War* (Hanover: Wesleyan University Press, 1990); Jarrett

Martineau and Eric Ritskes, "Fugitive Indigeneity: Reclaiming the Terrain of Decolonial Struggle Through Indigenous Art," *Decolonization: Indigeneity, Education & Society* 3, no. 1 (2014): i–xii; and Kyle P. Whyte, "Indigenous Science (Fiction) for the Anthropocene: Ancestral Dystopias and Fantasies of Climate Change Crises," *Environment and Planning E: Nature and Space* 1, nos. 1–2 (2018): 224–42.

5.     Mark Rifkin, *Settler Common Sense: Queerness and Everyday Colonialism in the American Renaissance* (Minneapolis: University of Minnesota Press, 2014).

6.     Iyko Day, *Alien Capital: Asian Racialization and the Logic of Settler Colonial Capitalism* (Durham, NC: Duke University Press, 2016); Beenash Jafri, "Refusal/Film: Diasporic-Indigenous Relationalities," *Settler Colonial Studies* 10, no. 1 (2020): 110–25; Juliana Hu Pegues, *Space-Time Colonialism: Alaska's Indigenous and Asian Entanglements* (Chapel Hill: University of North Carolina Press, 2021); Malissa Phung, "Asian-Indigenous Relationalities: Literary Gestures of Respect and Gratitude," *Canadian Literature* 227 (2015): 56–72; Rita Wong, "Decolonizasian: Reading Asian and First Nations Relations in Literature," *Canadian Literature* 199 (2008): 158–80.

# Bibliography

Allmendinger, Blake. *The Cowboy: Representations of Labor in an American Work Culture.* New York: Oxford University Press, 1992.

Althusser, Louis. "Ideology and Ideological State Apparatuses (Notes towards an Investigation)." In *Lenin and Philosophy and Other Essays,* 127–86. New York: Monthly Review Press, 1971.

Anderson, Benedict. *Imagined Communities: Reflections on the Origin and Spread of Nationalism.* London: Verso, 2006.

Anker, Elizabeth, and Rita Felski. "Introduction." In *Critique and Postcritique,* edited by Elizabeth Anker and Rita Felski, 1–28. Durham: Duke University Press, 2017.

Auerbach, Jonathan. *Male Call: Becoming Jack London.* Durham, NC: Duke University Press, 1996.

Bakhtin, Mikhail. "Art and Answerability." In *Art and Answerability: Early Philosophical Essays.* Translated by Vadim Liapunov, edited by Michael Holquist and Vadim Liapunov, 1–3. Austin: University of Texas Press, 1990.

———. "The *Bildungsroman* and Its Significance in the History of Realism." In *Speech Genres and Other Late Essays.* Translated by Vern W. McGee, edited by Caryl Emerson and Michael Holquist, 10–59. Austin: University of Texas Press, 1986.

———. "Epic and Novel." In *The Dialogic Imagination: Four Essays.* Translated by Caryl Emerson and Michael Holquist, edited by Michael Holquist, 3–40. Austin: University of Texas Press, 1981.

———. "Forms of Time and of the Chronotope in the Novel." In *The Dialogic Imagination: Four Essays.* Translated by Caryl Emerson and Michael Holquist, edited by Michael Holquist, 84–258. Austin: University of Texas Press, 1981.

Bateman, Geoffrey. "Queer Wests: An Introduction." *Western American Literature* 51, no. 2: 129–41.

Bebout, Lee. *Mythohistorical Interventions: The Chicano Movement and Its Legacies*. Minneapolis: University of Minnesota Press, 2011.

Beecher, Catharine, and Harriet Beecher Stowe. *The American Woman's Home: Principles of Domestic Science*. Bedford: Applewood Books, 2008 [1869].

Bentley, Nancy. "Marriage as Treason: Polygamy, Nation, and the Novel." In *The Futures of American Studies*, edited by Donald Pease and Robyn Wiegman, 341–70. Durham, NC: Duke University Press, 2002.

Berthoff, Warner. *The Ferment of Realism: American Literature, 1884–1919*. Cambridge: Cambridge University Press, 1981.

Bhabha, Homi. "DissemiNation: Time, Narrative, and the Margins of the Modern Nation." In *The Location of Culture*, 199–244. New York: Routledge, 1994.

Boag, Peter. *Same-Sex Affairs: Constructing and Controlling Homosexuality in the Pacific Northwest*. Berkeley: University of California Press, 2003.

Bold, Christine. *The Frontier Club: Popular Westerns and Cultural Power, 1880–1924*. Oxford: Oxford University Press, 2013.

———. "Malaeska's Revenge; or, The Dime Novel Tradition in Popular Fiction." In *Wanted Dead or Alive: The American West in Popular Culture*, edited by Richard Aquila, 21–42. Urbana: University of Illinois Press, 1996.

"A Brief History." 6th Cavalry Museum. Accessed July 31, 2023. https://www. 6thcavalrymuseum.org/regimental-history.

Brodhead, Richard. *Cultures of Letters: Scenes of Reading and Writing in Nineteenth-Century America*. Chicago: University of Chicago Press, 1993.

Brooks, Cleanth, R. W. B. Lewis, and Robert Penn Warren. *American Literature: The Makers and the Making, Volume II, 1861 to the Present*. New York: St. Martin's Press, 1973.

Brooks, Cleanth, and Robert Penn Warren. *Understanding Fiction*. New York: F. S. Crofts, 1943.

Brooks, Lisa. "The Primacy of the Present, the Primacy of Place: Navigating the Spiral of History in the Digital World." *PMLA* 127, no. 2 (2012): 308–16.

Brown, Bill. "About This Volume." In *Reading the West: An Anthology of Dime Westerns*, edited by Bill Brown, v–viii. Boston: Bedford/St. Martins, 1997.

———. "Reading the West: Cultural and Historical Background." In *Reading the West: An Anthology of Dime Westerns*, edited by Bill Brown, 1-40. Boston: Bedford, 1997.

Brown, Harry J. *Injun Joe's Ghost: The Indian Mixed-Blood in American Writing*. Columbia: University of Missouri Press, 2004.

Budick, Emily. "Sacvan Bercovitch, Stanley Cavell, and the Romance Theory of American Fiction." *PMLA* 107, no. 1 (1992): 78–91.

Byrd, Jodi. *The Transit of Empire: Indigenous Critiques of Colonialism*. Minneapolis: University of Minnesota Press, 2011.

Campbell, Donna. *Resisting Regionalism: Gender and Naturalism in American Fiction, 1885-1915*. Athens: Ohio University Press, 1997.

Campbell, Neil. *The Rhizomatic West: Representing the American West in a Transnational, Global, Media Age*. Lincoln: University of Nebraska Press, 2008.

———. "Wister's Retreat from Hybridity." In *Reading* The Virginian *in the New West*, edited by Melody Graulich and Stephen Tatum, 213–32. Lincoln: University of Nebraska Press, 2003.

Cawelti, John G. *The Six-Gun Mystique Sequel*. Bowling Green: Bowling Green State University Popular Press, 1999.

Chase, Richard. *The American Novel and Its Tradition*. London: G. Bell and Sons Ltd, 1957.

Chauncey, George. *Gay New York: Gender, Urban Culture, and the Making of the Gay Male World*. New York: Basic Books, 1994.

Clark, Katerina, and Michael Holquist. *Mikhail Bakhtin*. Cambridge, MA: Harvard University Press, 1984.

Cobbs, John. *Owen Wister*. Boston: Twayne, 1984.

Coffin, Tristram. "The Cowboy and Mythology." *Western Folklore* 12, no. 4 (1953): 290–93.

Cohen, Cathy J. "Punks, Bulldaggers, and Welfare Queens: The Radical

Potential of Queer Politics?" *GLQ* 3, no. 4 (1997): 437–65.

Coviello, Peter. *Tomorrow's Parties: Sex and the Untimely in Nineteenth-Century America*. New York: NYU Press, 2013.

Cox, J. Randolph. *The Dime Novel Companion: A Source Book*. Westport: Greenwood Press, 2000.

Cruz, Denise. "Reconsidering *McTeague*'s 'Mark' and 'Mac': Intersections of U.S. Naturalism, Imperial Masculinities, and Desire between Men." *American Literature* 78, no. 3 (2006): 487–517.

Darwin, Charles. *The Descent of Man, and Selection in Relation to Sex*, Vol. 1. New York: D. Appleton & Co., 1871.

Dawson, Hugh. "McTeague as Ethnic Stereotype." *American Literary Realism, 1870–1910* 20, no. 1 (1987): 34–44.

Day, Iyko. *Alien Capital: Asian Racialization and the Logic of Settler Colonial Capitalism*. Durham, NC: Duke University Press, 2016.

Deloria, Philip J. *Playing Indian*. New Haven, CT: Yale University Press, 1998.

D'Emilio, John. "Capitalism and Gay Identity." In *Powers of Desire: The Politics of Sexuality*, edited by Ann Snitow, et. al., 100–113. New York: Monthly Review Press, 1983.

Demos, John. *Circles and Lines: The Shape of Life in Early America*. Cambridge, MA: Harvard University Press, 2004.

Denning, Michael. *Mechanic Accents: Dime Novels and Working-Class Culture in America*. New York: Verso, 1998.

Derrida, Jacques. "The Law of Genre." Translated by Avital Ronell. *Critical Inquiry* 7, no. 1 (1980): 55–81.

Dillon, Grace. Introduction to *Walking the Clouds: An Anthology of Indigenous Science Fiction*, edited by Grace Dillon, 1–12. Tucson: University of Arizona Press, 2012.

Dimock, Wai Chee. *Through Other Continents: American Literature across Deep Time*. Princeton: Princeton University Press, 2006.

Dowd, Christopher. *The Construction of Irish Identity in American Literature*. New York: Routledge, 2011.

Duckett, Margaret. "Bret Harte's Portrayal of Half-Breeds." *American Literature* 25, no. 2 (1953): 193–212.

Duggan, Lisa. "The New Homonormativity: The Sexual Politics of

Neoliberalism." In *Materializing Democracy: Toward a Revitalized Cultural Politics*, edited by Russ Castronovo and Dana Nelson, 175–94. Durham, NC: Duke University Press, 2002.

Edelman, Lee. *No Future: Queer Theory and the Death Drive*. Durham, NC: Duke University Press, 2004.

Ens, Gerhard J., and Joe Sawchuk. *From New Peoples to New Nations: Aspects of Métis History and Identity from the Eighteenth to the Twenty-first Centuries*. Toronto: University of Toronto Press, 2015.

Ensor, Sarah. "Spinster Ecology: Rachel Carson, Sarah Orne Jewett, and Nonreproductive Futurity." *American Literature* 84, no. 2 (2012): 409–35.

Etulain, Richard W. *Calamity Jane: A Reader's Guide*. Norman: University of Oklahoma Press, 2015.

———. *The Life and Legends of Calamity Jane*. Norman: University of Oklahoma Press, 2014.

Fabian, Johannes. *Time and the Other: How Anthropology Makes Its Object*. New York: Columbia University Press, 2014.

Ferguson, Roderick. *Aberrations in Black: Toward a Queer of Color Critique*. Minneapolis: University of Minnesota Press, 2003.

Fetterley, Judith, and Marjorie Pryse. *Writing Out of Place: Regionalism, Women, and American Literary Culture*. Urbana: University of Illinois Press, 2003.

Fiedler, Leslie. *Love and Death in the American Novel*. New York: Criterion, 1960.

———. *The Return of the Vanishing American*. London: Cape, 1968.

Fisher, Philip. *Hard Facts: Setting and Form in the American Novel*. New York: Oxford University Press, 1985.

Fleissner, Jennifer. *Women, Compulsion, Modernity: The Moment of American Naturalism*. Chicago: University of Chicago Press, 2004.

"Following the Frontier Line, 1790 to 1890." United State Census Bureau. September 6, 2012. https://www.census.gov/dataviz/visualizations/001/#:~:text=In%201890%2C%20the%20Superintendent%20of,previous%20100%20years%20was%20complete.

Foote, Stephanie. *Regional Fictions: Culture and Identity in Nineteenth-Century American Literature*. Madison: University of

Wisconsin Press, 2001.

Foucault, Michel. *Discipline and Punish: The Birth of the Prison.* Translated by Alan Sheridan. New York: Vintage, 1995.

———. *The History of Sexuality, Volume 1: An Introduction.* Translated by Robert Hurley. New York: Pantheon, 1978.

———. *Society Must Be Defended: Lectures at the Collège de France, 1975–76.* Translated by David Macey, edited by Arnold I. Davidson. New York: Picador, 1997.

Freeman, Elizabeth. "Time Binds, or, Erotohistoriography." *Social Text* 23, nos. 3–4 (2005): 57–68.

———. *Time Binds: Queer Temporalities, Queer Histories.* Durham, NC: Duke University Press, 2010.

Freud, Sigmund. *Three Essays on the Theory of Sexuality.* New York: Basic, 2000.

Frye, Northrop. *Anatomy of Criticism: Four Essays.* Princeton: Princeton University Press, 2000.

Fusco, Katherine. "Brute Time: Anti-Modernism in *Vandover and the Brute.*" *Studies in American Naturalism* 4, no. 1 (2009): 22–40.

Gellner, Ernest. *Nations and Nationalism,* 2nd ed. Ithaca, NY: Cornell University Press, 2006.

Giddens, Anthony. *The Consequences of Modernity.* Stanford: Stanford University Press, 1990.

Giles, James. "Beneficial Atavism in Frank Norris and Jack London." *Western American Literature* 4, no. 1 (Spring 1969): 15–27.

Givens, Terryl. *The Viper on the Hearth: Mormons, Myths, and the Construction of Heresy.* New York: Oxford University Press, 1997.

Graulich, Melody, and Stephen Tatum, eds. *Reading* The Virginian *in the New West.* Lincoln: University of Nebraska Press, 2003.

Greenblatt, Stephen. "Invisible Bullets." In *Literary Theory: An Anthology,* edited by Julie Rivkin and Michael Ryan, 786–803. Malden: Blackwell, 1998.

Grey, Zane. *Riders of the Purple Sage.* New York: Modern Library, 2002.

Habegger, Alfred. *Gender, Fantasy, and Realism in American Literature.* New York: Columbia University Press, 1982.

Halperin, David M. *One Hundred Years of Homosexuality: And Other*

*Essays on Greek Love*. New York: Routledge, 1990.

Handley, William. "Introduction." In *Riders of the Purple Sage*, by Zane Grey. New York: Modern Library, 2002.

———. *Marriage, Violence, and the Nation in the American Literary West*. New York: Cambridge University Press, 2002.

Haraway, Donna J. *When Species Meet*. Minneapolis: University of Minnesota Press, 2008.

Harjo, Joy. *In Mad Love and War*. Hanover: Wesleyan University Press, 1990.

Harte, Bret. "The Idyl of Red Gulch." In *The Luck of Roaring Camp and Other Writings*, edited by Gary Scharnhorst, 58–67. New York: Penguin, 2001.

———. "The Iliad of Sandy Bar." In *The Luck of Roaring Camp and Other Writings*, edited by Gary Scharnhorst, 87–97. New York: Penguin, 2001.

———. "An Ingénue of the Sierras." In *The Luck of Roaring Camp and Other Writings*, edited by Gary Scharnhorst, 138–54. New York: Penguin, 2001.

———. "The Luck of Roaring Camp." In *The Luck of Roaring Camp and Other Writings*, edited by Gary Scharnhorst, 16–26. New York: Penguin, 2001.

———. "Notes by Flood and Field." In *The Luck of Roaring Camp and Other Sketches*, Portland edition, 198–234. Boston: Houghton, Mifflin Company, 1894.

———. "Tennessee's Partner." In *The Luck of Roaring Camp and Other Writings*, edited by Gary Scharnhorst, 49–57. New York: Penguin, 2001.

Hausladen, Gary. "Introduction." In *Western Places, American Myths: How We Think About the West*. Reno: University of Nevada Press, 2003.

Hegel, G. W. F. *Phenomenology of Spirit*. Translated by A. V. Miller. Oxford: Oxford University Press, 1977.

Higham, John. "The Reorientation of American Culture in the 1890s." In *The Origins of Modern Consciousness*, edited by John Weiss, 25–48. Detroit: Wayne State University Press, 1965.

Horsman, Reginald. *Race and Manifest Destiny: Origins of American Racial Anglo-Saxonism*. Cambridge, MA: Harvard University Press, 2009.

Howard, June. *Form and History in American Literary Naturalism*. Chapel Hill: University of North Carolina Press, 1985.

Hsu, Hsuan. "Chronotopes of the Asian American West." In *A Companion to the Literature and Culture of the American West*, edited by Nicolas Witschi, 145–60. Malden, MA: Wiley-Blackwell, 2011.

———. *Sitting in Darkness: Mark Twain's Asia and Comparative Racialization*. New York: New York University Press, 2015.

———. "Vagrancy and Comparative Racialization in *Huckleberry Finn* and 'Three Vagabonds of Trinidad.'" *American Literature* 81, no. 4 (2009): 687–717.

Hudson, Brian K. "Introduction: First Beings in American Indian Literatures." *Studies in American Indian Literatures* 25, no. 4 (2013): 3–10.

Hutton, Paul Andrew. *The Apache Wars: The Hunt for Geronimo, the Apache Kid, and the Captive Boy Who Started the Longest War in American History*. New York: Crown, 2016.

Jacobson, Matthew Frye. *Whiteness of a Different Color: European Immigrants and the Alchemy of Race*. Cambridge, MA: Harvard University Press, 1998.

Jafri, Beenash. "Desire, Settler Colonialism, and the Racialized Cowboy." *American Indian Culture and Research Journal* 37, no. 2 (2013): 73–86.

———. "Refusal/Film: Diasporic-Indigenous Relationalities." *Settler Colonial Studies* 10, no. 1 (2020): 110–25.

Jagose, Annamarie. *Orgasmology*. Durham, NC: Duke University Press, 2013.

Jameson, Fredric. "Magical Narratives: Romance as Genre." *New Literary History* 7, no. 1 (1975): 135–63.

Jewett, Sarah Orne. *The Country of the Pointed Firs and Other Stories*. New York: Signet Classics, 2009.

Johnson, Susan Lee. *Roaring Camp: The Social World of the California Gold Rush*. New York: W. W. Norton and Co., 2000.

Jones, Daryl. *The Dime Novel Western*. Bowling Green, OH: The Popular Press, 1978.

Kaplan, Amy. *The Anarchy of Empire in the Making of U.S. Culture*. Cambridge, MA: Harvard University Press, 2002.

———. "Nation, Region, and Empire." In *The Columbia History of the American Novel*, edited by Emory Elliott, 240–66. New York: Columbia University Press, 1991.

———. *The Social Construction of American Realism*. Chicago: University of Chicago Press, 1988.

Karuka, Manu. *Empire's Tracks: Indigenous Nations, Chinese Workers, and the Transcontinental Railroad*. Berkeley: University of California Press, 2019.

Katz, Jonathan Ned. *The Invention of Heterosexuality*. Chicago: University of Chicago Press, 2007.

Kipling, Rudyard. *Captains Courageous: A Story of the Grand Banks*. New York: The Century Co., 1919.

Klopotek, Brian. "'I Guess Your Warrior Look Doesn't Work Every Time': Challenging Indian Masculinity in the Cinema." In *Across the Great Divide: Cultures of Manhood in the American West*, edited by Matthew Basso, Laura McCall, and Dee Garceau, 251–73. New York: Routledge, 2001.

Knighton, Andrew Lyndon. *Idle Threats: Men and the Limits of Productivity in 19th-Century America*. New York: New York University Press, 2012.

Kolb, Harold, Jr. "The Outcast of Literary Flat: Bret Harte as Humorist." *American Literary Realism, 1870–1910* 23, no. 2 (1991): 52–63.

Kollin, Susan, ed. *Postwestern Cultures: Literature, Theory, Space*. Lincoln: University of Nebraska Press, 2007.

Kroeber, Theodora, and Robert F. Heizer. *Almost Ancestors: The First Californians*, edited by F. David Hales. San Francisco: Sierra Club, 1968.

Labor, Earle. *Jack London*. New York: Twayne, 1974.

Labor, Earle, and Jeanne Campbell Reesman. *Jack London*, rev. ed. New York: Twayne, 1994.

Lacan, Jacques. Écrits. Translated by Bruce Fink. New York: W. W.

Norton, 2007.

Lamont, Victoria. *Westerns: A Women's History*. Lincoln: University of Nebraska Press, 2016.

Latour, Bruno. *We Have Never Been Modern*. Translated by Catherine Porter. Cambridge, MA: Harvard University Press, 1993.

LeMenager, Stephanie. *Manifest and Other Destinies: Territorial Fictions of the Nineteenth-Century United States*. Lincoln: University of Nebraska Press, 2004.

Limerick, Patricia. *The Legacy of Conquest: The Unbroken Past of the American West*. New York: Norton, 1987.

Lockwood, J. Samaine. *Archives of Desire: The Queer Historical Work of New England Regionalism*. Chapel Hill: University of North Carolina Press, 2015.

London, Jack. *The Call of the Wild*. In *The Call of the Wild, White Fang & To Build a Fire*, 3–75. New York: Modern Library, 1998.

———. "In a Far Country." In *American Local Color Writing, 1880–1920*, edited by Elizabeth Ammons and Valerie Rohy, 374–89. New York: Penguin, 1998.

———. "The Other Animals." In *Revolution, and Other Essays 1910*. Ithaca, NY: Cornell University Library Digital Collections, 2010.

———. *The Sea Wolf*. New York: Grosset and Dunlap, 1904.

———. "To Build a Fire." In *The Call of the Wild, White Fang & To Build a Fire*, 255–71. New York: Modern Library, 1998.

Longstreet, Augustus Baldwin. "The Horse-Swap." In *Georgia Scenes*, 23–31. Nashville: J. S. Sanders & Company, 1992.

Luciano, Dana. *Arranging Grief: Sacred Time and the Body in Nineteenth-Century America*. New York: New York University Press, 2007.

Lukacs, Georg. "Narrate or Describe? A Preliminary Discussion of Naturalism and Formalism." In *Writer and Critic and Other Essays*, edited and translated by Arthur Kahn, 110–48. Lincoln, NE: iUniverse, 2005.

Lundblad, Michael. *The Birth of a Jungle: Animality in Progressive-Era U.S. Literature and Culture*. New York: Oxford University Press, 2013.

Lye, Colleen. *America's Asia: Racial Form and American Literature, 1893–1945*. Princeton: Princeton University Press, 2005.

Madley, Benjamin. *An American Genocide: The United States and the California Indian Catastrophe*. New Haven, CT: Yale University Press, 2016.

———. "Patterns of Frontier Genocide 1803–1910: The Aboriginal Tasmanians, the Yuki of California, and the Herero of Namibia," *Journal of Genocide Research* 6, no. 2 (2004), 167–92.

Marchand, Ernest. *Frank Norris: A Study*. Stanford: Stanford University Press, 1942.

Martin, Jay. *Harvests of Change: American Literature, 1865–1914*. Englewood Cliffs, NJ: Prentice-Hall, 1967.

Martineau, Jarrett, and Eric Ritskes. "Fugitive Indigeneity: Reclaiming the Terrain of Decolonial Struggle Through Indigenous Art." *Decolonization: Indigeneity, Education & Society* 3, no. 1 (2014): i–xii.

McClintock, Anne. *Imperial Leather: Race, Gender and Sexuality in the Colonial Contest*. New York: Routledge, 1995.

McElrath, Joseph R., Jr. "The Erratic Design of Frank Norris' 'Moran of the Lady Letty.'" *American Literary Realism* 10, no. 2 (1977): 114–24.

Meinig, D. W. "The Mormon Nation and the American Empire." *Journal of Mormon History* 22, no. 1 (1996): 33–51.

Merish, Lori. *Sentimental Materialism: Gender, Commodity Culture, and Nineteenth-Century American Literature*. Durham, NC: Duke University Press, 2000.

Michaels, Walter Benn. *The Gold Standard and the Logic of Naturalism: American Literature at the Turn of the Century*. Berkeley: University of California Press, 1987.

Mitchell, Lee Clark. *Westerns: Making the Man in Fiction and Film*. Chicago: University of Chicago Press, 1996.

Morgensen, Scott Lauria. *Spaces between Us: Queer Settler Colonialism and Indigenous Decolonization*. Minneapolis: University of Minnesota Press, 2011.

Morse, Kathryn. *The Nature of Gold: An Environmental History of the*

*Klondike Gold Rush*. Seattle: University of Washington Press, 2003.

Morson, Gary Saul. "Bakhtin, Genres, and Temporality." *New Literary History* 22, no. 4 (1991): 1071–92.

Morson, Gary Saul, and Caryl Emerson. *Mikhail Bakhtin: Creation of a Prosaics*. Stanford: Stanford University Press, 1990.

Newlin, Keith. "Introduction: The Naturalistic Imagination and the Aesthetics of Excess." In *The Oxford Handbook of American Literary Naturalism*, edited by Keith Newlin. London: Oxford University Press, 2011.

Nissen, Axel. *Bret Harte: Prince and Pauper*. Jackson: University Press of Mississippi, 2000.

———. "The Feminization of Roaring Camp: Bret Harte and *The American Woman's Home*." *Studies in Short Fiction* 34, no. 3 (1997): 379–88.

———. *Manly Love: Romantic Friendship in American Fiction*. Chicago: University of Chicago Press, 2009.

Norris, Frank. "The Frontier Gone at Last." In *Frank Norris: Novels and Essays*, edited by Donald Pizer, 1183–90. New York: The Library of America, 1986.

———. "The Literature of the West." In *Frank Norris: Novels and Essays*, edited by Donald Pizer, 1175–79. New York: The Library of America, 1986.

———. *McTeague: A Story of San Francisco*. Blacksburg, VA: Wilder, 2010.

———. "A Memorandum of Sudden Death." In *The Best Short Stories of Frank Norris*, 152–66. New York: Ironweed Press, 1998.

———. *Moran of the Lady Letty: A Story of Adventure off the California Coast*. New York: Doubleday, 1898.

———. "A Neglected Epic." In *Frank Norris: Novels and Essays*, edited by Donald Pizer, 1201–5. New York: The Library of America, 1986.

O'Sullivan, John L. "Annexation." *The United States Democratic Review* 17, no. 1 (1845): 5–10.

Owens, Louis. "White for a Hundred Years." In *Reading* The Virginian *in the New West*, edited by Melody Graulich and Stephen Tatum, 72–88. Lincoln: University of Nebraska Press, 2003.

Packard, Chris. *Queer Cowboys: And Other Erotic Male Friendships in Nineteenth-Century American Literature*. New York: Palgrave Macmillan, 2005.

Palmer, Stephanie. "Travel Delays in the Commercial Countryside with Bret Harte and Sarah Orne Jewett." *Arizona Quarterly* 59, no. 4 (2003): 71–102.

Parker, Andrew, et al. "Introduction." In *Nationalisms and Sexualities*, edited by Andrew Parker et al. New York: Routledge, 1992.

Pauly, Thomas H. *Zane Grey: His Life, His Adventures, His Women*. Urbana: University of Illinois Press, 2005.

Pegues, Juliana Hu. *Space-Time Colonialism: Alaska's Indigenous and Asian Entanglements*. Chapel Hill: University of North Carolina Press, 2021.

Penry, Tara. "Bret Harte: Celebrity, Commodity—New Views of an Old Western Mythmaker." *Western American Literature* 36, no. 1 (2001): 73–80.

Pérez, Hiram. *A Taste for Brown Bodies: Gay Modernity and Cosmopolitan Desire*. New York: New York Uuniversity Press, 2015.

Phung, Malissa. "Asian-Indigenous Relationalities: Literary Gestures of Respect and Gratitude." *Canadian Literature* 227 (2015): 56–72.

Pizer, Donald, ed. *The Literary Criticism of Frank Norris*. Austin: University of Texas Press, 2014 [1964].

———. *Realism and Naturalism in Nineteenth-Century American Literature*. Carbondale: Southern Illinois University Press, 1966.

———. *Realism and Naturalism in Nineteenth-Century American Literature*, rev. ed. Carbondale: Southern Illinois University Press, 1984.

Povinelli, Elizabeth A. *Economies of Abandonment: Social Belonging and Endurance in Late Liberalism*. Durham, NC: Duke University Press, 2011.

Pratt, Lloyd. *Archives of American Time: Literature and Modernity in the Nineteenth Century*. Philadelphia: University of Pennsylvania Press, 2010.

Puar, Jasbir. *Terrorist Assemblages: Homonationalism in Queer Times*. Durham, NC: Duke University Press, 2007.

Quay, Sara. "American Imperialism and the Excess of Objects in *McTeague*." *American Literary Realism* 33, no. 3 (2001): 209–34.

Reesman, Jeanne Campbell. *Jack London: A Study of the Short Fiction*. New York: Twayne, 1999.

———. *Jack London's Racial Lives: A Critical Biography*. Athens: University of Georgia Press, 2009.

Renan, Ernest. "What Is a Nation?" In *Nation and Narration*. Translated by Martin Thom, edited by Homi Bhabha, 8–22. New York: Routledge, 2003.

Rifkin, Mark. *Beyond Settler Time: Temporal Sovereignty and Indigenous Self-Determination*. Durham, NC: Duke University Press, 2017.

———. *Manifesting America: The Imperial Construction of U.S. National Space*. New York: Oxford University Press, 2009.

———. *Settler Common Sense: Queerness and Everyday Colonialism in the American Renaissance*. Minneapolis: University of Minnesota Press, 2014.

———. *When Did Indians Become Straight?: Kinship, the History of Sexuality, and Native Sovereignty*. New York: Oxford University Press, 2011.

Robinson, Forrest. *Having It Both Ways: Self-Subversion in Western Popular Classics*. Albuquerque: University of New Mexico Press, 1993.

Roediger, David. *The Wages of Whiteness: Race and the Making of the American Working Class*, new ed. New York: Verso, 2007.

Rohy, Valerie. *Anachronism and Its Others: Sexuality, Race, Temporality*. Albany: SUNY Press, 2009.

Roosevelt, Theodore. "Manhood and Statehood." In *The Strenuous Life: Essays and Addresses*, edited by Janet Kopito, 113–19. New York: Dover, 2009.

———. "Prefatory Letter from Theodore Roosevelt." In *The Woman Who Toils: Being the Experiences of Two Gentlewomen as Factory Girls*, by Marie Van Vorst, vii–ix. New York: Doubleday, Page & Co., 1903.

———. "The Strenuous Life." In *The Strenuous Life: Essays and Addresses*, edited by Janet Kopito, 1–10. New York: Dover, 2009.

Rossetti, Gina M. *Imagining the Primitive in Naturalist and Modernist*

*Literature*. Columbia: University of Missouri Press, 2006.

Scharnhorst, Gary. *Bret Harte*. New York: Twayne, 1992.

———. *Bret Harte: Opening the American Literary West*. Norman: University of Oklahoma Press, 2000.

Schuller, Kyla. *The Biopolitics of Feeling: Race, Sex, and Science in the Nineteenth Century*. Durham, NC: Duke University Press, 2018.

Sedgwick, Eve Kosofsky. *Epistemology of the Closet*. Berkeley: University of California Press, 1990.

Seltzer, Mark. *Bodies and Machines*. New York: Routledge, 1992.

Shah, Nayan. *Contagious Divides: Epidemics and Race in San Francisco's Chinatown*. Berkeley: University of California Press, 2001.

———. *Stranger Intimacy: Contesting Race, Sexuality and the Law in the North American West*. Berkeley: University of California Press, 2011.

Slotkin, Richard. *The Fatal Environment: The Myth of the Frontier in the Age of Industrialization, 1800–1890*. New York: Atheneum, 1985.

———. *Gunfighter Nation: The Myth of the Frontier in Twentieth-Century America*. Norman: University of Oklahoma Press, 1998.

Smith, Andrea. "Indigeneity, Settler Colonialism, White Supremacy." In *Racial Formation in the Twenty-First Century*, edited by Daniel Martinez HoSang, Oneka LaBennett, and Laura Pulido, 66–90. Berkeley: University of California Press, 2012.

Smith, Henry Nash. *Virgin Land: The American West as Symbol and Myth*. Cambridge, MA: Harvard University Press, 1970.

Smith, Victoria. *Captive Arizona, 1851–1900*. Lincoln: University of Nebraska Press, 2009.

Spillers, Hortense. "Mama's Baby, Papa's Maybe: An American Grammar Book." *Diacritics* 17, no. 2 (Summer 1987): 64–81.

Stegner, Wallace. "Western Record and Romance." In *Literary History of the United States*, edited by Robert E. Spiller, et. al., 862–77. New York: Macmillan, 1948.

Stenhouse, Fanny. *Tell It All: The Story of a Life's Experience in Mormonism*. Hartford, CT: A. D. Worthington & Co., 1875.

Stephens, Ann S. *Malaeska, the Indian Wife of the White Hunter*. New

York: Beadle & Adams, 1860.

Stevens, J. David. "'She War a Woman': Family Roles, Gender, and Sexuality in Bret Harte's Western Fiction." *American Literature* 69, no. 3 (1997): 571–93.

Stewart, George. *Bret Harte, Argonaut and Exile*. Boston: Houghton Mifflin, 1931.

Stoler, Ann Laura. *Race and the Education of Desire: Foucault's History of Sexuality and the Colonial Order of Things*. Durham, NC: Duke University Press, 1995.

Stoneley, Peter. "Rewriting the Gold Rush: Twain, Harte and Homosociality." *Journal of American Studies* 30, no. 2 (1996): 189–209.

Storey, Mark. "Country Matters: Rural Fiction, Urban Modernity, and the Problem of American Regionalism." *Nineteenth-Century Literature* 65, no. 2 (2010): 192–213.

Streeby, Shelley. *American Sensations: Class, Empire, and the Production of Popular Culture*. Berkeley: University of California Press, 2002.

Tatonetti, Lisa. *Written by the Body: Gender Expansiveness and Indigenous Non-Cis Masculinities*. Minneapolis: University of Minnesota Press, 2021.

Tatum, Stephen. "Postfrontier Horizons." *Modern Fiction Studies* 50, no. 2 (2004): 460–68.

Tengan, Ty P. Kāwika. *Native Men Remade: Gender and Nation in Contemporary Hawaii*. Durham, NC: Duke University Press, 2008.

Thomas, Brook. *The New Historicism and Other Old-Fashioned Topics*. Princeton: Princeton University Press, 1991.

Tompkins, Jane. *West of Everything: The Inner Life of Westerns*. New York: Oxford University Press, 1992.

Tuck, Eve, and K. Wayne Yang. "Decolonization Is Not a Metaphor." *Decolonization: Indigeneity, Education & Society* 1, no. 1 (2012): 1–40.

Turner, Frederick Jackson. *The Frontier in American History*. Tucson: University of Arizona Press, 1986.

Tuttle, Jennifer S. "Indigenous Whiteness and Wister's Invisible Indians." In *Reading* The Virginian *in the New West*, edited by Melody Graulich and Stephen Tatum, 89–112. Lincoln: University of Nebraska Press, 2003.

Twain, Mark. "Comments on the Moro Massacre." In *Mark Twain's Weapons of Satire: Anti-Imperialist Writings on the Philippine-American War*, edited by Jim Zwick, 170–78. Syracuse: Syracuse University Press, 1992.

Veracini, Lorenzo. *Settler Colonialism: A Theoretical Overview*. New York: Palgrave Macmillan, 2010.

Warner, Michael. *Fear of a Queer Planet: Queer Politics and Social Theory*. Minneapolis: University of Minnesota Press, 1993.

Watson, Matthew. "The Argonauts of '49: Class, Gender, and Partnership in Bret Harte's West." *Western American Literature* 40, no. 1 (2005): 33–53.

Wexler, Laura. *Tender Violence: Domestic Visions in an Age of U.S. Imperialism*. Chapel Hill: University of North Carolina Press, 2000.

"What 2,000 Years of Traditional Hopi Farming in the Arid Southwest Can Teach About Resilience." Environmental Defense Fund. December 20, 2019. https://blogs.edf.org/. growingreturns/2019/12/20/hopi-farming-resilience-southwest/.

Wheeler, Edward L. *Blonde Bill; Or, Deadwood Dick's Home Base. A Romance of the "Silent Tongues."* New York: Beadle & Adams, 1899.

———. *Deadwood Dick, the Prince of the Road; Or, the Black Rider of the Black Hills*. New York: Beadle & Adams, 1899.

———. *Deadwood Dick's Doom; Or, Calamity Jane's Last Adventure. A Tale of Death Notch*. New York: Beadle & Adams, 1881.

White, Donald. *The American Century: The Rise and Decline of the United States as a World Power*. New Haven, CT: Yale University Press, 1996.

Whyte, Kyle P. "Indigenous Science (Fiction) for the Anthropocene: Ancestral Dystopias and Fantasies of Climate Change Crises." *Environment and Planning E: Nature and Space* 1, no. 1–2 (2018): 224–42.

Wilderson, Frank B., III. *Red, White & Black: Cinema and the Structure of US Antagonisms*. Durham, NC: Duke University Press, 2010.

Will, Barbara. "The Nervous Origins of the American Western." *American Literature* 70, no. 2 (1998): 293–316.

Williams, Raymond. "Base and Superstructure in Marxist Cultural Theory." *New Left Review* 1, no. 82 (November/December 1973).

Wilson, Christopher P. *The Labor of Words: Literary Professionalism in the Progressive Era*. Athens: University of Georgia Press, 1985.

Wister, Owen. "The Evolution of the Cow-Puncher." *Harper's New Monthly Magazine*, September 1895, 602–17.

———. *The Virginian*. New York: Simon & Schuster, 2009.

Witschi, Nicolas. *Traces of Gold: California's Natural Resources and the Claim to Realism in Western American Literature*. Tuscaloosa: University of Alabama Press, 2002.

Wolfe, Patrick. *Settler Colonialism and the Transformation of Anthropology: The Politics and Poetics of an Ethnographic Event*. New York: Cassell, 1999.

"Women and Children Killed in Moro Battle: Mingled with Warriors and Fell in Hail of Shot. Four Days of Fighting: Nine Hundred Persons Killed or Wounded—President Wires Congratulations to the Troops." *New York Times*, March 11, 1906. https:// timesmachine.nytimes.com/timesmachine/1906/03/11/101768986.html?pageNumber=1.

Wong, Rita. "Decolonizasian: Reading Asian and First Nations Relations in Literature." *Canadian Literature* 199 (2008): 158–80.

Worden, Daniel. *Masculine Style: The American West and Literary Modernism*. New York: Palgrave Macmillan, 2011.

———. "Masculinity for the Million: Gender in Dime Novel Westerns." *Arizona Quarterly* 63, no. 3 (2007): 35–60.

Zagarell, Sandra. "Troubling Regionalism: Rural Life and the Cosmopolitan Eye in Jewett's *Deephaven*." *American Literary History* 10, no. 4 (1998): 639–63.

# Index

*Note: Character names are alphabetized by their first name or identifier. Example: Tommy Luck under "T"; Deadwood Dick under "D."*

# About the Author

**Ryan Tan Wander** has taught and researched at the University of California, Davis; Johannes Gutenberg University, Mainz; The College of Idaho; and Valdosta State University. During the 2021–2022 academic year, he was a visiting assistant professor of English at The College of Idaho, where he taught courses in US and British literature from the early modern period to the contemporary. His work has been published in the journals *Western American Literature* and *Settler Colonial Studies*, among other venues. He has been an assistant professor of English at Valdosta State University since the fall of 2022.